MYSTERIOUS DISAPPEARANCES
THEY NEVER CAME BACK!

Sean Casteel and Commander X (Retired Military Intelligence Operative)
With An Introduction By Timothy Green Beckley

MYSTERIOUS DISAPPEARANCES
THEY NEVER CAME BACK!

Sean Casteel

Introduction by

Timothy Green Beckley

Global Communications

Additional Source Material by Commander X

Copyright 2013 by Timothy Green Beckley

dba Global Communications/Inner Light Publications.

All Rights Reserved. No part of this book may be reproduced, stored in a retrieval system, or transmitted in any form, or by any means electronic, mechanical, photocopying or recording without permission of the publisher.

ISBN: 1606111477

ISBN 13: 9781606111475

Author: Sean Casteel

www.SeanCasteel.com

Commander X

Editorial Director, Timothy Green Beckley

Art and Layout, William Kern

Free weekly newsletter - www.ConspiracyJournal.com

For foreign and reprint rights contact:

Global Communications, Box 753, New Brunswick, NJ 08903

CONTENTS

Introduction by Timothy Green Beckley — iii

Part One — Chronicle Of The Missing—Sean Casteel

Chapter One — A Fortean Chronicle Of The Missing — 1

Chapter Two — Vanished! One By One And En Masse — 9

Chapter Three — Disappearances of the Rich and Famous — 19

Chapter Four – No Explanation! They Vanished Without A Trace — 35

Chapter Five – The Other Triangles — 42

Chapter Six – From Heaven To Earth—None Came Back — 48

Chapter Seven – The Strange Case Of Devil's Gate And Other Tales — 54

Chapter Eight – Disappearing Into Madness — 61

About the Author and Acknowledgements — 66

Part Two — Triangle of the Lost — Commander X

Chapter Nine — Warning! Stay Far Away From The Devil's Triangle — 69

Chapter Ten — Christopher Columbus in the Triangle of the Lost — 80

Chapter Eleven — Sea Serpents and Maritime Monsters — 92

Chapter Twelve — Have We Encountered Unidentified Undersea "Flying Saucers?" — 104

Chapter Thirteen — Does A Mysterious City Exist On The Ocean Floor? — 118

Chapter Fourteen — Bizarre Giants in the Triangle — 131

Chapter Fifteen — Shamballah: Land of the Smoky Gods — 143

Chapter Sixteen — Monsters, UFOs and Bizarre Beings — 161

Chapter Seventeen — Flights of Doom — 171

Chapter Eighteen — The Evidence For Alien Intelligence — 185

Chapter Nineteen — Will We Ever Unravel The Mysteries Of The Sea? — 201

Chapter Twenty — Psychics Predict Triangle Mysteries — 213

Chapter Twenty-One — Mysteries of The Devil's Island — 224

Chapter Twenty-Two — Ghost Ships In Satan's Sea — 235

Chapter Twenty-Three — What's Happening Out There? — 245

Chapter Twenty-Four — Is It Possible We Will Never Solve The Many Puzzles Of The Seas? — 253

Things That Disappear In The Blink Of An Eye

Introduction By Timothy Green Beckley, "Mr. UFO"

As a kid, I was mesmerized by stories of people who simply vanished into thin air. Picking up Charles Fort's works, I can recall reading cases of humans who disappeared just walking out their door, or getting into a coach, and never being seen again.

It's a damn eerie feeling to think that something like this could happen to any one of us and our friends, neighbors and loved ones will never know where we vanished to. I remember one of the stories I used to read over and over because I couldn't get it out of my mind. The story involves the Marie Celeste, a vessel found with all the plates set in place in the galley—for all of the ship's crewmembers—but there was no one in sight and no rational explanation for whatever became of these "mateys." It's like some huge mothership had come down and gobbled them all up.

So what can be the explanation for all these irrational stories involving the disappearance of sometimes one, sometimes hundreds of individuals, in the time spent taking a breath?

Some of the mysterious disappearances throughout history can be attributed to "criminal activity." I mean, we all know that Jimmy Hoffa was not abducted by a UFO (hey, come to think of it, there is a report I published in my "UFO Review" several years ago where someone claimed to have heard him shouting for help from inside a landed UFO—and I am not making this up, dear friends!), and there are some questions as to the whereabouts of Glenn Miller or Amelia Earhart, though it's iffy as to whether they might be hanging out somewhere in captivity on Mars or Uranus.

So what do we make of all these disappearances? There are thousands of new cases each year to contemplate. Odds are only a handful can be attributed to "supernatural forces." Some people just want to slip away and never be heard from again (bad debts—bad marriages). Others may wake up in another identity and not recall their name and then take on a new identity. There have been cases where people who have been "missing" for 15 or more years have finally "awakened" from a bad dream, recalled who they were and returned home as if nothing strange had ever happened. In the field of Ufology, we have close encounters where a person, after being stunned by a beam of light, might be taken onboard a craft and transported to somewhere (sometimes in front of others). They have vanished either never to be seen again or have shown up miles away from their departure sight, sometimes days or weeks later. The best-known episode of this type would be the abduction of Travis Walton, who was taken while cutting down trees in a forest near Snowflake, Arizona.

But what of those who don't fit into any of these categories? We know that hundreds of military personnel and private citizens have gone "poof" while traveling onboard a ship or plane inside one of the famous triangles that exist around the world. The most famous is the Bermuda Triangle, but there is also the Hoodoo Sea and other dark, sinister places that we need to stay clear of.

These, coupled with the many disappearances featured in this work by researcher Sean Casteel, should make your hair stand on end (of course, some days my hair stands on end without the benefit of anything bizarre associated with this effect). When we assigned Sean the task of going through our files and those of other astute students of the macabre, we knew we were in for a treat. This is the kind of stuff that page-turners are made of.

My bit of advice—if you feel your body start to tingle and you see your hands or feet start to become transparent, better grab onto someone nearby just like the sailors who disappeared during the Philadelphia Experiment. It may be the only thing that can save you from the kind of time displacement that could curtail your life!

I think you will agree after reading this timely manuscript that the saying "We may not be long for this Earth" takes on an entirely new and bolder meaning.

Timothy Green Beckley – MRUFO@webtv.net

MYSTERIOUS DISAPPEARANCES: THEY NEVER CAME BACK

CHAPTER ONE

A FORTEAN CHRONICLE OF THE MISSING

Charles Fort is a true legend among paranormal researchers. He laid so much of the groundwork for fields of study like Ufology and mysterious disappearances that it is impossible to imagine those disciplines existing without him.

Beginning around the turn of the century, in the early 1900s, Fort worked full time for twenty-seven years at the British Museum and the New York Public Library, pouring over scientific journals as well as old magazines and newspapers in order to gather material on the strange and paranormal. He used his research to write four books: ***The Book of the Damned***, ***New Lands***, ***Lo!*** and ***Wild Talents***.

In his books, Fort organized his findings and commented on a diverse range of phenomena, including flying saucer sightings that took place before the advent of man-made aircraft, strange noises in the sky, falls of red snow, frogs, fishes and worms, poltergeist phenomena, and countless other supposedly "fringe" subjects.

Fort would come to be embraced by other intellectuals of his day, like Clarence Darrow and Oliver Wendell Holmes. He also influenced a great deal of the science fiction that was to come later, which take up what are called "Fortean Themes."

NAPOLEON'S HANDS ARE CLEAN

But it is with Fort's research into the subject of mysterious disappearance that this chapter is concerned.

From Fort's book ***Lo!*** comes the following account of a mysterious disappearance:

MYSTERIOUS DISAPPEARANCES: THEY NEVER CAME BACK

"Upon November 25, 1809, Benjamin Bathurst, returning from Vienna, where, at the Court of the Emperor Francis, he had been representing the British Government, was in the small town of Perleberg, Germany. In the presence of his valet and his secretary, he was examining horses, which were to carry his coach over more of his journey back to England. Under observation, he walked around to the other side of the horses. He vanished."

Since much had been written at the time of Bathurst's disappearance, Fort said he chose not to repeat that material in his book, except to note that, in a newspaper from Hamburg, Germany, there was news not reported anywhere else. The item said that Bathurst had sent a letter to friends telling them he was safe. However, according to Fort's later research, no such letter had been sent. Was the item planted in order to make the authorities abandon the search? It was theorized at the time that Napoleon Bonaparte may have abducted the Englishman for political reasons, which Bonaparte even went to the trouble of publicly denying.

THE UNTOLD NUMBERS

The number of the missing is surprisingly large, even for such antiquated times. According to Fort, in the years from 1907 to 1913, London police records show that 170,472 persons mysteriously disappeared, and that nothing had been found out in 3,260 cases. Fort questions, however, just how many of the more than 160,000 cases for which at least some explanation allegedly existed were really explained at all. If it becomes a question of remarriage, for instance, or to collect insurance, then "half a dozen bereft ones may 'identify' a body found in the river or cast up by the sea." In other words, just how satisfactory were all those explanations?

THE TELEPORTATION FACTOR

Another interesting account recorded by Fort came from the London *Daily Chronicle*, dateline September 29, 1920.

"A young man, evening of September 27, walking in a street in South London. Magic—houses melting—meadows appearing—or there was a gap in perceptions. However he got there, he was upon a road, with fields around. The young man was frightened. He might be far away and unable to return. It was upon a road, near Dunstable, 30 miles from London, and a policeman finding him exclaiming, pacing back and forth, took him to a station house. Here he recovered sufficiently to tell that he

MYSTERIOUS DISAPPEARANCES: THEY NEVER CAME BACK

was Leonard Wadham, of Walworth, South London, where he was employed by the Ministry of Health. As to how he got to this point near Dunstable, he could tell nothing. Of a swish, nobody could tell much."

One of the more famous cases of a mysterious disappearance involved the writer Ambrose Bierce.

"Late in the year 1913, Ambrose Bierce disappeared. It was explained. He had gone to Mexico to join Villa, and had been killed at the Battle of Torreon. *New York Times*, April 3, 1915—mystery of Bierce's disappearance solved—he was upon Lord Kitchener's staff, in the recruiting service, in London. *New York Times*, April 7, 1915—no knowledge of Bierce, at the War Office, London. In March, 1920, newspapers published a dispatch from San Francisco, telling that Bierce had gone to Mexico to fight *against* Villa and had been shot. It would be a fitting climax to the life of this broad-minded writer to be widely at work in London, while in Mexico, and to be killed while fighting for and against Villa."

But Bierce at the time was an incurable invalid and more than 70-years-old, Fort says, then he pauses to wonder "whether Ambrose Bierce ever experimented with self-teleportation. Three of his short stories are of 'mysterious disappearances.' He must have been uncommonly interested to repeat so."

ABDUCTION BY MEANS OF TELEPORTATION

Another story involving teleportation is recounted in *Lo!* Fort says that he reconstructed this story from several fragments he came upon in his research.

"Perhaps in the year 1910, and perhaps not in this year, a Hindu magician teleported a boy from somewhere in England, perhaps from Wimbledon, London, perhaps not. The effect of this treatment was of mental obliteration; of profound hypnosis, or amnesia. The boy could learn, as if starting life anew, but mostly his memory was a void. Later the magician was dying. He repented, and his problem was to restore the boy, perhaps not to his home, but to his native land. He could not tell of the occult transportation, but at first it seemed to him that nobody would believe a story of ordinary kidnapping."

Kidnapping would be less believable than teleportation? Well, look at it this way.

"It would be a most improbable story: that in London a Hindu had

MYSTERIOUS DISAPPEARANCES: THEY NEVER CAME BACK

kidnapped a boy and, on the way to India, had spent weeks aboard a vessel with this boy without exciting inquiry, and with the ability to keep the boy from appealing to other passengers. Still, a story of kidnapping is a story in commonplace terms. No story of ordinary kidnapping could account for the boy's lapsed memory, but at the most some persons would think that some of the circumstances were queer and would then forget the matter."

In 1917, the Hindu abductor sent a confession to a Christian missionary organization in Nepal, India. A well-grown boy was found to be living with him, and the abductor again claimed to have kidnapped him without offering details about a voyage to India. The boy was taken to Gorakapur, and was given employment in a railway workshop. He could speak a small amount of English, but had no recollection of ever having been in England.

An item appeared in **Lloyd's Sunday News** on October 24, which said the "boy was not yet identified by Scotland Yard. An even more extraordinary development of the story is that quite a number of boys disappeared in Wimbledon ten years ago." The police had no way of tracing the boy because in Scotland Yard, all records of missing children were destroyed after a few years. Fort could find no further reports on the case, but it remains interesting as an example of the paranormal explanation being more believable than the prosaic one.

VANISHED IN AN INSTANT

There are many cases of people disappearing right before the eyes, or nearly so, of an observer. One such case presented by Fort was obtained from the **Journal of Psychical Research**, which tells of a vanishing event that took place in March of 1895 and was seen by a painter named John Osborne of Oxford in England.

"Osborne was walking along a road to Wolverton when he heard the sounds of a horse's hoofs behind him, and, turning, saw a man on horseback, having difficulty in controlling his horse. He scurried out of the way, and when safe, looked again. Horse and man had vanished."

An attempt was made to explain away what happened by claiming that the week before a man on horseback had been killed on this part of the road, and that the badly injured horse had been shot. The **Journal** later published a correction, which said that the accident with which this disappearance had been associated had not occurred a week before but years before, and was altogether different, having been an

MYSTERIOUS DISAPPEARANCES: THEY NEVER CAME BACK

accident to a farmer in a hay field.

"Several persons investigated, among them a magistrate, who wrote that he was convinced at least that Osborne thought he had seen the 'figures' disappear."

Once again, the paranormal explanation is much more satisfying than the conventional one, and the strangeness of what Osborne saw was attested to by a local magistrate, presumably a no nonsense official who does not suffer fools gladly.

Further speculation about the ability of some people to teleport themselves at will is offered by Fort with the following tale of a young woman who "was more than casually looked at, near the foot of Milton Hill, Massachusetts. She vanished. She was seen several times. So this is a story of a place that was 'haunted,' and the 'figure' was supposed to be a ghost. For a wonder, there was no story of a murder that was committed, years before, near this hill."

The absence of any typical back-story of a woman suffering a grievously unjust death and then being forced to wander the area as a restless spirit leads Fort to another possibility.

"For all I know, some young woman, living in Boston, New York, some distant place, may have had teleportive ability with an appearing point, or terminal of an occult current, at this hill, having been translated back and forth several times, without knowing it, or without being able to remember, or remembering dimly, thinking that it was a dream. Perhaps, sometime happening to pass this hill, by more commonplace means of transportation, she would have a sense of uncanny familiarity, but would be unable to explain, having no active consciousness of having ever been there before.

"Psychologists have noted the phenomenon," Fort continues, "of a repeating scene in different dreams, or supposed dreams. The phenomenon may not be of fancifulness, but of dim impressions of teleportations to one persisting appearing-point. A naive, little idea of mine is that so many ghosts in white garments have been reported because persons, while asleep, have been teleported in their night clothes."

SNATCHED FROM THE JAWS OF NOTHINGNESS

The concept of such portals is further examined by Fort.

"It may be that I can record a case of a man who was about to disappear, but was dragged back, in time, from a disappearing point. I

MYSTERIOUS DISAPPEARANCES: THEY NEVER CAME BACK

think of the children of Clavaux, who were about to be taken into a vortex, but were dragged away by their parents, who were not susceptible. Data look as if there may have been a transporting current through so-called solid substance, which 'opened' and then 'closed,' with no sign of a yawning. It may be that what we call substance is as much open as closed.... The greatest seeming security is only a temporary disguise of the abysmal. All of us are skating over thin existence."

To make his point more definitively, Fort told the story of a married couple who occupied good positions in Leeds, England. The two were arrested in a railroad station on December 9, 1873, in Bristol, and charged with disorderly conduct, both of them in their nightclothes, with the husband having fired a pistol. It was reported in the London **Times** that the husband had excitedly claimed that he and his wife had arrived the day before, from Leeds, and had taken a room in a Bristol hotel. Early the next morning, the floor had "opened" and that as he was about to be dragged into the "opening," his wife had saved him. Both of them were so terrified that they had jumped out the window and run to the railroad station, looking for a policeman.

The Bristol Daily Post subsequently published an account of the proceedings in police court. The husband's excitement was still so intense that he "could not clearly express himself." His wife testified that, early in the evening, they had heard loud, alarming sounds but had been reassured by the hotel landlady. The sounds were heard again around three or four the following morning. The couple jumped out on the floor, which they could feel giving way beneath them. Voices repeating their exclamations were heard, or their own voices echoed strangely.

"Then, according to what she saw, or thought she saw, the floor opened wide. Her husband was falling into this 'opening' when she dragged him back."

The landlady testified that she had also heard the strange sounds but was unable to clearly describe them. The police, upon examining the hotel room, could find nothing to justify the strange behavior of the couple from Leeds, and had labeled the matter a case of "collective hallucination." No one at any time suggested the couple had been intoxicated, and the dazed and bewildered pair were released in the custody of somebody who had come from Leeds to collect them.

Fort says the loud sounds heard in the above case are similar in nature to those heard in poltergeist hauntings.

MYSTERIOUS DISAPPEARANCES: THEY NEVER CAME BACK

"Spiritualists have persistently called poltergeist sounds 'raps,'" he writes. "Sometimes they are raps, but often they are detonations that shake buildings. People up and down a street have been kept awake by them. Maybe existences open and shut noisily."

Have these "noisy doorways" Fort refers to been the cause of countless thousands of bizarre disappearances? At this point, they are as good an explanation as any.

THE TWO DISAPPEARING AIRMEN

The disappearance of two pilots, similar to the story of Dr. Wallace Halsey, has also found a place in Fort's work. In **Wild Talents**, Fort begins the narrative by saying, "The story of these men is laid in a surrounding of hates of the intensity of oriental fanaticism." (So what else is new?)

"Upon July 24, 1924, at a time of Arab hostility, Flight Lieutenant W. T. Day and Pilot Officer D. R. Stewart were sent from British headquarters, upon an ordinary reconnaissance over a desert in Mesopotamia. According to schedule, they would not be absent more than several hours. I take this account from the London **Daily Express**, Sept 21, 28, 1924.

"The men did not return," Fort continues, "and they were searched for. The plane was soon found, in the desert. Why it should have landed was a problem. 'There was some petrol found in the tank. There was nothing wrong with the craft. It was, in fact, flown back to the aerodome.' But the men were missing. 'So far as can be ascertained, they encountered no meteorological conditions that might have forced them to land.' There were no marks to indicate the plane had been shot at."

The article Fort was working with speculated that there is perhaps some unknown way of plucking an airplane out of the sky, or for picking two men out of a desert. There were footprints left behind by Day and Stewart that extended for forty feet from the plane and then disappeared "as suddenly as if they had come to the brink of a cliff."

That it was impossible to explain the plane's landing was put aside as a minor mystery, and the theory was offered that the two men had been captured by hostile Bedouins, who had brushed away all trails in the sand starting at the point forty yards from the plane. But even hostile Bedouins could not go on brushing indefinitely, and a search was made to pick up the trail again.

MYSTERIOUS DISAPPEARANCES: THEY NEVER CAME BACK

"Aeroplanes, armored cars and mounted police searched. Rewards were offered. Tribal patrols searched unceasingly for four days. Nowhere beyond the point where the tracks in the sand ended abruptly were other tracks found."

Fort writes that according to the latest account of the disappearing pilots that he could find, from March of 1925, the mystery of the missing airmen was still unsolved.

* * *

Charles Fort died in 1932, having been the ground breaking pioneer for so much that we now take for granted about paranormal research. His legacy will be continued in the following chapters, some of which take a look at more recent instances of bizarre disappearances.

MYSTERIOUS DISAPPEARANCES: THEY NEVER CAME BACK

CHAPTER TWO

VANISHED! ONE BY ONE AND EN MASSE

As is the case with nearly every other subject under the sun, the Internet is full of information on the subject of mysterious disappearances. A quick trip through a search engine will yield innumerable cases of those who have vanished without a trace.

One unlikely but still very interesting source is the English online version of Pravda, the primary newspaper of the former Soviet Union. In a posting there, dated April 26, 2004, the following story of the disappearance of an entire battalion of soldiers was recounted.

"The event," the Pravda account begins, "which occurred on August 21, 1915, when an entire battalion was gone in the presence of other people, had been an official secret for over fifty years. Only in 1967 the documents containing the testimonies of twenty witnesses to this incident, which happened in Southern Europe near the Dardanelles, were made public. A long search for the vanished soldiers was mounted. But none of them had been found, neither among the dead nor among the POWs released by the Turks after the war."

THE FAMOUS ROANOKE COLONY INCIDENT

The posting goes on to say that mass disappearances are one of the hardest of historical mysteries to explain. For instance, the disappearance of about hundred men, women and children from an American colony on Roanoke Island in 1590 is just as baffling today as when it happened.

A more complete account of the Roanoke disappearance can be found on a site called "Unexplained Disappearances." According to the

MYSTERIOUS DISAPPEARANCES: THEY NEVER CAME BACK

unnamed author there, "In 1587, a colony of 114 men, women and children became one of the earliest attempts to colonize the new world—America. Traveling from Britain to Roanoke Island, on North Carolina's coast, they were the first true attempt at colonization of the New World. They also became one of the nation's great mysteries."

The group was led by John White, whose granddaughter Virginia Dare became the first Englishperson born on American soil. But life was hard for the colonists, and their hardscrabble survival necessitated the need for more supplies from home. Reluctantly, John White and a Portuguese sailor named Simon Fernandez sailed for England, and upon their arrival there, learned that England was in a serious war against Spain. White was forced to join the fighting and was unable to return to Roanoke for three years.

When White landed again in the Americas on August 18, 1590, "he could find not a single trace of the colony. No people, living or dead, could be found anywhere. All personal belongings were left in place, as if the people simply disappeared into thin air."

The only possible clue left behind was a carving on a tree, with the letters "CRO" being all he could decipher. The three letters matched the first part of the name of Croatoan, a nearby island. White sailed there to search for his family and countrymen, but no trace of the colonists has ever been found.

The Pravda account differs in some of the particulars. In their version, soldiers march into the village and find burning candles and tables set for a meal in the huts, but with no settlers around. "The first idea was that the Indians had killed them, but no drop of blood or dead body could be found anywhere. Only a few words were left carved, seemingly in great haste, on a tree near the priest's house reading, 'It doesn't look like...'"

In any case, the varying versions at least agree on the complete and unexplained disappearance of around one hundred people, and it is doubtful that any true understanding of what really happened will ever make itself apparent.

THEY SAW HIM DISAPPEAR!

Another case included in the "Unexplained Disappearances" posting involves a farmer from Selma, Alabama, named Orion Williamson. On a July day in 1854, with his wife and son and two other witnesses (neighbor Armour Wren and his son James) watching him intently, Wil-

MYSTERIOUS DISAPPEARANCES: THEY NEVER CAME BACK

son simply vanished into thin air.

"The Wrens, who'd been riding along a road on the other side of the field in a horse and buggy, immediately ran to the spot where Williamson had last been seen, idly swishing the ankle-deep grass with a small stick, but found nothing. Most of the grass was gone from the spot where Williamson had disappeared as well."

When the nearby town heard what had happened, a search party of 300 men was formed and began to comb the field, but their careful search yielded no clues. As news continued to spread, hundreds of the curious came to help in the fruitless search or merely to gawk at the scene.

"A geologist and a team of experts dug up the field to see if perhaps the ground underneath was unstable or abnormal at all. They found nothing unusual."

Newspaper reporters also inundated the area, and all were forced to report the same thing, that a man had vanished into thin air. Spookily enough, Mrs. Williamson and her son claimed to have heard the farmer's voice crying out for help from the region where he'd disappeared, but the voice weakened and faded away completely after a few weeks.

The writer Ambrose Bierce (who would eventually disappear himself, as recounted in Chapter Eight of this book) took an interest in the case, even interviewing members of the search party and studying the field where Williamson was last seen. Bierce also interviewed a German scientist named Dr. Maximilian Hern, who believed that there exists a kind of "universal ether" that could completely destroy any solid object it came in contact with and which may have caused the hapless farmer's bizarre exit from this plane of reality.

A reporter would eventually write a fictional version of the story, which included all the details of the real event, except that the farmer's name became David Lang, the story was set in Tennessee, and the date was changed to 1880. For some reason, it is this fictionalized version that has received more publicity, causing some degree of confusion over the years.

AN ENTIRE FAMILY VANISHES

The Rogue River National Forest Campground in Oregon was the scene of an entire family, the Cowdens, vanishing all at once. On September 5, 1974, the family of four was camping over Labor Day Week-

MYSTERIOUS DISAPPEARANCES: THEY NEVER CAME BACK

end. That Sunday morning, Richard Cowden was last seen buying some milk in nearby Copper, Oregon. When the family failed to show up for dinner with Richard's mother, the search began, with one of the local authorities comparing the deserted camp scene to something out of "The Twilight Zone." The Unexplained Disappearances website quotes Oregon Trooper Lee Rickson as saying, "That camp sure was spooky. Even the milk was still on the table." Investigators also found cooking utensils, fishing rods and the family car, as well as Richard's wallet and his wife's purse, with nothing apparently missing from them. There were no signs of a struggle, so it was impossible to pinpoint any kind of foul play.

ESKIMO VILLAGE IN CANADA COMPLETELY GONE

In the chilly month of November, in the year 1930, a Canadian fur trapper named Joe Labelle walked into what had long been a busy Eskimo fishing village located on shores of Lake Anjikuni in Canada. To his stunned surprise, he was greeted with an eerie silence. The normally noisy and bustling settlement of 2000 Eskimos was completely deserted. Labelle went to each hut and storehouse in turn, but none of the villagers were anywhere to be seen.

When he went to investigate a flickering fire seen in the distance, he found a smoldering pot of blackened stew. To increase the degree of mystery still further, there were absolutely no human footprints leading away from the village. Labelle knew something extremely strange had happened, and he hurried to the nearest telegraph office and alerted the Royal Canadian Mounted Police. Within hours the Mounties were at the scene and forced to confront the same baffling mystery. A huge search party was launched, but the villagers were never found.

Some weird remains were found, however. All the sleigh dogs that had belonged to the missing locals were discovered buried 12 feet under a snowdrift at the outer edges of the camp. All the animals had apparently been starved to death. However, the Eskimos' own provisions and foodstuffs had been left behind in their huts, which further mystified the searchers. Finally, in a chilling last detail, it was discovered that all the ancestral graves of the Eskimos were now empty.

"Whoever or whatever had taken all the living villagers," the Unexplained Disappearances website said, "had also dug up the dead as well, even though the icy ground around the graves was as hard as iron."

A bizarre blue glow lit up the horizon as the Mounties watched in awe. The strange light was not the northern lights, with which the

MYSTERIOUS DISAPPEARANCES: THEY NEVER CAME BACK

Mounties would have been familiar, but instead seemed "steady and artificial." The disappearance of the village was reported in the media worldwide, with many believing that a rational explanation would emerge in time. But the Anjikuni mass disappearance continues to be an unsolved mystery.

A POTPOURRI OF QUICK STORIES

In an excellent posting on the website "About: Paranormal Phenomena," writer Stephen Wagner offers up an interesting collection of brief accounts of mysterious disappearances, beginning with one he calls "The Vanishing Prisoner."

This first case is particularly interesting because it occurred in full view of witnesses.

"The year was 1815, and the location was a Prussian prison at Weichselmunde. The prisoner's name was Diderici, a valet who was serving a sentence for assuming his employer's identity after he died from a stroke."

Diderici was standing in line with other prisoners in the exercise yard, and as they began to walk, chains clanking noisily, Diderici began literally to fade before the eyes of everyone there. His body became increasingly transparent, until he was gone completely, leaving his manacles and leg chains empty on the ground. He was never seen again.

There is another case of a person disappearing in front of witnesses, this time in 1873 in Leamington Spa, England. James Worson was a simple shoemaker who believed himself something of an athlete. Worson made a wager with some friends that he could run from Leamington Spa to Coventry, a distance of 16 miles. His friends, believing that to be impossible, took him up on the bet and followed him on a horse-drawn cart to protect their wager. Worson did well the first few miles, but at one point he tripped on something and began to fall forward—but he never hit the ground. Instead, he completely vanished. Not believing what they were seeing, his friends made a thorough search of the area and then notified the police, whose investigation turned up nothing. "James Worson had run into oblivion," Wagner concludes.

GONE WITH NO FANFARE AT ALL

Some more recent cases of mysterious disappearances are also included in Wagner's postings, cases that seem on the surface to be more commonplace but which are nevertheless shrouded in enigmatic dark-

MYSTERIOUS DISAPPEARANCES: THEY NEVER CAME BACK

ness. One such case involved a man named Bruce Campbell, who was driving along with his wife from their hometown in Massachusetts to visit their son at some distance across the country. The date was April 14, 1959, and the couple made an overnight stop in Jacksonville, Illinois, checking into a motel for the night. In the morning, Mrs. Campbell awoke to find her husband had vanished, apparently in his pajamas. All of his belongings, including his car, clothing and money were still there, but Campbell was never seen again and his disappearance was never explained.

Another example that also took place in Illinois involved a couple in their 60s who were attending a convention in Chicago at the Sheraton Hotel in 1970. Other attendees to the convention noted that Edward Andrews, the husband, was complaining of a mild illness, which he ascribed to hunger because the party they were at was serving only drinks and small hors d'oeuvres. The couple soon left the party and went to the parking garage to retrieve their car. The parking attendant later told authorities that Andrews' wife appeared to be crying and that Edward didn't look so well either. As Edward drove the car away, he scraped the fender on the exit door but just kept driving. The attendant was the last person to see the couple before they vanished into the night. Police offered the opinion that Edward, in his sickness, may have driven the car off a bridge into the Chicago River, but were able to find no sign of an accident, even after dragging the river. The Andrews and their car were just gone.

A similar case involving the disappearance of both a couple and their car took place in 1980 and was even reported in the New York Times. Charles Romer and his wife Catherine were one of those retired couples that divided their time between homes in New York and Florida as the winter months came and went. It was on one such seasonal trip back to New York that the Romers met their mysterious fate. They begin their journey north on the morning of April 8, and late that afternoon they stopped at a motel in Brunswick City, Georgia, for the night. They checked in and took their luggage to their room, and then went back out again, possibly to get some dinner. But the couple never arrived at any restaurant nor did they return to the motel. Three days later, an investigation turned up the fact that they had never slept in their bed, and a thorough search found absolutely no trace of the Romers or their car. They simply vanished without a trace.

These last three cases, while they display no apparent paranormal overtones, do at least serve as examples of people gone missing to

MYSTERIOUS DISAPPEARANCES: THEY NEVER CAME BACK

little or no fanfare. Without a celebrity's claim to fame or the coincidental timing of a display of UFOs in the sky, their unspectacular disappearances still manage to throw a monkey wrench into our sense of the ordinary and the expected. Is there some other dimension at work here, some unknowable place that sucks average people into its otherworldly jaws for no discernible reason?

AN AUSTRALIAN PILOT DISAPPEARS

A website located at tinwiki.org offers a detailed account of the disappearance of a 20-year-old Australian pilot named Frederick Valentich. On Saturday, October 21, 1978, Valentich departed from Moorabbin Airport in Melbourne, Australia on what was expected to be a routine flight to King Island for the purpose of racking up some night flying hours as well as to pick up a crate of crayfish for friends back home.

"What happened instead would become one of the most disturbing cases in the history of Ufology," the site declares. "To this day, the Valentich disappearance remains as puzzling now as it was over 25 years ago."

Valentich's flight began at 6:19 P.M., with clear conditions, a few scattered clouds and a mild breeze. With such excellent visibility, the trip was expected to take an hour and ten minutes. Valentich would be crossing the Bass Strait, a small band of water between mainland Australia and Tasmania.

At 7:06 P.M., the young pilot radioed Melbourne Flight Service that he was being "harassed" by an unknown craft. He was also starting to have some kind of engine trouble, and the unknown craft was flying dangerously close to him.

Portions of the transcript of Valentich's pleas for help to Melbourne are quoted in the posting. Valentich first asks Melbourne whether they can see any traffic below 5,000 feet.

"No known traffic," comes the reply.

"There seems to be a large aircraft below 5,000," Valentich insists.

"What type of aircraft is it?"

"I cannot affirm. It is four bright—it seems to me like landing lights. The aircraft has just passed over me at least a thousand feet above."

"And is it a large aircraft, confirmed?" the voice from Melbourne asked.

"Er—unknown, due to the speed it's traveling. Is there any Air Force aircraft in the vicinity?"

"No known aircraft in the vicinity."

Valentich next says that the unknown craft is now approaching him from due east, and "it seems to me that he's playing some sort of game. He's flying over me two, three times at speeds I could not identify."

The conversation continues, with Valentich groping for words to describe what he's seeing.

"As it's flying past, it's a long shape (voice cuts out for a few seconds) cannot identify more than it has such speed. It's right before me now, Melbourne. It seems like it's stationary. What I'm doing right now is orbiting, and the thing is just orbiting on top of me also. It's got a green light and sort of metallic-like, it's all shiny on the outside. It's just vanished. Melbourne, would you know what kind of aircraft I've got? Is it a military aircraft? It's now approaching from the southwest."

At this point, the engine trouble becomes much worse.

"The engine is rough-idling," he says. "I've got it set at 23, 24, and the thing is coughing."

Melbourne then asks the pilot what he intends to do now.

"My intentions are—ah—to go to King Island, Melbourne. That strange aircraft is hovering on top of me again. It is hovering and it's not an aircraft."

That was the last that anyone would hear from Valentich.

IN THE AFTERMATH

A search and rescue effort was launched soon after Valentich's plane failed to arrive at its ETA of 7:28 P.M. The plane was equipped with both a life jacket and a radio survival beacon, and given that the plane's last reported position over water was known, it was thought that Valentich would be found without much difficulty. However, nothing was heard from the survival beacon.

The Royal Australian Air Force searched for two days straight, but no trace of Valentich or his aircraft were found. A few false clues turned up, like an oil slick discovered 18 miles north of King Island that was later determined to be marine diesel fuel and not related to an aircraft.

MYSTERIOUS DISAPPEARANCES: THEY NEVER CAME BACK

Debris was also found, which turned out to be packing crates from a ship, and not pieces of a plane.

The search process continued until October 25, but not a single trace of plane or pilot was uncovered. The only "witness," the air traffic technician who had spoken to Valentich by radio, was interviewed. He reported that after the last words Valentich spoke to him, there was an unusual 17-second period of metallic scraping noises and stop/start pulse sounds which had no apparent order. The technician tried to duplicate the sounds by rapid keying of the microphone, but that effect was very different than what is heard on the tape.

The story of the young pilot's disappearance made news worldwide, and there were various theories proposed about what had happened. "Some people believed that Valentich had been flying upside down and became disoriented," the website says, "and mistook the Cape Otway Lighthouse for a UFO. Certain persons in the Air Force and government officials favored this theory." However, that theory fails to account for the description of the unknown craft, its maneuvers, and Valentich's extremely disturbed state of mind while speaking to Melbourne.

Freak weather was also suggested as the cause, though this theory was mainly promoted by a UFO debunker named Harley Klauer, notorious in Australia for his views on the subject. There is little credence given to this one, however, as the weather at the time had been very mild and pleasant.

Klauer also offered even a less likely possibility: that the plane had been brought down by drug dealers using the Bass Strait to smuggle drugs onto mainland Australia. The drug dealers were known to use helium balloons with bags of drugs attached to their boats. If a patrol came, they could cut the helium balloons loose and get rid of evidence. Perhaps, Klauer said, the plane had been caught up in an invisible nylon string used to tow the drugs and thus brought down. This does not warrant serious consideration, as Valentich was flying at over 4,000 feet, an unlikely altitude for drug-filled balloons.

The most credible explanation, and the one that best fits the available evidence, is that pilot and plane were both abducted by a UFO. "It certainly is not the first case of a plane disappearing after coming into contact with a UFO," the website states.

In May of 1982, the Bureau of Air Safety Investigation released an

MYSTERIOUS DISAPPEARANCES: THEY NEVER CAME BACK

official report on the incident, in which the location of the occurrence, the time of the occurrence, and the apparent cause of the disappearance were all declared to be unknown, and Valentich himself was presumed dead.

Several separate, independent witnesses in the area from Cape Otway to King Island also reported seeing strange craft around the time of Valentich's sighting. A plumber who lived in the area even captured photos of an object he saw rising out of the sea about 20 minutes before Valentich radioed in his distress call. The photos are still unexplained.

"The Valentich Disappearance," the site concludes, "occurred during the biggest UFO flap in Australian history, activity which peaked the night of his disappearance, then strangely enough, began to drop off."

The Valentich case is typical of many others in this book in that, when the facts are closely examined, some sort of paranormal explanation, such as abduction by a UFO, makes more sense than the grasping for straws done after the fact by government officials and a bewildered media whose duty it is to present a "rational" account of events to the public that they serve.

MYSTERIOUS DISAPPEARANCES: THEY NEVER CAME BACK

CHAPTER THREE

DISAPPEARANCES OF THE RICH AND FAMOUS

It isn't only the occasional anonymous Midwestern farmer or Prussian diplomat who disappears. There have been numerous instances of famous celebrities from the music world, political personalities, even well known New York socialites who have vanished, never to be heard from again. This chapter will deal with some of these fascinating cases that prove that fame provides no protection from the vagaries of time and chance.

JIMMY HOFFA

Jimmy Hoffa was born in Brazil, Indiana, on February 14, 1913, to a poor coal miner. When his father died, Hoffa was forced to leave school and worked in a warehouse in Michigan. According to the Wikipedia Encyclopedia entry on Hoffa, "He developed a reputation as a tough street fighter who always stood up for his fellow workers against management."

When Hoffa was fired for his efforts, he took a job as an organizer for Local 299 of the International Brotherhood of Teamsters. Around that same time, Hoffa began using organized crime connections to shake down an association of small grocery stores, for which he was brought up on criminal charges and forced to pay a fine. He continued to rise in the ranks of the Teamsters' organization, as well as to work with crime syndicates in the Detroit area.

"Hoffa took over the presidency of the Teamsters in 1957," the Wikipedia entry continues, "when his predecessor, Dave Beck, was convicted on bribery charges and imprisoned."

MYSTERIOUS DISAPPEARANCES: THEY NEVER CAME BACK

By 1964, Hoffa had managed to bring nearly all North American truck drivers under a single national union. He next tried to bring the airlines and other transport employees into the Teamsters, which caused the federal government no small amount of concern, since a possible strike involving all transport systems would cripple the national economy.

Meanwhile, Hoffa's close association with the Mafia brought him under the scrutiny of Attorney General Robert F. Kennedy, who remained confident that Hoffa had pocketed large amounts of union money. Hoffa was convicted in 1964 of the attempted bribery of a grand juror and sentenced to 15 years. He was released by President Richard Nixon in 1971, who commuted his sentence on the condition that Hoffa not take part in union activities for ten years.

KEEPING HIS APPOINTMENT

Hoffa intended to sue to overturn the ten-year condition when he disappeared at around 2:30 pm on July 30, 1975. He was last seen in the parking lot of the Machus Red Fox Restaurant in Bloomfield Hills, Michigan, suburb of Detroit. He had been scheduled to meet a pair of known Mafia leaders, Anthony "Tony Jack" Giacalone, and Anthony "Tony Pro" Provenzano.

There are several theories that are still kicked around as possibilities. One is that Hoffa's assassination was allegedly ordered at Brutico's, an Italian restaurant in Old Forge, Pennsylvania. Another comes from Mafioso Bill Bonanno, who claimed in his book "Bound By Honor" that Hoffa was shot and put in the trunk of a car that was then put through a car compactor. Another Mafioso, Richard Kuklinksi said in a television interview that Hoffa was now a "car bumper." His story goes that Hoffa was stabbed in the back of the head and placed in a steel barrel. The barrel was buried, but then later dug up for fear the police would find it. The barrel, with Hoffa still inside, was next compacted, melted down, and then shipped to a Japanese carmaker as recycled steel.

It has been reported elsewhere that Hoffa is still alive, having taken a black striptease dancer to South America with him and set up housekeeping there. Still more theories are offered. According to one account, Hoffa was entombed in concrete at Giants Stadium in the New Jersey Meadowlands. Another claims that he was ground up and thrown to the fishes in a Florida swamp. Still another, that he was obliterated in a mob-owned fat-rendering plant that has since burned down.

MYSTERIOUS DISAPPEARANCES: THEY NEVER CAME BACK
A SERIES OF HIT MEN CONFESS

Some newer possibilities regarding the Hoffa disappearance are also recounted in the Wikipedia entry. In 2004, Charles Brandt, a former prosecutor and Chief Deputy Attorney General of Delaware, published a book called "I Heard You Paint Houses." The title comes from a coded conversation said to be routine among hit men and their prospective employers. "I heard you paint houses," to which the reply was, "Yes, and I do my own carpentry, too." The part about house painting is a reference to the splattering of blood on the walls, and "doing my own carpentry" is translated as disposing of the body.

In his book, Brandt reports a series of telephone conversations he had with Frank Sheeran, a Mafia hit man, truck driver, Teamster official and a close friend of Hoffa's. Sheeran wished to assuage his guilt as he confessed to his role as Hoffa's killer, acting on orders from the Mafia.

"He claimed to have used his friendship with Hoffa to lure him to a bogus meeting in Bloomfield Hills and drive him to a house in northwestern Detroit, where he shot him twice before fleeing and leaving Hoffa's body behind," the entry says. Hoffa's body was then cremated.

Another hit man, Gambino crime family member Louie Milito, told his wife during an argument in 1988 that he had killed Hoffa and dumped his body near Staten Island's Verrazano-Narrows Bridge in New York City. In April 2006, the aforementioned hit man Richard "The Iceman" Kuklinski told a writer that he had been part of a group of five men who had kidnapped and murdered Hoffa.

In May of that same year, the FBI began digging for Hoffa's remains outside of a barn on a farm in Milford Township in Michigan. The agency would not reveal who had tipped them off, though it was later reported to have been a 75-year-old federal prisoner in Lexington, Kentucky, who was trying to use his knowledge of Hoffa's disappearance to reduce his prison sentence. The search of the farm area was ended on May 30, 2006, without any remains being found.

None of these theories or confessions has ever been confirmed, and the whereabouts of Jimmy Hoffa's remains continues to be unknown.

MYSTERIOUS DISAPPEARANCES: THEY NEVER CAME BACK

GLENN MILLER

An article posted on the BBC's website does an excellent job of telling the story of the mysterious disappearance of revered bandleader Glenn Miller.

"Glenn Miller was a national darling," the article says. "The famous Glenn Miller orchestra, formed in 1938, had soared out of nowhere to incredible success, creating over 70 top ten records in four years, selling over a million records, and dominating the American airwaves."

When America entered the war in 1941, Miller quickly enlisted and was transferred to the Army Air Corps, given the rank of captain and allowed free rein to establish his own wartime band. He spent the next few years performing for Allied troops all over England.

It was now December, 1944, and with Christmas approaching, the Allies needed every possible morale boost. Miller was preparing to do a concert in Paris for the troops.

The original plan had been for manager Don Haynes to fly with Miller to Paris on December 15. However, Miller had made the acquaintance of Lt. Col. Norman B. Baessell the night before at the officer's club near Northampton.

"Baessell happened to mention that he would be departing for Paris the next day," the BBB article continues, "from an RAF airfield at Twinwood Farm, and upon hearing of Miller's plans, offered him a seat on the plane. Miller gladly accepted, and whiled away the night eating dinner and playing poker with Haynes and Baessell."

The morning of December 15 brought with it a heavy covering of fog. Haynes called Baessell to see if he still intended to make the flight, and Baessell promised him that the fog would lift after lunch. It was bitterly cold, and as Miller and Haynes waited in a car for the pilot, a man named John Morgan, Miller joked that Morgan would be unable to find the field at all since it was 24 degrees and "even the birds are grounded." Morgan landed the plane shortly thereafter, and when Miller saw that it had only one engine, he muttered, "Where the hell are the parachutes?"

In a strangely ironic moment of prescience, Baessell answered, "What's the matter with you, Miller? Do you want to live forever?" He pointed out that Charles Lindbergh had crossed the Atlantic on one engine, while their plane would only be going as far as Paris. Miller said nothing in reply.

MYSTERIOUS DISAPPEARANCES: THEY NEVER CAME BACK

Since there was no room for Haynes on the plane, he stayed behind. He was the last person to see them alive.

THEORIES ABOUT WHAT HAPPENED

The official explanation offered at the time was that the Norseman aircraft had crashed into the English Channel either because of iced-over wings or engine failure. However this failed to satisfy the majority of the populace, and multiple theories and speculations have been offered in the more than 60 years since.

Easily the most outrageous theory is that Miller and the two officers had safely crossed the Channel to Paris and had later died in "somewhat compromising conditions." This theory first surfaced through a German journalist in 1977, who had trawled through American and German intelligence documents while writing a book on German intelligence agencies. The writer claimed to have obtained, through the American Freedom on Information Act, evidence that Miller had arrived safely in Paris but had died while in the "dubious company of a French prostitute."

There were many holes in this theory, namely because it implied that the U.S. military had falsified Miller's death by planting a plane in the English Channel as "evidence," then neglected to plant bodies as well, but later managed to silence everyone involved, from Miller's manager Haynes to whoever moved Miller's body from the brothel and guarded the scene there. After which they somehow managed to leak it all to their German enemies.

The German reporter later claimed he had been misquoted and that he had never claimed to have found evidence of Miller dying in a brothel. He said the story had come to him from German intelligence specialists in an off-the-record conversation.

There are two different versions of the story of Miller dying for prosaic medical reasons. One story maintains that Miller died of gunshot wounds in Ohio in 1945, based on an anonymous letter from an unnamed medical doctor sent to a radio announcer named Dr. Chris Valenti, notorious for his Glenn Miller conspiracy theories.

The other story is told by Miller's younger brother, Herb, who broke a nearly 40-year silence in 1983 and announced that Miller had died of lung cancer in a hospital. When Miller landed in Paris on December 15, 1944, he reported feeling ill and was taken to a military hospital where the cancer took his life the next day.

MYSTERIOUS DISAPPEARANCES: THEY NEVER CAME BACK

To support his story, Herb Miller produced a letter from his chain-smoking brother that said, "I am totally emaciated, although I am eating enough. I have trouble breathing. I think I am very ill." Miller also suffered depression, irritability and exhaustion during his last months, all of which indicated that he had an underlying medical condition.

Miller's manager Doug Haynes confirmed that Miller had lost a great deal of weight and that his tailor-made uniforms "didn't fit him well at all. They merely hung on him."

Herb Miller could not furnish any information as to where his brother's last resting place was, though he offered the possibility that Miller had been buried in a mass grave somewhere in England. Herb said the story of a plane crash was fabricated so that Glenn could die a hero and not in a hospital bed.

THE FRIENDLY FIRE THEORY

In the mid-1980s, another theory surfaced, this one proposing that Miller's plane was downed by friendly fire. A navigator named Fred Shaw claimed that he was in the air on December 15, 1944, returning from an aborted bombing raid on Seigen in Germany. Because the squadron could not safely land with their huge load of bombs, the bombs had to be jettisoned over the English Channel. This was done in an area set aside for just this purpose, called the South Jettison Area, a ten-mile circle 50 miles south of Beachy Head, which was officially regarded as dangerous grounds to be avoided by all airplanes and ships.

"When the bombs were jettisoned from a safety height of 4000 feet," the BBC article says, "Shaw, who had never seen a bombing before, was driven by curiosity to look out the window. As the bombs exploded several feet above the surface of the sea, he saw a plane 2500 feet below, flying south."

Shaw would say years later that it was obvious the plane was in trouble, and so he watched intently to see what would happen.

"I saw it flick over to port in what looked like an incipient spin," he said, "and eventually I saw it disappear into the English Channel."

The bomb aimer had reported seeing the same thing moments before, and a rear gunner on Shaw's plane said over the intercom that "There's a kite just gone in down under."

Because they were technically not in enemy territory and the mission had already been reported, the men were not debriefed when they

MYSTERIOUS DISAPPEARANCES: THEY NEVER CAME BACK

landed and the downed plane remained unreported.

Shaw never made the connection between what he witnessed over the Channel that day and Miller's mysterious disappearance until 1956, when he saw the movie "The Glenn Miller Story." It would be another thirty years before he checked his old logbook and realized that the Norseman plane he saw plunge into the sea that day could have been Miller's.

When Shaw went public with his story, he was quickly dismissed as just another publicity seeker by many, but a later investigation by the British Defense Ministry's Air Historical Branch would lead to the conclusion that Shaw's version of events was not easily disproved. However, the disappearance of Glenn Miller remains officially unsolved.

MYSTERIOUS DISAPPEARANCES: THEY NEVER CAME BACK

PHILIP TAYLOR KRAMER

On February 12, 1996, Philip Taylor Kramer, at one time the bass player for the rock band Iron Butterfly (best known for their late 60s heavy metal hit, "In A Godda Da Vida), disappeared and has not been seen since.

In an online posting of an article from "Skeptic Magazine," author Frederic Rice presents a history of what is known about Kramer's disappearance.

Along with his skills as a musician, Kramer was also a scientist who claimed to have recently developed a form of faster-than-light communication. At the time of his disappearance, Ohio Representative James A. Traficant expressed public concern about Kramer's whereabouts because the ex-musician held nuclear-oriented security clearances tied to the MX Missile project as well as having conducted important mathematical research for the government.

Ron Bushy, one of the cofounders of Iron Butterfly, said that an Iron Butterfly reunion was in the works around the time of Kramer's disappearance. Bushy told the San Diego Union Tribune that, "I honestly believe that he has been abducted by our government or an agency that is part of it or maybe a foreign government or private company."

Bushy's remarks were prompted by the fact that just days before Kramer disappeared, he and his father believed they had worked out a mathematical breakthrough which would allow the nearly instantaneous transmission of matter and revolutionize the communications industry, technology similar to the "Beam me up, Scotty" device from the "Star Trek" television series.

THE EVENTS LEADING UP TO KRAMER'S VANISHING

Rice says there are conflicting reports about Kramer's final hours, but the scenario goes basically like this:

"Kramer either did or did not make an appointment to pick up an associate at the Los Angeles Airport, yet a $3 bill for 45 minutes of LAX parking was received by the Kramer residence ten days after his disappearance containing a receipt with Kramer's IOU written on it. Kramer, it seems, didn't have the cash on hand for parking, or, as it is considered by some, he didn't wish to waste $3 on parking knowing in advance that he was going to disappear. Being a computer executive, he would know how easily credit card and checking account transactions can be tracked

MYSTERIOUS DISAPPEARANCES: THEY NEVER CAME BACK

and, if one wishes to go underground, hanging on to three dollars when one can write an IOU instead makes good sense."

The article goes on to say that Kramer did not pick up his associate, and that something must have happened at the airport while he was waiting.

"Sometime during his wait," Rice writes, "something prompted him to simply walk back to his green van, leave an IOU for his 45 minutes of parking, then drive off into oblivion."

As he was driving away, Kramer called friends and family to express his love, then made one last call to 911, in which he said he intended to kill himself.

Rice speculates that if Kramer had been intent on making himself disappear, then planting the suggestion that he was going to kill himself would lead the investigators after the fact to assume that he had succeeded. It might also have been intended to help his wife financially in the aftermath, so that she would not have to wait several years before Kramer was declared legally dead.

There is general agreement that Kramer's mental stability was becoming questionable. Shortly before his disappearance, Kramer stated his belief that the Earth was going to end in a supernova; that his father, a Professor of Engineering at Youngstown University in Ohio, was really a god; and that his wife Jennifer was really Mother Earth. When house-hunting with his wife a few days earlier, he told her that he was frightened that someone would be coming for him.

Kramer had been becoming more involved in New Age mysticism, and was a genuine believer in the book "The Celestine Prophecy," about a middle-aged man who sets out to find the "nine insights" of life. After reading the book, Kramer asked his wife to eat only "the colors of the spectrum," and to refrain from eating meat or wearing black.

One theory kicked around by New Age believers is that Kramer's mathematical breakthrough that he and his father developed caused Kramer and his van to vibrate out of visibility, as happens in "The Celestine Prophecy." Meanwhile, Kramer's sister Kathy began to receive letters from self-professed psychics claiming to know the scientist's whereabouts.

"One such lead," Rice says, "which came through the mail, was from Austria, and it stated that her brother was the victim of an accident yet was alive and being worshipped as a deity among the Pechanga Indians on a reservation outside Los Angeles. Kathy Kramer went to talk with the tribe's council, yet they knew nothing about her missing brother."

When the aforementioned Representative James A. Traficant, Jr., twice called for an FBI investigation into Kramer's disappearance, the agency at first rejected the suggestion for an inquiry, but later reversed itself, admitting that, "It's a known fact that there are rogue nations like Iran working on nuclear weapons who could use someone with Philip Taylor Kramer's knowledge to make long-range missiles. Just because it's a remote possibility doesn't mean you shouldn't investigate it."

What is known for certain is that Philip Taylor Kramer obviously believed that his mathematical discovery was going to put his life and the lives of his family in danger. Whether he arranged his own disappearance or was abducted by aliens, a foreign government or a domestic agency that wished to exploit or suppress his scientific knowledge remains completely unknown.

AMELIA EARHART

Amelia Mary Earhart, the legendary pilot, was born on July 24, 1897, in Atchison, Kansas. While visiting the Iowa State Fair at age ten, she saw her first airplane, but was not much impressed.

"It was a thing of rusty wire and wood and not at all interesting," she would say later. It would be more than a decade before Earhart's interest in aviation would awaken.

According to a website devoted to Earhart (located at ellensplace.net), Amelia first took flight in 1920 at an "aerial meet" at Daugherty Field in Long Beach, California. Given a helmet and goggles, she boarded the open-cockpit biplane for a ten-minute flight over Los Angeles.

"As soon as we left the ground," she said, "I knew I myself had to fly!"

As her expertise as a pilot blossomed, she also developed a certain amount of celebrity. She would eventually fly solo from the Atlantic to the Pacific Coast in September of 1928, and worked to improve the image of aviation in general as well as to raise consciousness about female pilots. She soon became the first woman to fly solo across the Atlantic Ocean and the only person to fly it twice.

MYSTERIOUS DISAPPEARANCES: THEY NEVER CAME BACK

MYSTERIOUS DISAPPEARANCES: THEY NEVER CAME BACK

In 1935, Earhart began to work on plans for an around-the-world flight, which would accomplish two major firsts. Again, Earhart would be the first woman, and she would travel the longest possible distance, circumnavigating the globe at its waist. She would be accompanied by a navigator named Fredrick Noonan, and the first leg of the journey would be from Oakland to Hawaii on March 17, 1935. However, on takeoff from Luke Field near Pearl Harbor, she "overcompensated for a dropped right wing and the plane swung left out of control. The undercarriage collapsed and the aircraft slid along the runway on its belly." The plane was damaged, and had to be sent off for repair.

AMELIA'S LAST FLIGHT

After the plane was repaired and rebuilt, Amelia again attempted to fly around the world, departing from Miami, Florida, on June 1, 1937, and headed toward San Juan, Puerto Rico. From there to the northeast edge of South America before flying to Africa and the Red Sea.

Later stops included Calcutta, Bangkok, and Singapore. During this time, Earhart became sick with dysentery, which lasted several days. By June 29, she and Noonan had reached New Guinea. At this point, they had flown 22,000 miles and had 7,000 more to go, all of which were over the Pacific. Photos taken at the time show Earhart as looking very tired and still quite sick.

Earhart departed New Guinea at precisely 00:00 hours Greenwich Mean Time on July 2. It is believed that her plane was loaded with 1,000 gallons of fuel, enough for 20 or so hours of flying. At 07:20 hours GMT, Earhart radioed her position to the U.S. Coast Guard Cutter Itasca, which had been standing off Howland Island in order to provide radio contact for Earhart. At 08:00 GMT, she reported being on course for Howland Island and flying at 12,000 feet.

"No one saw or heard the plane fly over," the website states. "Several short transmissions were received by the Itasca with varying signal strengths, but they were unable to get a fix on her location because they were too brief."

At 19:30 GMT, Earhart radioed that, "We must be on you, but cannot see you. Gas is running low." At 20:14 GMT, Earhart's last voice transmission was an attempt to give positioning data. The ship continued to transmit on all frequencies until 21:30 hours GMT, when they concluded that Earhart must have ditched at sea and began to implement search procedures.

MYSTERIOUS DISAPPEARANCES: THEY NEVER CAME BACK

"It had been determined that the plane went down some 35 to 100 miles off the coast of Howland Island. A life raft was stored on board, but no trace has ever been found of it. Some experts felt that the empty fuel tanks could keep the plane afloat for a period of time."

President Franklin Delano Roosevelt authorized a search by nine naval ships and sixty-six aircraft at an estimated cost of over $4 million. The search was abandoned on July 18, having turned up absolutely nothing.

"Over the years," the website states, "many unconfirmed sightings have been reported and many theories abound. Among those theories: Amelia was on a spy mission authorized by President Roosevelt and was captured; she purposely dove her plane into the Pacific; she was captured by the Japanese and forced to broadcast to American GI's as 'Tokyo Rose' during World War II; or that she lived for years on an island in the South Pacific with a native fisherman. In 1961, it was thought that the bones of Amelia and Noonan had been found on Saipan, but they turned out to be those of Saipan natives."

But the search continues. An organization called The International Group for Historic Aircraft Recovery launched an investigation in 1988 to conclusively solve the mystery of Amelia Earhart's disappearance. The group has conducted four archeological expeditions to a remote, uninhabited Pacific atoll which have turned up what they believe is physical evidence that the Earhart flight may have landed there on July 2, 1937, after failing to find Howland Island.

MICHAEL ROCKEFELLER

Michael Rockefeller was the son of Nelson Rockefeller, one of the wealthiest and most powerful men in the United States. Michael had rejected the idea of following in his father's footsteps as a businessman and politician in favor of a life as an adventurer, and in 1961, the young man of 23 journeyed to New Guinea as part of a Harvard University expedition that sought to collect examples of native art.

Among the peoples of New Guinea are a group of primitives called the Asmat, who live in dense jungle conditions and have very limited contact with the outside world. They were said to have extreme warlike tendencies and in the past had been headhunters, though whether that was still true was uncertain.

MYSTERIOUS DISAPPEARANCES: THEY NEVER CAME BACK

Michael was an experienced outdoorsman, according to Daniel Cohen's book, "Missing! Stories of Strange Disappearances." But he was also known for taking chances, such as his decision to cruise the New Guinea coast in a less than sturdy boat, in spite of warnings that it was too fragile for the job. On the morning of November 16, 1961, Michael set off for the village of Atsj, accompanied by a Dutch scientist named Rene Wassing and two Asmat native helpers. Around noon, a large wave hit the boat, drowning the motor and setting the boat adrift. The two Asmats decided to swim to shore, while Michael and Wassing stayed with the boat. They tried for a day and a night to get the boat working again, to no avail.

The boat drifted out to sea until it was three miles from the coast. Michael assumed the Asmat natives had abandoned them, but they had instead contacted local authorities that were in fact sending help. Unaware that rescuers were on their way, Michael became impatient and decided to swim ashore. He made a float out of an empty gas can and began what should have been for him an easy three-mile swim. Wassing warned him about the sharks and crocodiles infesting the waters, but Michael dove in anyway. Wassing was the last person to see Michael Rockefeller alive.

Wassing was picked up a short time later by a rescue seaplane. When he inquired as to Michael's whereabouts, the pilots said they had not seen or heard anything. Word of the young man's disappearance spread quickly, and his father Nelson Rockefeller, at the time the Governor of New York, chartered a plane for New Guinea to search for his son. The massive effort included helicopters scanning the jungles and searchers on the ground visiting Asmat villages, with a reward offered for any information about the missing man. Finally, Nelson Rockefeller called a press conference in which he said he no longer expected to find his son alive, then flew back to New York.

POSSIBLE EXPLANATIONS

Although interest in the case soon subsided, a local New Guinea doctor named Ary Kemper expressed his doubts that Michael had simply been attacked by sharks or crocodiles.

"That young man was a powerful swimmer," the doctor is quoted as saying by Cohen, "and with those floats on his back he could not have drowned."

Dr. Kemper also said that in all his years in New Guinea he had

MYSTERIOUS DISAPPEARANCES: THEY NEVER CAME BACK

never heard of a single person being attacked by sharks or crocodiles and that the sea creatures at least along that particular coastline did not seem to be man-eaters. Kemper's own theory was that Michael had reached the shore and then been murdered by Asmat warriors.

Meanwhile the local government continued to state their belief that Michael had drowned, and seemed to be motivated to protect the local natives from criminal charges and a possibly very embarrassing trial. And why would the natives have killed Michael to begin with? Did he offend them somehow, being both a white man and a stranger?

Rumors continued for some time afterwards, including a story told by someone claiming to have seen Michael's skull being carried by an Asmat warrior, and another claimed to have seen an Asmat wearing Michael's shorts. Still another rumor was that Michael had not been killed but was instead being held prisoner by the Asmats.

In 1967, an admitted smuggler named John Donahue told a leading New York magazine that he had met a white man on a small island near New Guinea who had a long sandy beard and was partly crippled. The man told Donahue that he was Michael Rockefeller and that he had successfully swum ashore that day in 1961 but had broken both of his legs in the jungle and had never healed properly. The natives had considered him to be some sort of magician or sorcerer and had held him captive as a kind of good luck charm. Donahue said he didn't tell his story to the local authorities in New Guinea, as that would have entailed admitting he was a smuggler, so he waited until he reached America where he could relate the events safe from criminal prosecution. The location of the island and its inhabitants could not be verified when the magazine tried to check Donahue's story out.

A journalist named John Godwin said that in December of 1972, an Australian sailor claimed to have met Michael Rockefeller the previous month when he visited the Asmat region where the young man had reportedly last been seen. "He had straight blond hair and a big straggly beard. The Asmats can't grow beards. He was taller than the rest." According to the sailor, this white man made no attempt to speak to him, and when the group turned to go, the white man went with them. The sailor tried to follow them, but some of the natives raised their spears and he thought better of it.

When the sailor returned to Australia, he looked up old newspaper stories with pictures of Rockefeller. He said that if he hadn't seen Michael himself, then he had seen his double. Godwin, the journalist,

MYSTERIOUS DISAPPEARANCES: THEY NEVER CAME BACK

upon hearing the sailor's tale, wondered if Michael Rockefeller was not simply a captive but rather had willingly abandoned his wealth and civilization and freely chosen to live among the Asmats.

In any case, more than forty years later, the whereabouts of Michael Rockefeller are still unknown.

MYSTERIOUS DISAPPEARANCES: THEY NEVER CAME BACK

CHAPTER FOUR

NO EXPLANATION! VANISHED WITHOUT A TRACE!

Researcher and author Troy Taylor has written extensively about ghosts, but he also has an interest in tales of mysterious disappearances.

"That's always been a fascination of mine," Taylor said, "as far as people who just walked away one time and never came back."

Taylor said he came to his current field of research in an unusual way—without any paranormal experiences of his own.

"Everybody thinks that because I do this for a living," Taylor said, "that there must have been some sort of revelatory experience, like my Mom died and came back to haunt me or something like that. But really it was just something I was interested in my entire life. And now it's my day job."

Taylor conducts guided tours of haunted locations on his home turf in Illinois, and has published several books, including *The Ghost Hunter's Handbook* and *Haunted Illinois*.

In an interview conducted exclusively for this book, Taylor related many stories of mysterious disappearances, both paranormal and prosaic.

STRANGE EVENTS IN VERMONT

"Off the top of my head," Taylor began, "there are a few stories that have really gotten to me more than others. Probably the number one story would be not about a particular person, but more about a place, I guess you would say.

"It's the stories you hear about the Long Trail in the Green Moun-

MYSTERIOUS DISAPPEARANCES: THEY NEVER CAME BACK

tains in Vermont," he continued. "For some reason, there has been a rash of disappearances that have taken place there, starting around 1945. This is an outdoor area, and obviously it's a rough area. But we're talking about Vermont, which is not that big of a state, and even in this modern day, people have disappeared out there who shouldn't have."

The first in the series of disappearances in the Green Mountains involved an older man who worked as a hunting and fishing guide. He had lived in the area for many years and was extremely experienced with being in the wild.

"He went out one day with a group of hunters into the woods," Taylor said. "He got just a little bit ahead of them on the path, then he turned a corner in the trail and vanished. They looked for him everywhere and couldn't find him. The state police came, the National Guard, Boy Scouts, local residents—they combed the woods for hours and never saw him again. That was in November of 1945."

A year later, a young woman enrolled at Bennington College went out for a walk.

"Although, oddly, in very cold, bad weather," Taylor said, "in early December of 1946. She started up the Long Trail and just vanished. She was last seen around 5 P.M. and just never came back. Nobody was able to explain it. Her parents were pretty prominent people, and had a lot of money to put behind an investigation. The police came in, but it was the same situation as before."

The search included bloodhounds and helicopters, and several hundred volunteers, but absolutely no trace of the young woman was ever found. Three years later, in December of 1949, another man disappeared.

"He was on a bus," Taylor said, "and got off the bus near the trail. He started walking and was never seen again. The next one took place in 1950. A little boy disappeared from a town dump near where the trail ran, never seen again. Two weeks later, another woman disappeared. She was actually an outdoorswoman who had lived in the area her entire life. She had taken a group out hiking and just disappeared. And again it was a case of nobody knew why."

Taylor said that hindsight might provide a possible explanation.

"To look at it now," he said, "we kind of have to wonder. You're talking about a different time there, the late 40s and early 50s, when

MYSTERIOUS DISAPPEARANCES: THEY NEVER CAME BACK

people hadn't yet used a term like 'serial killer.' And you've kind of got to wonder if maybe there wasn't one operating in the area that was responsible for these disappearances. But if that's the case, no evidence that there was any other person involved ever came to light. The disappearances just sort of stopped and to this day remain unsolved. No clues have ever, ever been found about any of the people who vanished."

HONEYMOONERS GONE MISSING

"Another favorite story of mine would have to be the one about Glenn and Bessie Hyde," Taylor said, "who vanished into the Grand Canyon. Now the Grand Canyon has certainly seen its share of problems over the years anyway, in terms of people trying to run the river and that sort of thing and just never coming back."

Glenn and Bessie were newlyweds who in the late 1920s decided to take a rafting trip in the Grand Canyon area as part of their honeymoon.

"They started downstream in what seemed to be a reliable craft," Taylor said, "and they seemed to know what they were doing."

Brothers Emory and Ellsworth Cole, a pair of photographers/writers, lived in the Canyon and operated a kind of trail guide system, according to Taylor. They were the last to see the young couple alive.

"They said the honeymooners seemed to be competent as far as navigating the raft, but that Bessie was very hesitant about the fact that they were going to make this voyage downriver. And again they just disappeared. People searched for them for years, and no trace of them ever turned up. I know it's a rough area and it can be a dangerous area, but it just seemed like somebody should have spotted something and nobody ever did."

PULLING A CRATER

Taylor also talked about the case of Judge Joseph Crater, who disappeared one August night in 1930.

"This was a case that got major headlines at the time," Taylor said. "He was last seen just walking out of a restaurant one evening. He was recognizable, and people remembered him. They knew him for who he was. He'd been a very successful man, president of the Democratic Party, appointed to the New York State Supreme Court.

"And although he had recently withdrawn about $20,000 from the

MYSTERIOUS DISAPPEARANCES: THEY NEVER CAME BACK

bank, he didn't have any money troubles. He seemed to be happy in his private life."

While vacationing with his wife in Maine that summer of 1930, Crater received a mysterious phone call asking him to return to New York, which he did. He was known to have visited his office that day and rifled through some of his files.

"I guess there were some issues," Taylor said, "but no one seems to know exactly what they were. He went off that evening to see a play. He had dinner and was in a good mood, sitting around with friends and talking. He left the restaurant around nine o'clock, waved goodbye to his friends, got into a taxi that he'd called and that was it. They never saw him again."

The long hunt for Judge Crater began.

"Obviously, the police searched," Taylor said, "the authorities searched for him for a long time. The entire nation was kind of captivated by the whole thing. The grand jury that looked into the case ended up calling around 95 witnesses, and there were a thousand pages of testimony about his disappearance.

"Most people thought he dodged out of something, as far as business or political dealings. For a long time, as a slang term for ducking out on your responsibilities, people would say that 'You pulled a Crater.'"

Crater was declared dead in 1939, but sightings of him continued, nonetheless. He was supposedly seen in Canada, Europe and the Caribbean.

"But nobody could ever prove that he was actually there," Taylor said, "and that was pretty much the end of it."

THE BEAUTIFUL SOCIALITE

The 1910 disappearance of socialite Dorothy Arnold is another case that interests Taylor.

"You look at photographs of her," Taylor said, "and she's an absolutely just beautiful young girl. And it was a case where she had everything going for her. She had all the money you could ask for, an upscale family. She was a graduate of Bryn Mawr. She went out shopping one afternoon in Manhattan in December of 1910 and was never seen again.

"When she left her house," he continued, "she stopped and talked

MYSTERIOUS DISAPPEARANCES: THEY NEVER CAME BACK

to a lot of people who knew her. Clerks remembered seeing her throughout the day. Then that was it. She just never came home."

Arnold's family did not immediately report her absence.

"As everybody always says, the rich are a different kind of animal, I guess," Taylor said. "Her parents and her family kept the entire thing secret. They didn't call the police and didn't tell anybody that she'd disappeared. They called in the Pinkerton Detective Agency, and spent thousands of dollars but never found anything."

The Arnold family employed an attorney who used to appear from time to time with Dorothy on his arm.

"He used to take her to a lot of functions and social events," Taylor said. "He spent thousands of dollars of his own money. He searched hospitals, morgues, jails, all over the East Coast, thinking that maybe she had amnesia or something. Some people thought she might have been attacked in Central Park and her body thrown in the river. When they finally called the police in, the river was dragged."

A man whose attentions Dorothy had refused was considered a suspect for a time.

"He had been what we would call a 'stalker' today," Taylor said. "They thought that maybe he was involved, but he had an alibi. When the story made the newspapers, because the family was very well known, sightings came in from all over the country. Literally hundreds of thousands of dollars were spent, and that's in 1910 dollars, trying to find her. Her father died in 1922, heartbroken, and never ever was there any trace of Dorothy Arnold."

FACT AND FICTION BLEND

What about disappearance stories with paranormal overtones?

"Some of the best ones," Taylor answered, "cases where a lot of people have been quoting them for years, turned out to be the work of Ambrose Bierce. Like the Oliver Larch story and the story about the kids that go out to the well one day, leaving a trail of footprints, and just vanish. People go out and look in the snow where the footprints were and find the footprints simply came to an end. Sometimes the story goes on to say that they heard voices coming out from the fields or from the sky and they find there's nobody there.

"I've seen a couple of versions of that story and it actually turns

MYSTERIOUS DISAPPEARANCES: THEY NEVER CAME BACK

out that those were little pieces of fiction that Ambrose Bierce wrote about and a lot of people took them as fact. But interestingly, though, he wrote those stories about people who just disappear without a trace based on a true story that happened in 1854."

Taylor next related his version of the story of a farmer named Orion Williamson, who lived in Selma, Alabama. (See Chapter Nine.)

"One day Williamson was sitting on his front porch," Taylor said. "It was a hot day. He sat with his wife and child drinking lemonade. A passing carriage went by, a neighbor of his, and waved. Williamson next got up and walked out into an open field, just a grassy field, toward the carriage. As he got halfway across the field, he just vanished. I mean literally vanished into thin air. His wife saw it, the child saw it, and the two neighbors saw it. They were just completely stunned."

They searched the area and found nothing but open ground.

"They called the authorities," Taylor continued, "and they had 300 volunteers who came out from Selma to help look. They went all over the field. They lined up, holding hands, walking across the field a step at a time. They searched for caves and openings and holes dozens of times. Night finally fell and the next day they brought in a couple of hundred more volunteers, along with a group of geologists who came in searching for any kind of cave-ins or crevices or holes, but they found not a single trace of Williamson."

Then, to ratchet up the spookiness still more, Williamson's wife found something strange in the field the following spring.

"According to the story," Taylor said, "his wife said that there was an odd circle of dead grass that formed in the field in the exact same spot where he'd disappeared. And apparently she was so traumatized by the event that she didn't tell anybody for quite some time that in the months that followed her husband's disappearance, she would sometimes hear his voice calling to her from in the dark at night.

"Now whether or not she imagined it, as far as the voice goes, we'll probably never know. But in front of those witnesses, this guy just simply walked across the field and disappeared."

THE APPEAL OF THE UNKNOWN

What is it that keeps us so fascinated by these cases of mysterious disappearance?

MYSTERIOUS DISAPPEARANCES: THEY NEVER CAME BACK

"This stuff is so interesting," Taylor said, "because it is unsolved. I've written about the Jimmy Hoffa case, for instance, with the idea of 'nobody knows,' that kind of thing. I wish I had some other theory. Obviously, in Hoffa's case, there's a guy who definitely crossed the wrong people. People make jokes about it. Just recently they dug up a football field in Michigan thinking that they'd finally found Jimmy Hoffa. But I imagine he's other buried somewhere where we're never going to find him or he's in such small pieces that they'll never be put back together again. That's a classic case of messing with the wrong people.

"But again I think that the reason that we have such a fascination with this stuff is because they are unsolved. I think it's the reason why, after 120 years, we're still talking about Jack the Ripper, because we don't know. We don't know who he was, and at this point it's unlikely that we'll ever find out. Most of these people who disappear are gone for good. We'll never find out what happened to them.

"But people love a mystery," he said.

There are thousands of people listed as missing every year throughout the United States. While most of them turn up later, there are still many cases where they do not. Where did those other people go?

"We think that because it's the 21st century," Taylor said, "that we've charted all there is to chart in our country and in the world, and there's no place left to go. There are no more final frontiers. But I think, when it comes to disappearances, that unfortunately most of those people meet an untimely and usually murderous end. I think there are a lot more places to hide bodies than we think there are in these modern times.

"And I think a lot of people walk away on their own. And again, it gets into the same thing. We think because it's the 21st Century that we've got it all down and we can find anybody, but that's not the case. People walk away all the time, and vanish completely without a trace, and start over again as somebody else or someplace else, and I think that accounts for a lot of the unsolved disappearances. But I think unfortunately most of them meet bad ends. I think there are a lot more killers out there than we like to think, which is not something that helps people sleep at night, probably."

While Taylor's theory is but one among countless others, it remains a very real though unhappy possibility.

MYSTERIOUS DISAPPEARANCES: THEY NEVER CAME BACK

CHAPTER FIVE

THE *OTHER* TRIANGLES

The Bermuda Triangle is easily the most famous "triangle area" known for the mysterious disappearances of ships and planes, but the reader may be less familiar with a pair of triangles in far divergent parts of the world that have also swallowed up pilots, sailors and the occasional hiker.

THE BENNINGTON TRIANGLE

While some of this material was presented in the previous chapter, as told by Troy Taylor, there are significant details not included in Taylor's treatment of the subject. The area in the Green Mountains of Vermont that Taylor described has also been called the Bennington Triangle, a term first coined by New England author Joseph A. Citro during a 1992 radio broadcast in which he talked about the weird events there. Citro marked the area in southwestern Vermont as centering around Glastenbury Mountain and extending to include most of the towns surrounding it, such as Bennington, Woodford, Shaftsbury and Somerset. The area once contained moderately thriving logging and industrial areas, which began declining toward the late 19th Century, leaving Glastenbury and Somerset essentially ghost towns now.

Citro wrote a series of books on the area, which told of strange events happening prior to the 1940s, when the rash of disappearances was first said to have begun. Other sources confirm that there are bizarre stories and folklore about the region dating back to the late 19th century. For example, there was a local folk belief that Native Ameri-

MYSTERIOUS DISAPPEARANCES: THEY NEVER CAME BACK

cans regarded Glastenbury as cursed and took great pains to avoid it. There were also frequent sightings of hairy "wild men" and other weird creatures in the woods there.

A Wikipedia entry on the subject of the Bennington Triangle lists the same five disappearances that Taylor touched on, but adds an interesting detail. Of all the missing people, the remains of only the last to vanish were ever found—that of 53-year-old Frieda Langer, who was an experienced woodswoman and gun-handler.

"Most sources on the subject view the circumstances as mysterious," the Wikipedia entry says, "as her body turned up in some tall grasses in an area that had been searched extensively a number of times in the seven months between her disappearance and the discovery of the corpse, making it unlikely that the search teams had simply missed her."

However, the Wikipedia writer differs from Taylor's belief that a serial killer may have been responsible for the disappearances, since the victims varied widely in age and were both male and female, none of which conforms to the usual limited choice of victims-types found in most serial killing cases.

"This, combined with a lack of any evidence to offer support for any more prosaic explanation, has led many to speculate on possible paranormal causes, including abduction by UFO occupants, 'inter-dimensional trapdoors,' or attack by the 'Bennington Monster,'" the Wikipedia entry says.

MORE ON THE BENNINGTON MONSTER

In a blog entitled "The Beast of Bennington," writer Joe Durwin provides some background on just what the Bennington Monster is alleged to be. Incidents as recent as September of 2003 are recounted in the blog, one of which involved the experience of a writer visiting from San Francisco as he drove along Route 7 in the Bennington area.

On Tuesday, September 16, Doug Dorst, was headed south on Route 7 on his way to deliver a lecture at Bennington College. Near the highest elevation point, east of Glastenbury, he watched a large figure cross the road ahead of him. Dorst described the creature as being covered in dark hair, with a lighter brown face.

The same creature was seen eight days later along the same exact stretch of road, this time by at least three people, including a man named

MYSTERIOUS DISAPPEARANCES: THEY NEVER CAME BACK

Ray Dufresne, who saw it walking off to the east, away from the highway and into the woods. Though he was 140 feet away from the mysterious interloper, he estimated that the creature was over six feet tall, around 270 pounds, covered in dark hair with long ape-like arms. Two Bennington women reported driving past the same creature a minute or so before Dufresne. Their descriptions were basically the same as the two men's, but they added the detail that the creature appeared to have a tail.

All three insisted that what they saw was not a bear, but that was exactly what a wildlife official declared it to be to the local media, in the standard form of denial of those whose job it is to debunk this sort of thing. The possibility that a hoax was responsible was also considered, though a man known locally as a prankster denied any involvement and stated that he had never owned an ape suit.

According to Durwin, sightings of such creatures in the Vermont area go back to the early 1600s, when Native Americans told of a bear-like monster that walked like a man. Early settlers in the northern part of the state called it "Slippery Skin," because it evaded all their attempts to capture it. In 1815, Marion Daley, a local historian wrote that, "He was a mean animal, and evidently had a grudge against humans. He destroyed their fences, ripped up their gardens, frightened cows and sheep, tromped through corn fields and caused no end of mayhem."

Sightings of Sasquatch-like creatures in the Bennington area go back to the 19th century. There is even a New York Times article from 1879 that refers to an old story about hair-covered, man-like creatures seen frequently along the southern part of the Green Mountain area. Another 19th century story tells of a stagecoach traversing what was at the time the Glastenbury plank road.

"It was a stormy night," Durwin writes, "and the road was full of washouts. On the last part of the trip, the driver started having trouble controlling the horses. They lurched and bucked frantically, then stopped altogether. Figuring that a bobcat might be around, the driver grabbed his gun and hopped down. As he did, he looked down to behold a series of enormous tracks, unlike those of any animal he knew. He called out to the passengers, and as they disembarked, the horses went into a completely frenzied state. Suddenly, something slammed into the coach, toppling it. An enormous creature with 'great glinting eyes' stared at them, then, with a deafening roar, tromped back into the woods."

Durwin concludes by saying that sightings of something strange

MYSTERIOUS DISAPPEARANCES: THEY NEVER CAME BACK

and hairy in the Bennington Triangle area continue to this present day with no completely satisfactory explanation. Is an apelike "monster" the culprit in the Bennington Triangle disappearances?

THE DRAGON'S TRIANGLE

On nearly the exact opposite side of the planet from the Bermuda Triangle, in the Pacific Ocean, lies what has come to be called the Dragon's Triangle. The Japanese call it the Ma-no Umi, or the Sea of the Devil. The area has been designated as a Danger Zone by the Japanese government, and even the United States Air Force has expressed concern over aircraft disappearances there.

In an online posting located at everything2.com, and credited to a person called only "Corwin," the Dragon's Triangle in the Western Pacific indeed forms a generally triangular pattern. It follows a line from western Japan north of Tokyo to a point in the Pacific at approximately latitude 145 degrees east. It then turns west-southwest past the Bonin Islands, then down to Guam and Yap, west to Taiwan and finally returns north-northeast back to Japan.

Corwin mainly relies on material published by linguist and author Charles Berlitz in his 1989 book "The Dragon's Triangle." Berlitz begins by describing the area in general terms and noting some of the strange phenomena found there, including mysterious lights, unexplained disappearances, sudden fogs and storms, and so on.

Berlitz makes the obvious comparison between the anomalous Pacific area and the Bermuda Triangle on the opposite side of the world, pointing out that both areas are located on the eastern edges of continental shelves, where the ocean floor drops off into deep trenches and strong currents sweep over actively volcanic areas. Both spots also mark nodal points where major surface and tidal currents turn, usually in opposite directions. Berlitz says that since both the triangles share those characteristics, the disappearances of planes and ships in the two areas may be more than coincidental.

In the next section of Berlitz's book, he details some of the craft that have disappeared in the Dragon's Triangle. In most cases, no wreckage, oil slicks or flotsam was ever found to indicate a sinking. The missing craft included tankers weighing over 200,000 tons, Japanese and American warships, airplanes (including one that was carrying an early version of the atomic bomb), and Soviet nuclear missile submarines. Some of these ships later turned up as ghost vessels, with no crew on

MYSTERIOUS DISAPPEARANCES: THEY NEVER CAME BACK

board, but most of them vanished completely and without a trace.

Berlitz also speculates that aviator Amelia Earhart may have been a victim of the Dragon's Triangle, saying that Earhart had perhaps deviated from her established flight plan and flown north, at the request of the U.S. government, to spy on Japanese islands in the area. Evidence he sites includes a transmission from Earhart about bad weather, though her intended flight path was clear all the way. There was also a report that the Marines, soon after capturing the island of Saipan, secretly disinterred the bodies of Earhart and her navigator Fred Noonan and transported them back to America.

In a short article called "The Dragon's Triangle," and posted on Mystery Magazine's website, writer Ade Dimmick, discusses the idea that strange events in the area may be due to an ever-changing seascape. "Islands and land masses have formed and disappeared literally overnight," Dimmick writes, "through volcanic activity and seaquakes. Records of islands were charted by experienced navigators and documented as having been visited; yet years later no trace of these places could be found!"

LEGENDS AND PARANORMAL EXPLANATIONS

Dimmick also recounts legends more than a thousand years old in which the Japanese tell of restless dragons surfacing from the depths and taking unfortunate mariners back to their underground lairs. Other legends report underwater places inhabited by dragons and of a great "slumbering dragon" that haunted the region.

"However, it wasn't until the late 1960s that western attention was drawn to this eastern phenomenon," Dimmick writes, "and connections made to the Bermuda Triangle. Despite frequent coverage in the Japanese media of disappearances, reports rarely made the international press. Language barriers and racist attitudes may have had a lot to do with this. One wonders how well known the Bermuda Triangle might have been if it wasn't situated off the coast of the United States?"

Dimmick continues by saying that in ancient times such happenings were explained by the interventions of gods, demons and mythical creatures, whereas today the mystery might be explained as alien abduction, or even as a kind of disappearance into a "black hole," or a gateway into another dimension, time or parallel universe. It could also be a manifestation of human covert military or scientific experimentation, or abduction by "unfriendly forces." Even an elaborate game of

MYSTERIOUS DISAPPEARANCES: THEY NEVER CAME BACK

insurance fraud has been suggested, in which a ship is actually taken to some "rust-bucket" shipyard but is reported as missing in the triangle.

In any case, the Bennington and Dragon's Triangles continue to elude any final explanation for the mysterious disappearances that have taken place there.

MYSTERIOUS DISAPPEARANCES: THEY NEVER CAME BACK

CHAPTER SIX
FROM HEAVEN TO EARTH—NONE CAME BACK

British researcher and author Brian Haughton brings a unique combination of two very different disciplines to bear on his work. He is both an archeologist and an unabashed researcher of "fringe" subjects, to include mysterious disappearances. Haughton presents a great deal of his impressive research in a book called ***"Hidden History: Lost Civilizations, Secret Knowledge and Ancient Mysteries,"*** published in 2007 by New Page Books, as well as on his website at mysteriouspeople.com

Haughton gave an exclusive interview for this book in which he talked about such strange instances of disappearance as Flight 19 of Bermuda Triangle fame and the ghost ship the *Mary Celeste*.

"Mysterious disappearances have a profound hold on the imagination," Haughton said. "Occurring without apparent reason or cause, these unexplained vanishings can involve people, animals, ships and airplanes. Some researchers, such as John Keel and Nandor Fodor, have suggested possible paranormal explanations for these cases, while others believe the vast majority are the result of hoaxes or incomplete research. If the latter is true, how many infamous cases are genuinely mysterious? Are there tall tales lurking amongst actual accounts of real events?"

ARE UFOs THE CULPRIT?

Haughton said that there are a number of unexplained disappearances connected with the UFO phenomenon.

"One of the most mysterious of these," he said, "occurred over Lake Superior, on the American-Canadian border, on the night of No-

MYSTERIOUS DISAPPEARANCES: THEY NEVER CAME BACK

vember 23, 1953. Lieutenant Felix Moncla, Jr. and Lieutenant Robert L. Wilson had been sent up from Kinross Air Force Base in their Northrup F-89C jet aircraft to identify an unidentified craft that had been tracked on Air Defense Command Ground Intercept radar at Truax Air Force Base. Moncla pursued the object, which had been flying over restricted airspace at the Soo Locks, for about half an hour, flying at 30,000 feet over the middle of Lake Superior."

As the ground control radar operator was tracking both objects, he noticed that the images on the radar screen were extremely close to each other.

"Then the unidentified object suddenly reversed its course," Haughton said, "and the two objects appeared to merge into one. The radar operator was stunned. The unidentified blip remained on the screen for a few moments before it flew off north and disappeared from the radar, leaving the screen empty. Where was Moncla's plane?"

Attempts to contact Moncla on his radio failed. A search and rescue operation was mounted as quickly as possible but proved fruitless and no trace was ever discovered of the crewmembers, the F-89C, or the unknown machine. In 2006, a company called the Great Lakes Dive Company claimed to have located an F-89C on the bottom of Lake Superior in roughly the same area as Moncla's last known position.

"However, investigations into this claim have revealed that it was probably a hoax," Haughton said.

Haughton also commented on the case of Australian pilot Frederick Valentich (which is also discussed in chapter nine of this book), saying it is perhaps the best known of the stories of UFO-related disappearances.

The 20-year-old Valentich took off on October 21, 1978, at 1819 hours, from Moorabin Airport in Melbourne, in his freshly refueled single-engine Cessna 182, heading for King Island, located in the Bass Strait between Victoria and Tasmania.

"Visibility was clear during the flight," Haughton recounted, "and at 1906 hours, Valentich contacted Melbourne Flight Station and reported he was being followed by an unknown aircraft."

During the next six minutes, Valentich described the object as being "a long shape with a green light and sort of metallic-like . . . it's all shiny on the outside." His last transmission at 1912 hours was that "a strange aircraft is hovering on top of me again . . . it is hovering and it's

MYSTERIOUS DISAPPEARANCES: THEY NEVER CAME BACK

not an aircraft." The microphone remained open for another 17 seconds, during which time several "metallic, scraping sounds" were heard before the signal was lost.

"No further transmissions were received," Haughton said, "and despite a full-scale search and rescue operation, nothing more was ever heard of Frederick Valentich or his Cessna 182. Reports from witnesses on the ground at the time of Valentich's disappearance, who saw the Cessna accompanied by a large green unidentified flying object, support the fact that something seems to have forced Valentich's plane down, probably into the Bass Strait, where it presumably still lies.

"In a desperate effort to ignore the UFO-related aspects of this case," Haughton continued, "some researchers have come up with explanations more bizarre than any 'extraterrestrial' theory. These include that Valentich stumbled upon a drug smuggling operation—presumably the drug smugglers were in possession of highly advanced technology—or that he was struck by lightning from a lenticular cloud, or that he was so disoriented that he was flying upside-down, and mistook lighthouse lights for a strange aircraft.

"Vanishings involving UFOs," he went on, "are perhaps the most fascinating and unexplainable of all disappearance cases, particularly as there are often eye witness reports and radar evidence for the incidents, and no question that something out of the ordinary occurred."

DISAPPEARING PLANES AND SHIPS

No book on mysterious disappearances would be complete without some mention of the Bermuda Triangle, an area in the Atlantic Ocean roughly bounded by Miami, Bermuda and Puerto Rico. Haughton talked about two particular incidents among numerous others.

"The most famous vanishing within the Bermuda Triangle," Haughton said, "occurred on December 5, 1945. At around 2:10 in the morning, Flight 19—consisting of five TBM Avenger Torpedo Bombers carrying 14 men, took off from the U.S. Naval Air Station in Fort Lauderdale, Florida. Led by instructor Lieutenant Charles Taylor, they headed out over the Atlantic on the first leg of a routine navigational training mission, but soon became hopelessly lost as the weather rapidly deteriorated."

Apparently, both of the compasses on Taylor's plane were malfunctioning, and he decided that as soon as the first plane's fuel level dropped below ten gallons, all five planes would ditch into the sea.

MYSTERIOUS DISAPPEARANCES: THEY NEVER CAME BACK

"Attempts to contact Flight 19 by radio failed," Haughton said, "and two rescue airplanes were sent out to search for the lost flight. But the five Avenger aircraft were never found. During the rescue mission, one of the seaplanes also disappeared, never to be heard from again."

According to Haughton, while some have suggested supernatural elements were involved in the disappearance of Flight 19, the most widely accepted explanation is that a combination of malfunctioning compasses, inexperienced pilots and adverse weather conditions were responsible for the disappearance.

Another incidence of a lost plane in the Bermuda Triangle occurred on Halloween Day, 1991, when John Verdi and his copilot Paul Lukaris were flying a Grumman Cougar jet toward Tallahassee. They were in radio contact with the flight center and were being tracked on radar.

"All of a sudden," Haughton said, "the radar signal faded from the screen. The Cougar and its two-man crew had disappeared, never to be seen again."

Haughton also told the story of a navy coal ship called the *"USS Cyclops"* which had set out from Rio de Janeiro on March 4, 1918. The ship was headed for Baltimore when it disappeared with all 306 crew and passengers without a trace.

"A detailed search was undertaken," Haughton said, "but nothing was ever discovered and the cause of her loss remains unknown.

"Around 1700 ships and planes," he continued, "have apparently been lost within the area of the Bermuda triangle. Although the majority of those losses have been explained, that still seems an inordinately high amount of disappearances. Popular theories put forth to account for the Bermuda Triangle vanishings include a death-ray from Atlantis, abduction by UFOs, a parallel dimension and giant sea monsters. Some of the more orthodox explanations are freak waves caused by underwater earthquakes, hurricanes, human error, piracy and equipment malfunction."

A recent explanation blames periodic eruptions of methane hydrate, which would apparently cause ships to suddenly plunge to the bottom of the Atlantic. However, this theory is not widely accepted.

"Distressingly," Haughton said, "disappearances are continuing in the Bermuda Triangle and until there is a scientific expedition launched to investigate the area, we will never know the truth of the matter."

MYSTERIOUS DISAPPEARANCES: THEY NEVER CAME BACK

THE MARY CELESTE

"One of the most intriguing of all disappearances," Haughton said, "and certainly the most interesting sea mystery, is that of the *Mary Celeste*. The *Mary Celeste* was a brigantine, which set sail from New York Harbor for Genoa, Italy, on November 7, 1872, carrying a cargo of 1701 barrels of industrial alcohol. The ship was under the command of Captain Benjamin Briggs, who was accompanied by his wife Sarah, two-year-old daughter Sophia Matilda, and seven crew members."

Which sets the stage for what happened next.

"On December 4, the *Mary Celeste* was sighted by a vessel called the *Dei Gratia*, apparently drifting out of control midway between the Azores and the Portuguese coast. The *Dei Gratia* was captained by Captain David Reed Morehouse, who knew Captain Briggs. After receiving no reply when he signaled the ship, Morehouse ordered Oliver Deveau, the chief mate of the *Dei Gratia*, to lead a party in a small boat to board the *Mary Celeste*."

They found that the vessel appeared to be in generally good condition, but there was no sign of the ten people who had been sailing in her.

"The presence of the crew's pipes and oil skin boots and a missing lifeboat," Haughton said, "indicated that the *Mary Celeste* had been abandoned in a hurry, perhaps because it was believed to be sinking. The chronometer and sextant were missing, which supports the theory that the ship had been deliberately abandoned. The last entry in the Captain's logbook was for November 25, when the ship had reached the Island of Saint Mary in the Azores."

The crew of the *Dei Gratia* sailed the *Mary Celeste* to Gibraltar where, after prolonged admiralty court hearings, they were awarded the prize money for salvaging the ship.

"After the hearings," Haughton said, "the recovered ship enjoyed somewhat of a cursed reputation among seamen and ship owners, and over the next twelve years changed hands frequently. During her last journey from Boston, the *Mary Celeste* was wrecked off the coast of Haiti, probably on purpose to claim the insurance money. In August 2001, the remains of the *Mary Celeste* were recovered in an expedition headed by Clive Cussler of the National Underwater and Marine Agency."

None of the *Mary Celeste's* crew or passengers was ever found,

MYSTERIOUS DISAPPEARANCES: THEY NEVER CAME BACK

and speculations as to what happened to them have been rife for over 130 years. One of the first to speculate on the mystery, and one whose fictional account of the disappearance has been used as fact by a number of subsequent authors and journalists who wrote on the subject, is Arthur Conan Doyle, author of the Sherlock Holmes stories.

"Conan Doyle's 1884 short story, *'J. Habakuk Jephson's Statement,'* established many of the popular elements of the vanishing," Haughton said, "including the name *'Marie Celeste'* rather than *Mary Celeste*, and the myth that the crew's tea was still warm and breakfast was cooking when the vessel was discovered abandoned."

POSSIBLE EXPLANATIONS

There has been no shortage of theories to explain the mystery of the *Mary Celeste*, ranging from the mundane to the fantastic.

"These include," Haughton said, "mutiny, poisoned food, insurance fraud, pirates, a waterspout, which is a tornado-like storm encountered over water, a seaquake, the Bermuda Triangle, though the ship was nowhere near the Bermuda Triangle when found, sea monsters and alien abduction. No evidence has been found to support any of these explanations.

"What does seem probable," he continued, "from the evidence found onboard the vessel, is that the *Mary Celeste* was abandoned because Captain Briggs believed she was about to sink. Briggs may have believed the cargo of alcohol was about to explode, panicked and abandoned the ship. Whatever happened, all mariners agree, it must have been something life-threatening for an experienced captain and crew to abandon ship, an extreme measure taken only as a last resort."

"It must be admitted," Haughton concluded, "that many supposed 'mysterious' disappearances have mundane explanations, like foul play or amnesia in the case of missing people, and bad weather conditions, human error or equipment failure in the case of ships and planes. Other mysterious disappearances have their origin in fiction and there is no factual basis for the stories at all. The puzzling question of the Bermuda Triangle must remain open, pending further scientific investigation."

So open questions and unsolved mysteries continue to be the order of the day as Brian Haughton soldiers on in his effort to separate fact from fiction—wherever possible—in the realm of unexplained disappearances and anomalous historical oddities.

MYSTERIOUS DISAPPEARANCES: THEY NEVER CAME BACK

CHAPTER SEVEN

THE STRANGE CASE OF DEVIL'S GATE

AND OTHER UNEXPLAINABLE TALES

For five decades, award-winning writer Brad Steiger has been devoted to exploring and examining unusual, hidden, secret and otherwise strange occurrences. Since 1956, Steiger has published more than 2000 articles with paranormal themes, as well as writing more than 162 books, including *"Mysteries of Time and Space,"* and one particularly relevant to the subject at hand, *"Strange Disappearances."*

In an interview conducted exclusively for this book, Steiger talked about numerous cases of bizarre vanishings, as well as some of the theories offered to explain them.

WALKING THROUGH THE DEVIL'S GATE

"One of the cases that I've always been fascinated with," Steiger said, "happened at the Devil's Gate Reservoir section, above the City of Altadena, not far from Azusa. That's in California's Angels National Forest. On March 23, 1957, eight-year-old Tommy Bowman is walking just a few feet ahead of six members of his family. He just walks around a little bush and disappears. Now, within hours after little Tommy disappears, they had over 400 volunteer searchers in the area. Rescue dogs, mounted patrol, bush-beaters. Every crevice into which he might have fallen— the forest trail was crossed and re-crossed. Helicopters, everything."

Needless to say, the search effort yielded no trace of Tommy Bowman.

"The family had been just a few steps behind him," Steiger said, "and they didn't hear him cry out, as he would have if had tripped or

MYSTERIOUS DISAPPEARANCES: THEY NEVER CAME BACK

fallen. He didn't shout. He was just gone."

Tommy Bowman was actually part of a long list of children who had vanished in that same Devil's Gate region. Little Donald Lee Baker and Brenda Howell disappeared on the morning of August 5, 1956, adding to the grim statistics.

"Bruce Kremen disappeared just nine days before his seventh birthday," Steiger said. "It was his first YMCA hike, July 13, 1960. He was so excited, brimming with enthusiasm. The adult leader was walking with Bruce and everyone was laughing and marching and having a good time. When they were a few yards from the camp's perimeter—as I said, this is the YMCA—the leader told Bruce to go on ahead and report to one of the other leaders. That leader then went back to rejoin the main group. He turned around to go, expecting Bruce to walk the few yards to the camp's perimeter. But little Bruce never made those last steps. He simply disappeared."

For twelve days, 300 volunteers combed every foot of the forest for ten square miles before they finally gave up. Steiger next told about a more recent but similar occurrence that happened in Colorado in the early years of the 21st century.

"There was an incident where a little boy was just a few feet in front of his father and disappeared," Steiger said. "Now what do we have as an explanation? A mountain lion? That just jumps and takes the child away? It can't be a mountain lion. They're quiet, they're fast, but the kid is at least going to scream.

"This is so eerie to me, as a father," Steiger continued. "I think of all the times the kids have wandered off and you have that moment of panic, but there they are again. But just feeling for the parents, to just be a few feet behind the kid. He goes around the corner and that's it. The last you see of him is just walking a few feet ahead of you."

Steiger said the Devil's Gate area where so many kids were lost has since been nicknamed *"The Forest of Disappearing Children."*

As for further possible explanations, Steiger was asked about the idea of doorways to other dimensions.

"This is one of the explanations we can talk about," he said. "If there are little vortices or portals to another dimension that just kind of open and close for no reason that we can understand, then theoretically someone could walk into one and not be seen. Or the other thing is that

MYSTERIOUS DISAPPEARANCES: THEY NEVER CAME BACK

this is the machinations of some entity from another dimension.

"Remember the movie *'Predator,'* the one with Arnold Schwarzenegger, a few years ago? The predator was invisible unless you caught him at just the right angle. I know that's a gruesome scenario," Steiger continued, "but we could have one of those things. What if entities from other dimensions come in and hunt and fish and pluck one of us out? These are very disconcerting kinds of thoughts."

THE SALESMAN WHO HAD IT ALL

The story of a 25-year-old salesman who disappeared under mysterious circumstances is another case Steiger finds interesting.

"At six P.M., on March 19, 1964," Steiger said, "Lawrence Kolarik called his wife from Luddington, Michigan, to tell her he was about to leave on a ferryboat called *'The City of Saginaw,'* a Chesapeake and Ohio railway car ferry. He was on his way from Grand Rapids, Michigan to pick up his wife and five children, who were still living in Wisconsin. He had just bought a home in Grand Rapids, and he was eager for his family to see it."

Kolarik drove his car onto the ferry at about 5:15 P.M., checked into a cabin, left his belongings there and went to make the call to his wife. The ferry left Luddington, bound for Manitowoc, Wisconsin, at 7:15 P.M. It reached the Wisconsin side of Lake Michigan at 11:30 P.M.

"An hour later," Steiger said, "a crewman aboard *'The City of Saginaw'* reported that one car remained in the dock parking lot. They checked the passenger manifest and verified that the car belonged to Lawrence Kolarik. But he was not in his cabin. His suitcase and belongings were there, but the bed hadn't been slept in and he wasn't anywhere around."

The ferryboat's skipper thought at first that Kolarik had been left behind in Luddington, but the Mason County Sheriff's office could find no evidence of the missing salesman having been there.

"Several days later," Steiger said, "when they called off the search, the authorities were forced to admit that Lawrence Kolarik was the eighth person to disappear under mysterious circumstances in Luddington within a period of a few years. Although police officials had classified each of the disappearances as accidental drownings or suicides, not a single body was ever found."

The police contended that the absence of any corpses was easy to

MYSTERIOUS DISAPPEARANCES: THEY NEVER CAME BACK

account for. Strong lake currents had simply swept the bodies away, and the water is just too cold to endure for even a few minutes without a wet suit.

Steiger said that in the case of Kolarik suicide was highly unlikely.

"He'd just purchased a new home," Steiger said, "he was happy in his work, he'd been praised by his superiors, and he'd just telephoned his wife to express his eagerness to rejoin his family. His wife told reporters, 'He was in such good spirits. He said he was happy in his new location, his bosses had told him what a good job he was doing, and he could hardly wait to bring us back with him.'"

DID BUTCH AND SUNDANCE SURVIVE?

On a lighter note, Steiger had picked up a story about Butch Cassidy and the Sundance Kid, two western outlaws immortalized in the movie with Paul Newman and Robert Redford.

Steiger said he heard the story from a close friend of his who claimed that the Sundance Kid was his uncle.

"They allegedly died in South America," Steiger said, "but that was pure fiction. They had to have an ending for the movie. Meanwhile, my friend said that both Butch and Sundance made it back to New York City and lived the rest of their lives in very pleasant, peaceful obscurity."

Steiger's friend added another interesting wrinkle to the tale.

"Etta James, the woman played by Katherine Ross in the movie, was the girlfriend of both Butch and Sundance," Steiger continued, "or that's the way it appears in the movie. Anyway, she had an appendicitis attack, according to this story. So they packed her in ice and took a ship all the way back to New York, where she had surgery. Then she married Sundance and they just disappeared. I mean they *arranged* their disappearance.

"As I say, this person was a very good friend of mine and we would always laugh when we'd bring up the Paul Newman/Robert Redford movie, because that just isn't the way it was. They really pulled it off. They pulled off this strange disappearance that they had manufactured."

A LAUNDRY LIST OF FAMOUS DISAPPEARANCES

Steiger ran down a list of other disappearances involving the rich and infamous.

MYSTERIOUS DISAPPEARANCES: THEY NEVER CAME BACK

"The big mystery," he said, "which people will be arguing about for generations, is the Lindbergh baby."

Charles A. Lindbergh became a national hero when he flew solo nonstop from New York to Paris in 1927. In 1932, his baby son was kidnapped and killed. A man named Bruno Richard Hauptmann was arrested in 1934, convicted in 1935, and executed in 1936.

"The thing is," Steiger said, "some conspiracy theorists claim that they never found the body of Lindbergh's baby boy. And Hauptmann went to his demise on a completely trumped up charge. The body of the baby was never found and his remains have never been identified. So one of the theories is that the child was kidnapped but not killed, and then they railroaded Hauptmann so they would at least have an explanation. But there's a whole school of thought that says Charles Lindbergh III is still out there. He's still living somewhere, probably unaware of his own identity."

In his book *"Conspiracies and Secret Societies, The Complete Dossier,"* Steiger has a section dealing with the Nation of Islam, founded in Chicago in 1930 by Wallace Dodd Fard, which began as a social group working to improve the political and economic lives of blacks throughout the local community. Changing his name to Wali Fard Muhammad, he de-emphasized the Bible and began introducing his followers to the Koran, as well as teaching that the white race is the devil and that black people are the cream of planet Earth.

"By 1934," Steiger writes, "Wali Fard Muhammad had gathered about 8,000 members into his flock, and then, in June of that year, he mysteriously disappeared. His most dedicated minister, Elijah Muhammad, took over the Nation of Islam. Elijah was so dedicated to his predecessor that he believed Wali Muhammad was God incarnate."

Steiger talked about why the story so intrigues him now.

"It was after Fard says, or they say he said, 'Elijah Muhammad, you shall now be my protégé,' that he disappeared," Steiger explained. "And of course it's been suggested that either he was murdered by Elijah Muhammad or, as the Nation of Islam claimed—they accused the Chicago police of killing him. But their official story is that Fard was so spiritual that he just ascended to Mecca. He did disappear, and there has been no trace, no body found."

Steiger also touched on the case of Sean Flynn, the son of legendary movie star Errol Flynn and Lilly Dimeta.

MYSTERIOUS DISAPPEARANCES: THEY NEVER CAME BACK

"Sean Flynn was a photojournalist and was as daring in real life as his father was in the movies," Steiger said. "It was big news when he was believed captured by the Vietcong or the Khmer Rouge while covering the war. They believe that he was executed in Cambodia in 1971."

And then of course there is the famous D. B. Cooper, the subject of a couple of movies in his own right.

"He skyjacked a Boeing 727," Steiger said, "and jumped from the plane over the Pacific Northwest on November 21, 1971, and disappeared. Either he did the perfect robbery by skyjacking and jumping out of an airplane, or he died parachuting and got impaled on a pine tree. No one has ever found him."

Another case recounted in *"Conspiracies and Secret Societies"* is that of Congressman Hale Boggs.

"Boggs, the House Majority Leader," Steiger writes, "was the only Warren Commission member who publicly expressed doubt about their findings that Oswald and Ruby were not part of any conspiracy. Boggs accused FBI director J. Edgar Hoover of lying about Oswald, Ruby and their associates. Boggs disappeared on a flight from Anchorage to Juneau, Alaska, on October 16, 1972. Neither the plane nor any bodies were ever found."

WHERE HAVE SO MANY PEOPLE GONE?

There are hundreds of thousands of people reported missing every year. While most of them are eventually accounted for, what about that core of people whose disappearance remains unexplained?

For Steiger, the answer is uncomfortably grim.

"First of all, we have to make note of the terrible, horrible sex slavery rings that exist, the child pornography rings that exist, and that are worldwide," he said. "So many of these people can literally be kidnapped for those kinds of evil, nefarious purposes. The young and the beautiful of both sexes. And then there are people who obviously have had it with their life and arrange their own disappearances.

"It's horrible to contemplate," Steiger continued. "Women disappear in this Canadian town and then they find a bunch of barrels in a pig farmer's lot where he had been feeding people, as disgusting as it is, to the hogs. It's hard to be an optimist. The world is filled with evil people who obviously kill wantonly.

MYSTERIOUS DISAPPEARANCES: THEY NEVER CAME BACK

"Hundreds of thousands," he went on. "When you see the figures, I don't know if they can ever be accurate. It's just incredible how many people disappear every year. Again, we can talk about cosmic inter-dimensional hunters or kidnappers, or we can talk about the truly evil people that exist in this world who, without another thought, kidnap and exploit and use people. We've found out about women who are kept in dungeons and not fed. This happens in major cities, where it's been uncovered more than once.

"This is a tricky subject. It's fascinating, it's eerie, it's haunting, and it's captivating to the imagination," Steiger concluded, "because you know there are a host of explanations."

MYSTERIOUS DISAPPEARANCES: THEY NEVER CAME BACK

CHAPTER EIGHT

DISAPPEARING INTO MADNESS

Like the Bermuda Triangle mystery discussed previously, the *Philadelphia Experiment* has long been a legend in the annals of paranormal and conspiracy theory. But a brief summary of the story may still be useful here.

According to Brad Steiger's 1990 book on the subject, *"The Philadelphia Experiment and Other UFO Conspiracies,"* in October 1943, the U.S. Navy secretly accomplished the teleportation of a warship from Philadelphia to a dock near Norfolk by successfully applying Einstein's Unified Field Theory.

"The experiment also caused the crew and officers to become invisible," Steiger writes, "during which time they were sent to a time-space warp in another dimension. The majority of the crew continued to experience devastating 'side effects' the rest of their lives, becoming invisible and catching on fire."

Strange technology indeed! Other sources say the method used was simply to bombard the ship with huge amounts of electromagnetic energy.

TOTAL INVISIBILITY ACHIEVED?

"The result," according to an alleged witness to the event, Carlos Miguel Allende, whom Steiger quotes, "was complete invisibility of the ship and all of its crew while at sea. The electromagnetic field was effective in an oblate, spheroidal shape, extending 100 yards out from each beam of the ship. Any person within that sphere became vague in form, but he too observed those persons aboard that ship as though they were

MYSTERIOUS DISAPPEARANCES: THEY NEVER CAME BACK

in the same state yet were walking upon nothing."

The effects on the crew of the ship extended beyond simple invisibility, however.

"Half of the officers and the crew are at present mad as hatters," Allende said. "A few are even yet confined to certain areas where they may receive trained scientific aid when they either 'go blank' or 'get stuck.'"

Allende explained that "to go blank" was an aftereffect of a human having been within the field too long. When a person went "blank," he suddenly found himself fading into invisibility. Meanwhile, "to get stuck" meant that a sailor/victim could not move of his own volition. If two or more of his fellow crewmembers could not help him by the laying on of their hands, the unfortunate sailor would "freeze." Restoring the sailor's ability to move might take an hour or it might take six months in the strange limbo that held the sailors captive.

Along with being frozen, the luckless sailors might also catch on fire for no apparent reason. When a pair of sailors began to smolder for eighteen days, the remainder of the crew began to lose their faith in the method of laying on of hands and descended hopelessly into utter madness, but not before one sailor managed to walk through the walls of his quarters in full view of his wife and child and then was never seen again.

While the story of the *Philadelphia Experiment* has never been completely authenticated and proven to be fact, it is at least a fascinating urban legend of the mysterious disappearance, probably by teleportation, of both a mammoth warship and the hapless crew onboard. One can only imagine now the lengths the U.S. Navy was willing to go to in order to get an edge on our World War II enemies, and sending a few sailors to a strange netherworld might be listed as "acceptable losses."

THE MISSING AND MYSTERIOUS ANASAZI

In a February 2007 review of the book *"House of Rain,"* by Craig Childs, **Los Angeles Times** reviewer Judith Lewis describes the mysterious Anasazi tribe of Native Americans and their disappearance this way:

"They lived on the edge of the world, in the red mountains of the desert Southwest, in houses with T-shaped doorways tuned to arcane celestial events. They fashioned elaborate pottery, grew corn and beans in stubborn soil, built ceremonial chambers (called kivas) dedicated to

MYSTERIOUS DISAPPEARANCES: THEY NEVER CAME BACK

sun, stars and gods. By the 11th century, they were a highly evolved, technological society. And then suddenly they were gone."

Lewis quotes Childs from the book as saying, "Farming implements were left in the fields. Ceramic vessels remained neatly stowed in their quarters; ladles rested in bowls as if people had been swept from their land by an ill and sudden wind."

Or so the story goes. According to Childs, no one really knows what happened to the ancestral tribes of the Southwestern canyons now lumped together as the Anasazi. Lewis writes that, "Their disappearance has captivated modern explorers, professional and casual. It is a mystery pieced together from tree-ring patterns in fallen roof beams, pottery shards, human bone fragments unearthed by archeologists and hikers (one of them a Boy Scout whose flashlight fell down a hole). Any number of solutions to the mystery could be true."

The term "Anasazi" is sometimes translated as meaning "the old ones," but lately it is said to be more accurately translated as "enemy ancestors."

THE CANNIBALISM THEORY

In an online posting at LookSmart, entitled *"Eating Them Out of House and Home,"* writer John Elvin leads a lively discussion of the cannibalism theory offered to explain the mysterious disappearance of the Anasazi.

"One of history's most perplexing riddles," Elvin writes, "involves the disappearance of the cliff-dwelling Anasazi Indians, known popularly as a remarkably advanced, mystical, peaceful and agrarian culture that once inhabited the parched, desolate vast Four Corners region of present Colorado, Utah, Arizona and New Mexico in the late pre-Colombian era. The stark and stunning sandstone pueblos they abandoned are among America's great wonders.

"What happened?" Elvin continues. "Why did the Anasazi clear out as though vaporized, leaving a treasure trove of worldly goods behind?"

The answer, according to Christy G. Turner II, a bio-archeologist at Arizona State University, is cannibalism.

"Turner theorizes that the American Southwest in the centuries around the turn of the first millennium was the stomping ground of a band of Charles Manson-type cannibals," Elvin writes, "Toltec thugs from

MYSTERIOUS DISAPPEARANCES: THEY NEVER CAME BACK

Mexico who ate their way through the local population. In his book, Turner states point blank that 'cannibalism was practiced intensively for almost four centuries' in the region inhabited by the Anasazi. The public, shall we say, seems to be eating it up."

While Elvin's little pun acknowledges that this is the kind of sensational story the public tends to latch onto, he says there are numerous archeologists in the field working to disprove Turner's cannibalism theory. But there are also other scientists who are willing to back him up.

Elvin quotes David Wilcox, the curator of the Museum of Northern Arizona, as saying, "We are in a period where everything Native American is seen as spiritual, sensitive and wonderful. We would like to believe that all of the nasty stuff was introduced by the Europeans, and before that it was all truth, beauty and love. Sorry, that's just not so."

Paleo-anthropologist Tim D. White also studied an Anasazi site and found evidence of the cooking of 17 adults and 12 children.

"They skinned them, roasted them, cut their muscles off, severed their joints, broke their long bones on anvils with hammer stones, crushed their spongy bones, and put the pieces in pots," White said.

Another archeologist, Brian Billman, found evidence of humans processed in the same manner as deer or elk, including cutting tools with residue of human blood. He sent off an ancient human stool sample for testing, and it came back positive for myoglobin, which should only have been present if human skeletal muscles or hearts were eaten. Billman believes cannibalism was used as a terror tactic among competitors for the scarce resources in the area.

The whole cannibalism theory is considered to be extremely politically incorrect, and is seen as shattering cozy New Age beliefs about the Anasazi as a spiritually advanced people. And even some scientists feel compelled to back away from the grotesque violence implied by the theory.

"There is tremendous social pressure not to study certain things, even among scientists," says Robert Pickering, curator of anthropology for the Denver Museum of Natural History. "Cannibalism is one of those things. There are taboos."

The many unanswered questions about the Anasazi have puzzled archeologists for many decades, and will probably do so for many years

MYSTERIOUS DISAPPEARANCES: THEY NEVER CAME BACK

to come.

MYSTERIES ON TOP OF MYSTERIES

This book has endeavored to provide a cross-section of so many unsolved cases of mysterious disappearance. From Charles Fort's chronicles of the missing to Jimmy Hoffa's rumored whereabouts to man-eating Indians of the desert Southwest, there stretches a long line of historical material about people who were literally gone in the blink of an eye. While it is always possible that new evidence could turn up in any of the cases in this book, it is much more likely that the majority of the histories recounted here will never have a complete explanation.

Which is a fundamental part of the fascination that these stories hold for us, of course. As Troy Taylor says in the pages of this book, "People love a mystery." And perhaps it also true that, while curiosity about learning the facts of what actually happened is a primary human response to these stories, we also love maintaining that state of "not-knowing" just as much.

MYSTERIOUS DISAPPEARANCES: THEY NEVER CAME BACK

About the Author

Sean Casteel received his B.A. in Journalism from the University of Oklahoma in 1985. He has written about UFOs, alien abduction and other paranormal subjects since 1989. He is currently a contributing editor to *"UFO Magazine"* and a regular contributor to *"Open Minds Magazine."* Casteel's previous books for Inner Light/Global Communications include ***UFOs, Prophecy and the End of Time, The Excluded Books of the Bible,*** and ***Signs and Symbols of the Second Coming***. He is the coauthor, with Timothy Green Beckley, of ***Our Alien Planet: This Eerie Earth***. Casteel's work has also been published in the UK, Italy and Romania.

MYSTERIOUS DISAPPEARANCES: THEY NEVER CAME BACK

Troy Taylor

Brian Haughton

Brad Steiger

Acknowledgments

Thanks so much to the researchers and authors who granted us interviews for this book:

Troy Taylor, whose website is located at prairieghosts.com

Brian Haughton, website located at mysteriouspeople.com

Brad Steiger, who has a website located at bradandsherry.com

Troy, Brian and Brad provided invaluable assistance with their stories and insights and helped to educate us further about mysterious disappearances throughout history. This book would not be possible without them.

MYSTERIOUS DISAPPEARANCES: THEY NEVER CAME BACK

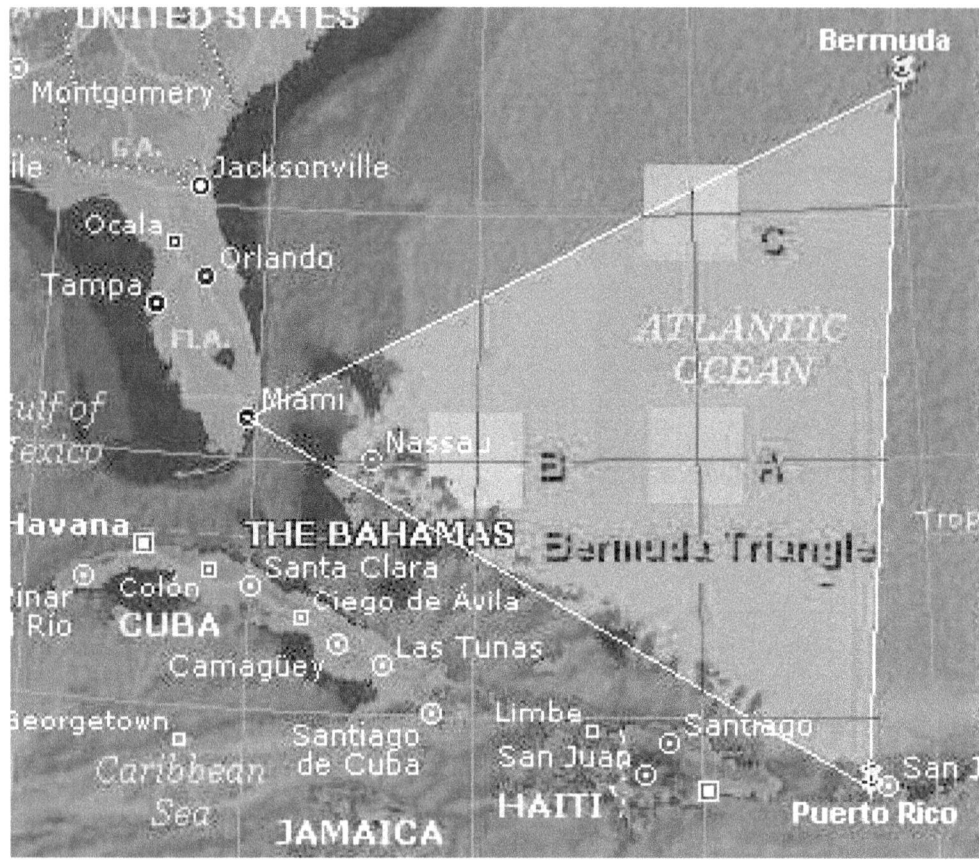

TRIANGLE OF THE LOST

Commander X and The Committee of Twelve

AN UNDERWATER BASE FOR ALIEN SPACECRAFT?

THE SITE OF THE LOST CONTINENT OF ATLANTIS?

KIDNAPPINGS BY OTHER WORLDLY BEINGS?

OR A VIOLENT HURRICANE CENTER?

How do you explain why thousands of people, hundreds of ships and planes, have mysteriously vanished in that deadly, enigmatic stretch of the Atlantic Ocean known as the *Bermuda Triangle?*

Incredible as it seems, there is data to support all of the above possibilities. Geological and archeological findings, eyewitness accounts of UFOs in the Triangle, reports from true psychics, even the logs of Christopher Columbus, have contributed towards the unraveling of the most unfathomable mystery ever!

MYSTERIOUS DISAPPEARANCES: THEY NEVER CAME BACK

CHAPTER NINE

WARNING! STAY FAR AWAY FROM THE DEVIL'S TRIANGLE

Join me for a voyage into the Triangle of the Lost. This is a deadly, enigmatic stretch of water in the Atlantic Ocean known as a maritime graveyard. Thousands of doomed people and hundreds of ships and airplanes have vanished inside the Triangle of the Lost. They have sailed or flown to their unknown doom without leaving a clue to their fate. The purpose of our journey into this zone of disaster is to obtain a factual, unprejudiced account of these unexplained mysteries.

During our trip we will probe the growing evidence that the Triangle of the Lost is a dangerous menace to aerial and sea navigation. We will learn that some researchers believe the waters of the Triangle of the Lost cover the sunken continent of *Atlantis*. Others speculate the Triangle is a "time-space warp" where people and machines are sucked into another dimension. Still other UFO researchers claim the controversial Triangle of the Lost is an underwater base for alien spacecraft from other worlds.

Incredible?

Unbelievable?

Let's look at the facts:

"I wouldn't go back out there for a million dollars," is the way 62-year-old Samuel Otis described his frightening night in the Triangle of the Lost. Otis, a retired clerk from New York State, moved to Florida in 1967. Following the death of his wife and daughter in an automobile crash, Mr. Otis became depressed.

MYSTERIOUS DISAPPEARANCES: THEY NEVER CAME BACK

"I visited a doctor for my depression," Otis related. "Instead of writing a prescription for pills, he suggested that I take up fishing. He felt this would get my mind away from my grief. On the afternoon of July 7, 1973, I rented a small boat and sailed from Miami along the coast line. I planned to spend a week fishing close in along the coast, camping at night in some secluded cove."

The first two days and nights were uneventful. "It was really pleasant and I was enjoying the outdoors," said Otis. "On the third night I camped in a small bay, put out my fishing lines, and cooked my evening meal. After eating, I prepared to retire when it happened. I was putting out the campfire when a huge, glowing ball of fire materialized near my boat."

Otis claims the fiery ball was approximately the size of a large ranch home. "I'd judge it to be about seventy feet long, maybe two stories high," he related. "The light was brighter than anything I'd ever seen. I had to turn away because of the intensity. The color was reddish-orange."

The fisherman started to run to his boat. "I didn't know what this thing was," he admitted, "but it was getting dangerously close to my anchored boat. Just as I reached the boat, the light dimmed and the whole thing took on the appearance of an old sailing ship."

Even today, Samuel Otis has difficulty in describing the phenomena. "I've never been a person who believed in ghosts, phantoms or anything like that," he related. "You can imagine my shock and surprise when the outlines of a ghost ship appeared on the waters of the bay."

Otis declared the image of a ghost ship was outlined in the darkness. He emphasized this was a transparent image. "I mean the thing could be seen by anyone," he related. "Yet, I could see the outlines of the trees across the bay through the image. I was terrified by then and my heart caught for a moment. I stepped back from the shore and watched as the ship's image moved slowly past my boat. The incredible part is that I could see images of people on the ship. These ghosts-which is what I guess you call them-were moving around on the deck as if preparing for battle. I could seethe outlines of cannons and the men carried swords or lances."

As the ghost ship moved slowly toward the open sea, Otis noticed that the image was unaffected by the rise and fall of ocean water. "The ship's image didn't ride the waves as a normal ship," he related. "In-

MYSTERIOUS DISAPPEARANCES: THEY NEVER CAME BACK

stead, the image seemed to glide across the surface without moving up and down."

After reaching the mouth of the bay, the ghostly ship turned south and struck a course toward the Triangle of the Lost. Otis watched in slack-jawed amazement as the image was suddenly transformed back into the glowing ball of fiery intensity. Seconds later, the entire phenomenon vanished. Otis was left with trembling hands, a troubled mind, and dozens of unanswered questions. Finally, he composed himself and quickly moved his camp to a site across the bay.

"I spent a very restless night," he admitted. "I sat around the campfire and watched the bay for the reappearance of the ghost ship. I was bleary-eyed when daylight arrived."

What was the unexplained materialization? Like everything else in life, the account by Mr. Otis is either true or false. Like many other witnesses to such events, Mr. Otis was not a believer in the occult.

"Since then I've done some research into the hoodoo sea out there," he stated recently. "I'm now a firm believer in the Triangle of the Lost. There's a dangerous scenario at work there. It may be something from outer space. It could be something or someone from another dimension. I don't know what it is. I do know that I don't spend any more nights out there. I used to think that ghost ships and such things were a figment of someone's imagination. Now, I'm a firm believer in these mysteries."

The Triangle of the Lost is a large stretch of the Atlantic ocean. It starts at the port of Norfolk, Virginia and crosses the Atlantic ocean to the 40th parallel. From there, it moves down to Venezuela and Trinidad, then over to the Florida peninsula. The Triangle of the Lost is not a true triangle, its western edge being disrupted by the coastline of Florida. Inside the Triangle of the Lost is the deadly Bermuda Triangle, formed by lines connecting Bermuda, Puerto Rico, and Miami.

The sorrowful events that have occurred within this zone of doom are staggering to the imagination. Since the first mariner sailed into these seas, they have been the subject of sailor's folklore and superstition, The earliest seafarers to the New World were extremely leery of these waters. Few sailors have changed their minds despite the passage of hundreds of years. Many modern mariners avoid the Triangle as effective insurance for a long and healthy life.

There have been hundreds of unexplained disappearances of

MYSTERIOUS DISAPPEARANCES: THEY NEVER CAME BACK

ships inside the Triangle. One of these enigmatic events occurred in June, 1950, when the freighter *Sandra* sailed from Savannah, Georgia, bound for Puerto Cabello, Venezuela. The ship was heavily loaded with a cargo of 350 tons of insecticide. The ship was well-equipped with up-to-date navigational equipment. Radio transmitting and receiving equipment was also on board.

The captain planned to sail south along the Florida coastline. The *Sandra* is known to have passed Jacksonville, Florida, bound for Miami. Without a distress call or any cries for help; the *Sandra* vanished. The U.S. Coast Guard launched an intensive aerial and sea search for some sign of the missing ship. There was not a single clue to the freighter's fate. Seemingly, the *Sandra* sailed into oblivion.

"There's many unexplained things in the *Sandra* case," reported a spokesman for the Coast Guard. "First, a ship's captain usually has advance warning about a possible disaster. This occurs when you lose engine power, punch a hole in the bottom or something like that. A ship doesn't sink in a moment or two. There's always enough time to get a radioed message off before abandoning the vessel."

The spokesman also wondered about the lack of debris from the *Sandra*. "She was fitted out with plenty of life preservers, lifeboats, and other life-saving equipment," he continued. "There's usually plenty of floating debris around the site of a sunken ship. In the disappearance of the *Sandra*, nothing was found to indicate what happened to the ship."

One of the largest loss of lives within the Triangle of the Lost was the 1,080-ton *City of Glasgow*. There was a holiday air of gaiety on the docks of Liverpool, England on the morning of March 1, 1854. Thirteen ships were sailing for America that day; their passengers were happy, enthusiastic immigrants who hoped to find new opportunities and a possible fortune in the United States.

As they moved into the ship, the passengers chatted amicably. "To a new land and a new chance in life," said a grinning passenger. He handed his ticket to the purser.

"I can hardly wait to get there," said an Irishman.

"You'll get there all right with time to spare," said an agent for the Liverpool and Philadelphia Steamship Company. "*The City of Glasgow* is one of the best ships in the world. She's got an iron hull for safety. She's got plenty of strong sails. And if the wind dies out, we have steam engines for auxiliary power."

MYSTERIOUS DISAPPEARANCES: THEY NEVER CAME BACK

The City of Glasgow sailed that afternoon with 480 crewmen and passengers aboard. It was expected that the passage across the Atlantic ocean would require approximately six weeks. By mid-April, anxious friends and relatives watched the Delaware Bay for some sign of the *City of Glasgow*. Newsmen heard rumors about the missing ship and questioned the ship's agents, Richardson Brothers Company..

"Don't worry, said Amos King, speaking for the Richardson Brothers. "*The City of Glasgow* is a safe ship. The engines may have broken down. The Captain is probably bringing her in by sails."

By mid-May, rumors were at a fever pitch in Philadelphia. Newspapers printed daily articles on the possible fate of the ship. One editor printed a lurid account the ship being plundered by murderous pirates. Another newsman published a tip that the ship was run aground off the coast of South America, that the crew and passengers had been captured by a tribe of cannibalistic natives. Another newspaper printed a report that the *City of Glasgow* had been seen near the island of Bermuda.

None of the reports proved to be true. Whatever her ultimate fate, the *City of Glasgow* entered the Triangle of the Lost and vanished forever. No trace was ever found of her 399 passengers or the sailors who crewed the ship. To this day, no one knows what happened to the queen ship of the Liverpool-to-Philadelphia run.

The five men aboard the *Driftwood* were also in a festive mood when they sailed out of Dania, Florida, for a week-long fishing trip around the island of Bimini, in the Bahamas. The *Driftwood* was a thirty-six-foot cabin cruiser, a charter boat captained by Johnny Pellet.

After purchasing supplies at the dock, the cruiser sailed off into the Triangle on January 14, 1949. Besides Captain Pellet, the passengers included Logan Eisle, a businessman from Nashville, Tenn., and his friend, Dr. Albert Sullivan, a surgeon from Nashville. Also on board was Paul Heckert, a building inspector and his friend, Bert LeBree, a businessman. Both men were residents of Dania. These passengers knew that Captain Johnny Pellet was one of the best seamen in the Florida to Bimini run.

"Johnny had made more than a hundred trips to Bimini and back," a friend told newsmen. "He had a good cruiser and he kept the ship in top condition. Before the trip, the *Driftwood* had been in the boat yard for repairs. Johnny had the bottom of the hull painted and the engines

MYSTERIOUS DISAPPEARANCES: THEY NEVER CAME BACK

overhauled. The *Driftwood* had two powerful Chrysler engines that were tuned to a perfect pitch."

Despite these precautions, the fishing party failed to return to Florida on schedule. A message was radioed to the authorities at Bimini. "The *Driftwood* hasn't been here," was the reply. A search of the islands was launched, but no trace of Captain Johnny Pellet and his passengers was ever found. It seemed as if the small cruiser had sailed into another dimension.

Flying through the Triangle of the Lost has always been a dangerous undertaking. Some of the first aviators to vanish in this part of the ocean were rum-running pilots during the wild days of the Prohibition era. Many military planes were also lost in the Triangle during World War II. In late December, 1943, seven U. S. Air Force bombers roared down the runways at Kindley Field, Bermuda, for a flight to Italy. About three hundred miles from the island, the bombers encountered strong headwinds. Suddenly, the squadron ran into a series of unusual air currents. The storm lasted no longer than a minute, yet the terrifying force caused two planes to turn back to the Bermuda air field.

MYSTERIOUS DISAPPEARANCES: THEY NEVER CAME BACK

"One moment we were flying along in formation," a survivor of the incident reported. "The next minute, we were in an area of tremendous aerial turbulence. Some of the planes were forced upward, others downward for a thousand feet or more. It happened so fast that we were not prepared to handle it. I can remember hearing the entire plane shaking and making loud popping noises from the tremendous force of the wind."

The two planes waited overnight in Bermuda, then resumed their flight the next day. The five bombers that had flown on into the Triangle of the Lost were never seen again. Despite an extensive search by air-sea rescue units, nothing was located to pin-point where they might have gone down. "They had radios, life jackets, and plenty of inflatable life rafts," a survivor stated. "The crews who ferried planes across the oceans were well trained in how to handle ditching procedures at sea. It's incredible that five planes and their crews could just disappear."

Following the war, commercial airliners began to vanish in the Triangle. One of the first was the *Star Tiger*, a large four-engine Avro luxury Tudor IV airliner en route to Kingston, Jamaica. The plane had left London, England, on January 27 with stops at Lisbon, Portugal, and the Azore Islands. Landing time in Jamaica was scheduled for midnight on January 29, 1948. Twenty-five passengers and six crew members were aboard the plane.

At approximately 10:30 p.m., the air controller in Bermuda received a radio message from Captain David Colby. "This is the *Star Tiger* of British South American Airways," Colby stated. "We're about four hundred miles from you. We expect to arrive on schedule as the weather and performance of the plane is very good."

This was the final message from the plane.

When the *Star Tiger* was known to be overdue, the United States Air Force Base at Kindley Field launched a massive aerial search. By dawn, Commander Tom Ferguson had forty planes sweeping the sea for some sign of the missing plane. More than a dozen ships were steaming at full speed to rescue any survivors. At the height of the search more than eleven hundred men were looking for the *Star Tiger*.

Tired and frustrated after a month of fruitless looking, the searchers ended their unsuccessful quest to find the plane or any survivors. More than 200,000 square miles of ocean had been carefully scanned during the search. Planes from as far away as Mitchell Field, New York,

MYSTERIOUS DISAPPEARANCES: THEY NEVER CAME BACK

had joined in the rescue operation.

The search was resumed on February 4 after a mysterious radio signal was received by several amateur Ham radio enthusiasts. The message "t-i-g-e-r" was picked up. A short interval of silence interrupted the message, then "g-a-h-n-p" was heard. Canadian Air Force radiomen in Halifax, Nova Scotia, were among those receiving the message.

All planes and ships in the Triangle of the Lost were alerted to the possibility that the message would be repeated. The U. S. Federal Communications Commission rushed high-powered directional finding equipment into the area. They hoped to pick up any new message and obtain a "fix" on the position. Unfortunately, no additional messages were received. The *Star Tiger* remained missing. "We can only conclude that the message was a ghoulish hoax," declared a spokesman for the British South American Airways. "It would seem impossible that a plane could remain afloat in the ocean for more than a month. The radio equipment aboard the *Star Tiger* was much too heavy to be carried away from the plane on a raft. If someone survived the crash, they would have a light transmitter aboard the raft for sending emergency signals."

In England, the Minister of Civil Aviation appointed a court of inquiry into the fate of the *Star Tiger*. Results of their investigation were published as a white paper that concluded ". . . it can truly be said that no more baffling problem has ever been presented for investigation."

The report's last paragraph read: ". . . In the complete absence of any reliable evidence as to either the nature or cause of the disaster to the *Star Tiger,* the court has been unable to do more than suggest possibilities, none of which reaches the level of possibility. What happened in this case will never be known."

Despite this tragic mystery, the Triangle of the Lost was not finished with British South American Airways. The sister ship of the *Star Tiger* was another luxurious airliner, the *Star Ariel*. Like other Tudor IV planes, the *Star Ariel* was a commercialized version of the British Lancaster bomber used in World War II. This design was considered one of the most reliable among propeller driven bombers. Four 1700-horsepower Rolls-Royce engines enabled the plane to cruise at speeds up to 300 m.p.h.

On the calm, beautiful morning of January 19, 1949, the *Star Ariel* rolled down the runway and soared into the skies above Bermuda. Forty-five minutes later, Captain J. C. McPhee contacted the Bermuda Air Ra-

MYSTERIOUS DISAPPEARANCES: THEY NEVER CAME BACK

dio Control Tower. "I'm about two hundred miles south of Bermuda," said Captain McPhee. "The weather is beautiful and the plane is excellent in performance. I'm going to change my radio frequency to air control at Nassau, Jamaica."

This was the last message ever received from the *Star Ariel*. The plane carried enough fuel to cruise until 6:00 p.m. that evening. On board were twelve passengers and six crew members. A wide-spread air and sea search swept across the Triangle of the Lost. Like her sister airliner, the *Star Ariel* vanished without a clue to her ultimate fate. During the night, one of the most massive searches in maritime history was organized. U. S. Coast Guard planes from Massachusetts, New York, and Georgia were rushed to Bermuda. The U. S. Air Force brought in a B-29 Superfortress bomber and a B-17 to aid in operations. Coast Guard rescue planes from Florida, Texas, and Louisiana were flown to the island during the night. The U. S. Navy added the *U.S.S. Kearsarge* and *U.S.S. Leyte*, two huge aircraft carriers. These two vessels, along with the *U.S.S. Missouri*, a battleship, joined another six U. S. destroyers already in the Triangle of the Lost.

Within hours of the plane's disappearance there were scores of ships, an estimated 100 airplanes, and more than 14,000 men looking for the *Star Ariel*. They were unable to find an oil slick, a bit of debris, or some part of the plane to indicate that the plane might have gone down.

"We're mystified that the captain McPhee couldn't have sent out an S.O.S. signal," a spokesman for the airliner stated. "Search planes have criss-crossed this part of the ocean without finding a single piece of debris. After the loss of the *Star Tiger*, we felt certain that survivors would be found."

Reaction to the *Star Ariel's* disappearance was swift. In London, Sir Roy Dodson, president of A. V. Roe and Company, Ltd., held a press conference. "I'm convinced that the Tudor IV is a safe plane," he announced. "My firm believes that sabotage may be the real reason behind these disappearances."

Lord Pakenham, then Minister of Civil Aviation, was asked about Dodson's statement. "If there was sabotage it would be in the form of a bomb or some sort of explosive aboard the *Star Ariel*," he claimed. "An explosion of any sort would mean there would be a sizable amount of debris found floating on the surface of the ocean. As no debris was discovered during the search, we'll have to dismiss the possibilities of sabotage."

MYSTERIOUS DISAPPEARANCES: THEY NEVER CAME BACK

A newsman inquired, "What does your commission plan to do?"

"We're placing the Tudor IV under temporary grounding," Lord Pakenham answered. "'We want to make a special examination of the plane to determine if there are flaws in the design."

On December 20, 1949, Air Commodore Vernon Brown, Chief Inspector of Accidents for the Ministry of Civil Aviation, released his report. "Through lack of evidence due to no wreckage being found, the cause of the accident to the *Star Ariel* is unknown. The *Star Ariel* was lost almost exactly a year after a sister aircraft, the *Star Tiger*, had disappeared in equally mysterious circumstances. These two losses have led to the withdrawal of Tudor IVs for carrying passengers, and they have not been employed for this purpose by the corporation since, even though they have operated successfully on the Berlin airlift and elsewhere."

The report stated that the *Star Ariel* was in excellent mechanical condition before departing from Bermuda. Captain McPhee was an experienced pilot and had flown the route on many previous flights. The plane's crew was competent, well-trained and above average in their flight experience. All equipment aboard the plane had passed a recent inspection, including the radio transmitters and receivers.

". . . and there are no indications that the accident was caused by abnormal meteorological conditions," the report summed up.

Both Tudor IVs were presumed lost at sea. The disappearance of the two airliners in the Triangle of the Lost was a severe blow to British South American Airways. The firm had started serving the Caribbean islands and the west coast of South America on September 2, 1946. BSAA

MYSTERIOUS DISAPPEARANCES: THEY NEVER CAME BACK

was absorbed by the British Overseas Airways Corp. (BOAC) in a merger. Mid-Atlantic service was not resumed until March, 1950, when BOAC airliners started flying to Bermuda.

What has been happening to airplanes in the Triangle of the Lost?

No one has an answer to this day. As we'll see in a chapter to follow, there have been even more mysterious disappearances of planes. The story of their disappearances was often the same-no debris, no S.O.S. messages, no survivors. Some researchers have suggested that a "rip" between the dimensions exists in the Triangle of the Lost. Airplanes and ships speed through this opening and find themselves in another world, possibly another dimension.

The frightening implication is that the inter-dimensional "rip" operates as a one-way door. No one has ever returned to prove or disprove the theory.

MYSTERIOUS DISAPPEARANCES: THEY NEVER CAME BACK

CHAPTER TEN

CHRISTOPHER COLUMBUS IN THE TRIANGLE OF THE LOST

As incredible as it may sound, the Triangle of the Lost led Christopher Columbus to make his four voyages to the New World!

Let's start by taking a walk back in time to the reign of King Ferdinand of Aragon and Queen Isabella of Castile. They were joint rulers of Spain after their marriage on January 7, 1469, although the Queen always wielded the strongest power. Before their vows were exchanged, Ferdinand signed a lengthy articles of marriage that allowed his subjects to be considered foreigners in Castilian Spain. He also swore to make no appointments without the Queen's consent and gave his wife the right to make ecclesiastical nominations to the Catholic Church.

Isabella, who was the patroness to Christopher Columbus, has been treated generously by our historians. She was far from the sweet, pious woman that we've read about. In reality, Isabella was a tough, sadistic woman who used any tactics to fill her purse and increase her power. "She was under the influence of the Catholic priesthood from an early age," reported a historian. "At the age of sixteen she was brought to the court of Castile. It was nothing more than a brothel with the loosest morals imaginable."

Once installed on the throne, a suitable king was sought for the teenage queen. She was frequently engaged to men who died mysteriously if they didn't yield to her demands. "She was raised to the throne by scandalous testimony against her brother's wife," the historian continued. "Her lies put the brand of illegitimacy on her niece. The fires of the Inquisition were glowing in Spain and it was Queen Isabella who

MYSTERIOUS DISAPPEARANCES: THEY NEVER CAME BACK

fanned them into a bonfire."

Queen Isabella petitioned the Pope in Rome to appoint Torquemada as Grand Inquisitor. Once the appointment was made, whole towns and villages were depopulated. The wealth of the victims was added to Queen Isabella's royal treasury. Even the dead were persecuted. Graveyards were looted, bodies, exhumed and burned, and the wealth of the dead men taken from their heirs.

"I have caused great calamities and depopulated towns, lands, provinces, and kingdoms," wrote Queen Isabella. "But this was done for the love of Christ and his Holy Mother!"

Despite her protests, Isabella was burning whole communities to confiscate property. Typical among them was the case of a man known as Peeho of Xerez who was condemned to burn at the stake for heresy. The queen grabbed his fortune of two hundred thousand maravedis, then "donated" twenty thousand maravedis to the victim's widow and children.

In his *Introduction to Spanish Papers*, historian G. A. Bergenroth wrote: ". . . She used corruption on a large scale, larger even, as she declared, than was agreeable to herself. The final result was that the courts of Spain and Rome came to an understanding respecting the person who was to be sent as legate to investigate the proceedings of the Inquisition. He received rich donations in Spain, and his inquiry was reduced to a mere form . . . The queen was implored to relent, but she answered that it was better for the service of God and herself to have the country depopulated than to have it polluted with heresy."

This then is the queen who allegedly financed the first voyage of Columbus to the New World. Columbus is believed to have been about fifty years old when he approached the Spanish court with a proposal to finance his voyages. Columbus is said to have arrived in Lisbon, Portugal, after pirates attacked and destroyed several Venetian merchant ships during an assault at sea. Shortly after his arrival in Portugal, Columbus married a moderately wealthy widow and moved to the island of Madeira.

Authors who were living during the time of Columbus place much credence on the story of the "lost pilot." The historian, Spotorno, says in his *"Historia Memoria,"* "...as to the idle tale which was current in Spain that he had taken the idea of the New World from a pilot of whom a number of fables are told, I shall not stop to refute it."

MYSTERIOUS DISAPPEARANCES: THEY NEVER CAME BACK

The story of the lost pilot is also recounted in *Gomarra's History of the Indies* which was published in Spanish and sanctioned by the Archbishops of Saragossa. Gomarra was a priest who represented Columbus as a saintly person. He reported that "rude crosses erected by Columbus healed the sick and performed many miracles after his death."

Garcilasso de la Vega also gives credence to the story of the pilot. In his *The Royal Commentaries of Peru*, written in Spanish, we find the following story of how the Triangle of the Lost influenced Columbus to set sail for a new land. It reads:

"About the year 1484, a certain pilot who was a native of Helva in the province of Niebia, was named Alonso Sanchez. He usually traded in a small vessel from Spain to the Canary Islands, and there picked up merchandise from that country and sailed to Madeira. There he sold his cargo and loaded up with sugar and other items for his return voyage home.

"This was his constant traffic course. During one of his voyages he met with a most violent storm, and not being able to bear sail, was forced to put before the wind for an interval of 28 or 29 days. He knew not where or whither he went because, in all of that time, he was unable to take an observation of the height of the sun. And so powerful was the storm that the mariners could neither eat nor sleep with any convenience.

"At last, after so many long and tedious days, the wind abated. They found themselves near an island which is not certainly known. It is believed to be Santo Domingo since that lies just west of the Canary Islands. The Master of the ship landed on the shore and observed the height of the sun, and so noted particularly in writing what he had seen. Once he was supplied with fresh water and wood, the mariners put out to sea again for the voyage home. But they had not observed their course well during the storm and their return was very difficult. Their voyage lasted so long that they began to need both water and provisions. Members of their crew fell sick and died. Of the seventeen people who sailed from Spain, there remained but five alive when they arrived at Madeira. The Master of the ship and four of his crew members came to lodge at the house of Christopher Columbus. He received them with such kindness and treated them with all things necessary, that so he might learn from them the particulars which occurred, and the discoveries they had made in their long voyage.

"However, they brought a languishing distemper with them, caused by their suffering at sea, and they could not recover even under

MYSTERIOUS DISAPPEARANCES: THEY NEVER CAME BACK

the kind treatment of Columbus. They all happened to die at his house leaving their labors for his inheritance, the which he improved with such readiness of mind that . . . he bestowed the New World, with all of its riches, on Spain. . .

"In this manner the New World was first discovered, for which greatness Spain is beholden to the little village of Helva, which produced such a son as gave Columbus the information of things not known or seen. Like a prudent person, Columbus took these secrets and concealed them until under the assurance of silence he disclosed them to such persons of authority as the Catholic kings. His designs could never have been laid or chalked out, neither by the art of Cosmography, or the imagination of man, had not Alonso de Sanchez given the first light on this great discovery." It was a storm that drove the Sanchez vessel into the Triangle of the Lost, the first discovery of land in the West Indies. Columbus corroborates that he sailed by the charts and logbook of the unfortunate mariner who died at his home by writings in his logbook. In his journal for September 25, 1492, we read: "Martin Alonzo Pinzon conferred with the admiral on the chart in which lands were laid down, as the ships were then in their neighborhood and had been for three days- in which the admiral agreed; but, as the ships had not seen them, it was considered that they had drifted northward of them by the current . . . The admiral directed that the course be altered to the southwest."

"October 3, 1,492: The Admiral considered the ships were to the westward of the islands marked on the chart."

With his charts and logbooks from the Sanchez voyage, Columbus approached several kings with his proposal to sail westward to reach the new land. The story is told of how he came to the royal court in Spain and was rudely rejected by King Ferdinand. Then, the supposedly generous Queen Isabella pawned her jewels to a Jewish merchant in order to raise money for the voyage.

What actually happened is that Queen Isabella's royal treasury was swollen with the ransoming of Moorish captives during the prolonged war. After extracting millions in tribute for the prisoners' release, she sold the captives into slavery. With nothing to lose, Isabella made the following royal order:

Requisition on the Municipality of Palos

"In consequence of the offense which we received at your hands, you were condemned by our council to render us the service of two

MYSTERIOUS DISAPPEARANCES: THEY NEVER CAME BACK

caravels, armed at your own expense, for the space of twelve months, whenever and wherever it should be our pleasure to demand the service."

The poor fishing village of Palos didn't greet Columbus like a visiting dignitary when he strode into their town square. He was probably as welcome as a hound dog at a cat show. Knowing the Queen's reputation for sadistic behavior, the Finzon family agreed to loan Columbus enough money to outfit a third ship. When the local fishermen refused to follow Columbus, Martin Alonzo and Vincent Yanez agreed to captain the Nina and the Pinta. Columbus dubbed himself as "admiral" and took charge of the larger *St. Mary* caravel.

Once his ships were inside the Triangle of the Lost, Columbus was plagued with a surly crew, vast stretches of uncharted ocean, and a sea of drifting seaweed now known as the Sargasso Sea. His ship was also apparently visited by a spookish light.

Calling his crew to attention one morning, Columbus told them he knew sighting land was imminent. "I want you to keep a sharp eye out for land," Columbus said.

"Whoever makes the first cry of 'land ho!' will get a doublet made of the finest velvet and a pension of thirty crowns a year from the King and Queen."

At ten o'clock that same night of October 11, Columbus later claimed he saw a light bobbing in the distance. Although he failed to mention the fact to the crew, he called Roderigo Sanchez de Segovia to the side of the ship. Segovia failed to see the light and, according to Columbus, did so "through malice and a desire to rob me of my well-earned fame." Columbus reported later that he called Peter Gutierrez, groom to King Ferdinand, who was accompanying Columbus on the voyage. Gutierrez was reported by Columbus to have seen the light.

By two o'clock in the morning, the *Pinta* was sailing far ahead of Columbus' ship, the *St. Mary*. Land was sighted by *Pinta* crewman Juan de Triana. Historians have been baffled by this incident since then. Some claim Columbus lied to cheat Triana out of his reward. Later Columbus did receive the thirty crowns as a pension from the royal Spanish treasury.

According to Columbus' log books, the *Pinta* was sailing two leagues ahead of the *St. Mary*. At an estimated speed of ten miles per hour, the *St. Mary* was almost fifty miles behind the *Pinta*. The curvature

MYSTERIOUS DISAPPEARANCES: THEY NEVER CAME BACK

of the earth, the rolling swell of the ocean waves would have prevented Columbus from sighting a light on land. In addition, the ships in which Columbus sailed were small. It is doubtful that a small light on shore could have been seen at half that distance.

In his ***Columbus: His Life and Voyages***, (G. F. Putnam's & Son; New York; 1905) author Washington Irving had difficulty with the inconsistencies about the light. He observed: ". . . had Columbus seen a light ahead, four hours' swift sailing would have brought him high and dry upon the shore; while on the other hand had he seen a light in any other direction, it was scarcely probable that he would have sailed from it." In addition, Columbus did not mention his sighting until after the signal from the *Pinta*.

Before we label Columbus as an opportunistic liar, we might explore other unexplained lights in the Triangle of the Lost. In 1954, R. B. David of Cedar Key, Florida, set out for some fishing on the Gulf Coast of Florida. He was accompanied by his brother, Tilden David, and Oliver Holmes, a retired railroad man. Out at sea, the three men discovered a strong wind moving in. The wind increased the size of the waves until a large swell swamped the boat and it started to sink.

MYSTERIOUS DISAPPEARANCES: THEY NEVER CAME BACK

An experienced and quick-thinking individual, R. B. David quickly released the mounting bolts on the boat's outboard motor. This enabled the boat to remain afloat in a capsized position. The three men hung onto the overturned vessel as they drifted through the dark ocean.

"They became concerned when they lost their sense of direction," a newsman reported. "The ocean and sky were extremely dark. None of the three men knew in which direction they should go to return to land."

Around midnight, a red light suddenly materialized out in the darkness. The light bobbed up and down, to and fro, as if asking the three men to move toward it. Using a seat from their boat as a makeshift paddle, they gradually moved towards the light. When they seemed to reach the light, it moved away from them. Dawn was breaking over the ocean when the three grateful men felt land beneath their feet. "And," reported Rube Allyn in the *St. Petersburg Times*, "they never did locate the source of the light."

The incident was covered by author Vincent Gaddis in his remarkable book, ***Mysterious Fires and Lights*** (David McKay Company; N. Y., 1967; and Dell paperback edition; 1968). Gaddis covered other enigmatic lights and fires in his book, including a light that guided searchers to a crashed airliner in the hills of Tennessee.

Could Columbus have seen a supernatural light? UFO buffs frequently point out that such mysterious glowing globs of light are often associated with flying saucers. Could we stretch our imaginations to consider that Columbus might have been guided by spacecraft from alien worlds? Before we accept the truth of the admiral's statements, let's look at what he discovered in the Triangle of the Lost. In his journal, he reported seeing three mermaids during his voyage to the New World. He also claimed to have discovered two islands opposite each other inhabited by Amazonian women with a ferocious, warlike nature. The other island was held by men. Columbus said the men were allowed to visit the Amazon's island one day each year to perpetuate their race. Boy babies were sent to the male island for raising, while the females were retained by their mothers.

Columbus also said the small island of San Salvador had a harbor large enough to hold all the "ships in Christiandom." Another of his fantasies was the alleged sighting of men with dog's heads, people with tails, lions, elephants, and tigers. He also claimed to have seen a griffin, a legendary animal with the head and wings of an eagle and the body of a lion. His Journal also told of sighting a group of people with single,

MYSTERIOUS DISAPPEARANCES: THEY NEVER CAME BACK

cyclopean eyes and of hearing the song of the nightingale—a bird that was unknown in the Western Hemisphere.

On his return to Spain, Columbus was given a hero's welcome. After enjoying the splendor of the royal court, and the company of the King and Queen, he sailed three more times to the New World. On his third voyage, Columbus was replaced as head of the government in the New World. Bobadilla, his successor, had Columbus arrested and the man who was known as "Admiral of the Ocean, Viceroy and Governor-General of the Indies," was sent back to Spain in chains.

Columbus successfully defended himself before the King and Queen and, on May 19, 1502, sailed on his fourth and final voyage into the Triangle of the Lost. Upon his arrival in the New World, Columbus tried to dock his ship on Hispaniola (now Haiti and the Dominican Republic) although he'd been forbidden to do so by the Queen. Thirty-two caravels rode low in the water of the harbor at Santo Domingo, a vast treasure fleet with riches for the Spanish treasury. Flagship of the armada was the *El Dorado*, commanded by Admiral Antonio de Torres.

Columbus had many enemies in Hispaniola and he was forbidden to land on the island he had discovered. Instead, he rowed to the *El Dorado* for a conference with Admiral Torres.

"One of my ships is in bad shape," Columbus reported. "I'd like to trade you for one that can hold full sail." Admiral Torres shook his head. "Impossible! Every ship is loaded and ready to sail this evening." Columbus looked shocked. "Surely you're not sailing with the wind blowing in from the west."

"We've got a priceless treasure stored aboard," replied Admiral Torres. "Governor Bobadilla has retired. His gift for the royal family is a table crafted from pure gold. It weighs more than three thousand pounds. We've waited far too long to get these ships loaded."

"The west wind can get stormy in minutes," Columbus insisted.

The Spanish Admiral was considering the explorer's proposal when the door opened and retired Governor Bobadilla entered the cabin. Columbus repeated his warning to the man who had sent him back to Spain in chains.

Bobadilla laughed. "The wind isn't too high," he snorted. "We'll need a strong wind to get us back to Spain. These ships are loaded with gold. Normally we would have to fight against an east wind. We should

MYSTERIOUS DISAPPEARANCES: THEY NEVER CAME BACK

make it back to Spain in record time."

Columbus shook his head sadly. "You'll be carried too far out into the ocean," he insisted. "If the wind gets higher, you'll be in trouble."

Admiral Torres sided with Bobadilla and, as Columbus left the *El Dorado*, the ships' crew was hoisting their sails. Columbus returned to his ship and, pacing the deck, watched Spain's first treasure armada sail toward home. Three days later, the fleet sailed into Mono Passage, a stretch of water separating Hispaniola from the island of Puerto Rico.

Admiral Torres strode the deck, warily watching the rising gusts of wind from the west. Suddenly, a cry rang out from the crow's nest. "Storm a-coming!" yelled the lookout. Moments later, the storm struck with the fury of hell unleashed. The alarm was sounded and sailors rushed to their emergency positions.

The howling wind pushed against the caravels with tremendous force. Timbers creaked and masts plunged to the deck. Whole sheets of sail were ripped away. Falling timbers crushed the frightened crew members against the deck. Millions in gold smashed through ship's bottoms and plunged into the sea.

When the storm was over, the *El Dorado* and twenty-six other caravels were missing. Ten storm-smashed ships were driven ashore on the reefs off Hispaniola and Puerto Rico. The other seventeen ships vanished, undoubtedly sunk beneath the sea. Bobadilla, the man who arrested Christopher Columbus, vanished along with his massive gold table he intended to give the Spanish King and Queen. Strangely enough, the only ship which reached Spain safely was the poorest, weakest vessel in the fleet. On board was four thousand pieces of gold that belonged to Christopher Columbus!

On his fourth and final journey to the New World, Columbus sailed slowly down the coast of Honduras, then along the Mosquito Coast to the Village of Cariari. Once again, he describes an unusual animal he allegedly encountered. He wrote in his journal:

"I had, at the time, two pigs and an Irish dog, who was always in great dread of them. An archer had wounded an animal like an ape, except that it was larger and had the face of a man. The arrow had pierced it from the neck to the tail, which made it so fierce that they were obliged to disable it by cutting off one of its arms and a leg. One of the pigs grew wild on seeing this, and fled; upon which I ordered the begare (as the inhabitants call him) to be thrown to the pig, and though the animal was

MYSTERIOUS DISAPPEARANCES: THEY NEVER CAME BACK

nearly dead, and the arrow had passed quite through his body, yet he threw his tail around the snout of the pig, and then, holding him firmly, seized him by the nape of the neck with his remaining hand, as if he were engaged with an enemy. The action was so novel and extraordinary that I have thought it worthwhile to describe here."

What was a begare? A half-man, half-ape like the abominable snowman of the Himalayan mountains? A cousin of the Big Foot allegedly found in the mountains of the western United States? Or was Christopher Columbus merely dreaming up new fantasies to thrill his readers back at the royal court? We can only be left to wonder about this sadistic account of savage treatment to animals, whatever they may be.

During the last century there was an organized effort to have Christopher Columbus canonized as a saint in the Catholic Church. One of his would-be canonizers was M. de Lourges, who told of how Columbus performed a miracle by saving his ships from a storm. M. de Lourges explained:

"It was one of those waterspouts that seamen call fronks, which then so little known, and which have "since submerged so many vessels. . . at the cries of distress, he rises with wonted vigor in order to survey and weigh the peril. He also perceived the formidable thing that was approaching. The sea appeared to be sucked up into the heavens. For this unknown phenomenon he saw no remedy. Art was useless and navigation powerless; besides, there was no steering any longer.

"Immediately Columbus, the adorer of the Word, suspected in this terrific display of the brute force of Nature, some satanic maneuver. He could not exorcise the power of the air, according to the rites of the Church, fearing to usurp the authority of the priesthood; but he called to mind that he was the chief of a Christian expedition, and that his object was a holy one; and that he desired in his way, to compel the spirit of darkness to yield the passage to him.

"He had blessed wax-candles immediately lighted and put in lanterns; then he girdled himself with his sword over the cord of St. Francis, and, taking the book of the gospels, standing in the face of the waterspout, which was coming near, accosted it with the sublime declaration which commences the gospel of the well-beloved disciple of Jesus, St. John, the adoptive son of the Blessed Virgin.

"Trying to raise his voice above the howling tempest, the messenger of Salvation declared to the Typhoon that in the beginning was

MYSTERIOUS DISAPPEARANCES: THEY NEVER CAME BACK

the Word; that the word was with God, and that the word was God, that all things have been made by Him, and that without Him was not anything made that was made; that in Him was life, and that the life was the light of men; and that the word was made of flesh, and that he dwelt among us.

"Then, in the name of the divine word, Jesus Christ, whose words calmed the winds and appeased the billows, Christopher Columbus commands the waterspout to spare those who carry the cross to the extremities of the earth, and navigate in the name of the thrice Holy Trinity. Then, drawing his sword with a full and ardent faith, he traces the air with the steel, the sign of the cross, and describes a circle around him with the sword, as if he had already severed or intercepted the waterspout. And in fact—O prodigy!—the waterspout which was coming straight toward the caravels, appeared to be pushed obliquely, passed between the caravels and went bellowing off to lose itself in the immensity of the Atlantic Ocean."

This interesting passage is from *"Christopher Colombo,"* by M. de Lourges, volume two, chapter two.

During that same voyage, Columbus set down in his journal that he fell asleep one night on the deck of his ship and, during his sleep, held a conversation with God. As Columbus wrote, the Diety seemed displeased that Queen Isabella and others had deprived the mariner of his just rewards for discovery of the New World. "Thus I have told Thee what the Creator has done for thee." Columbus wrote of his vision, "and what He does for all men. Even now He partially shows thee the reward of so many toils and dangers incurred by thee in the service of others."

After further adventures in the Triangle of the Lost, Columbus sailed back to Spain to petition the royal family for his share of plunder from the New World. The King and Queen were slow in granting Columbus his titles and royalties on these riches. He wrote to them and stated: "Gold is the most precious of all commodities; gold constitutes treasure, and he who possesses it has all he needs in this world, and also the means of rescuing souls from purgatory and restoring them to the enjoyments of paradise."

Knowing that death was near, Columbus donned the garb of the Franciscan monks. He redoubled his prayers and fasting. In the first two weeks of May, 1506, he prepared his will. He passed away on the 20th day of that same month. His adventures in the Triangle of the Lost were over. His efforts to find new land in the west led Pope Alexander the

MYSTERIOUS DISAPPEARANCES: THEY NEVER CAME BACK

Sixth to confer title to the new continent on the Spanish royal family. Regardless of his motives' and the truth o his adventures in the Triangle of the Lost, Columbus was assured a place in history.

MYSTERIOUS DISAPPEARANCES: THEY NEVER CAME BACK

CHAPTER ELEVEN

SEA SERPENTS AND MARITIME MONSTERS

It was July, 1893, and the freighter *Umfli* fought against the swelling waves of the turbulent Atlantic Ocean. It was almost noon on a clouded, misty morning when the ship entered the Triangle of the Lost. Suddenly, a breathless first mate dashed into the cabin of Captain Joseph Cringle.

"Sir, the lookout has spotted a sea serpent," shouted the first mate,

"Mister! Have you been drinking?" snapped the captain. He sniffed at his mate's breath. "You've been on board at sea long enough to realize there's no such thing as a sea serpent."

Moments later Captain Cringle, his officers, and the crew of the *Umfli* revised their thoughts about maritime monsters. While the crewmen and the ship's passengers watched, a large barrel-bodied creature with three sharp humps rose up a few yards away from the ship. The creature's weird head rose fifteen to twenty feet out of the water atop a long serpentine neck.

The astonished sailors and their passengers observed the unusual sea serpent for more than an hour. They sighed audibly when this strange creature sank beneath the surface and vanished into the ocean depths.

A man acquainted with the superstitions of the sea, Captain Cringle knew that sailors have been reporting the appearance of sea monsters since the first mariner sailed on the first voyage over the oceans. He also was well acquainted with the old tales told in waterfront bars about sailors who claimed our seas hide monstrous sea serpents. These ancient legends prevented the exploration of much of the world until Christopher Columbus sailed to the New World.

MYSTERIOUS DISAPPEARANCES: THEY NEVER CAME BACK

Realizing the importance of the sighting, Captain Cringle assembled his crew and the ship's passengers. "We've just witnessed a creature that is unknown to science," Captain Cringle told the group. "I would appreciate each of you writing down your account of what happened. I would like you to sign documents to authenticate what we've seen this morning."

These statements and documents were promptly prepared, notarized, and signed. The first mate collected these accounts and placed them in the purser's safe.

"Those pieces of paper aren't going to help us," the first mate told the captain, in a dour tone. "I don't think anyone's going to believe us if we had a shipload of signed documents."

The first mate's pessimistic statement was truly prophetic. Scientists refused to seriously consider the possibility of a sea serpent. One scholar suggested to Captain Cringle that a string of porpoises had been mistakenly identified as a sea serpent, pointed to the nearness of the Sargasso Sea and said the *Umfli* had spotted a floating island of seaweed. One outraged expert on marine life penned a scathing article in a scientific journal. He stated that Captain Cringle and the other witnesses had seen a combination of sharks, seaweed, and porpoises while under the influence of mass hallucinations.

"I do not know what it was," admitted Captain Cringle. "I don't believe an island of seaweed can move along at fourteen knots. I know a porpoise can't keep his head fifteen feet out of water on a slender neck. After the controversy about the sighting, I wish some other ship had spotted the serpent. I've been ridiculed by everyone. I know what I saw and, until my dying day, I'll believe that creature was from some prehistoric time. There are more wondrous creatures in the ocean than our scholars would like to admit. Their cynical attitudes may amuse their readers and followers, but it doesn't change the truth."

Throughout the world over the past few centuries, many respected people have sighted sea serpents and enormous maritime monsters. The bodies of huge, unknown creatures have been washed ashore in Scotland England, France, and several other countries. The carcass of one massive monster was beached in Tasmania a few years ago and to date, scientists have been unable to identity this baffling creature.

Captain George Hope sailed through the Triangle of the Lost in 1883 and sighted a weird marine animal. Captain Hope reported the creature had "the head of an alligator, except that the neck was considerably longer. Instead of legs, the creature had flippers."

Everyone had a good laugh at the captain's claims until a scientist revealed that his description matched perfectly with that of a prehistoric animal called the Plesiosaurus. In recent years several zoologists have suggested that these beasts and many of their companions may have moved to the depths of the oceans when life upon land became dangerous. Humanity evolved from cellular life in the sea and dinosaurs and other prehistoric creatures may have reversed the process. Dinosaurs ruled the earth for several million years, then vanished unexplainably. Perhaps, beneath the waves of the Triangle of the Lost and other ocean waters reigns a band of gilled dinosaurs.

During a meeting of the International Geographic Congress at the United Nations recently, a scientist stated that prehistoric creatures still exist in the ocean. He explained that scientists have discovered sharks' teeth that measure a foot in length. "To hold teeth of that size" a shark would have to have a jaw span of from 15 to 22 feet," said one oceanographer. "We have barely begun to catalogue the many forms of marine life in our oceans. What we may ultimately find in the deepest regions of the seas is beyond any man's imagination."

One remarkable scientist is not only a believer in marine monsters but he has often fished for these creatures. Dr. Robert Menzies, of Columbia University, used a fishing line with a 2-1/2-ton breaking point. He attached this line to the ship's wench. The fishhook was a three-foot steel shank that was baited with squid.

On one occasion Dr. Menzies was fishing in the waters of the extremely deep Peru-Chile Ocean trench along the coast of South America. His hook had been lowered to a depth of 1200 feet ". . . when 'something' grabbed the bait. There was a brief moment of furious action along the line, then the cable slackened. When he pulled his line to the surface, Dr. Menzies discovered that his three-foot steel hook had been completely straightened by some enormous creature from the ocean's depth."

Author J. B. Holder, writing in *Century Magazine's* issue of June, 1892, told of a monstrous carcass that had been washed ashore near the New River Inlet in Florida. He wrote: ". . In the spring of 1885 the Rev. Gordon of Milwaukee, president of the United States Humane Society, chanced to visit, in the course of his duties, a remote and obscure portion of the Atlantic shores of Florida.

MYSTERIOUS DISAPPEARANCES: THEY NEVER CAME BACK

"While lying at anchor in New River Inlet, the flukes of the anchor became fouled with what proved to be a carcass of considerable length. Mr. Gordon quickly observed that it was a vertebrate, and at first thought it was probably a cetacean, but, on examination it was seen to have features more suggestive of saurians. Its total length was 42 feet. Its width was six feet. The head was absent; two flippers, or forelimbs, were noticed, and a somewhat slender neck . . . six feet in length. The carcass was in a state of decomposition; the abdomen was open, and the intestines protruding.

"The striking slenderness of the thorax as compared with the great length of body and tail very naturally suggested to Mr. Gordon, whose readings served him well, the form of the great saurians, whose bones have so frequently been found in several localities along the Atlantic coast. No cetacean known to science has such a slender body and such a well-marked and slender neck . . . Appreciating the great importance of securing the entire carcass, Mr. Gordon had it hauled above the high-water mark, and took all possible precautions to preserve the bones until they could be removed . He counted without the possible treacherous hurricane, the waters of the ocean—recalled the strange waif!"

MYSTERIOUS DISAPPEARANCES: THEY NEVER CAME BACK

Whatever the strange monster in Florida may have been, we know that it was found in the Triangle of the Lost.

On the morning of March 23, 1830, Captain Eugene Delan directed the schooner *Eagle* southward out of Charleston, South Carolina. Captain Delan and his crew said that about 11 o'clock that morning a large creature like an alligator approached their ship. They said the creature was swimming on the surface of the water.

The *Eagle* sailed to within an estimated twenty yards of the beast. The monster seemed curious and remained motionless as the ship approached. A crewman on the *Eagle* aimed a musket at the creature and fired. Several bullets struck the beast and it immediately dove under the ship. Sailors cried out in fear as the beast pounded the bottom of their ship several times with its tail.

Newspapers reported the incident and a description of the beast. One report said: "All of the sailors had an excellent opportunity to see their enemy and agreed that its length was about 70 feet. The body was as thick as, or possibly thicker, than a 60 gallon keg. The unknown creature was grayish in color, eel shaped, without any visible fins and was apparently covered with scales. The head and beak resembled an alligator, but the head was ten feet long and as big as a hogshead."

An unusual sea serpent was spotted in the Triangle of the Lost on March 20, 1873. The report was not published until 1906 when the **Illustrated London News** printed an astonishing account of the sighting by two expert zoologists. Encouraged by this report, retired Naval Commander Reginald Yonge sent the newspaper an excerpt from his log book which was written aboard *H.M.S. Orontes:*

"March 20, 1873, 3:15 a.m. Air pump rod carried away. Stopped engine. 7:20 a.m. as Captain Ferry and myself were walking on the upper bridge, we saw something, which first attracted my attention through being white, rise gradually out of the water, and remain stationary for a few seconds. It was the head of an immense monster. The shape looked to me very much like an eel's head. It rose about five feet out of the water, but what was its length under water I was unable to see. The ship was drifting toward it. I rushed down to the chart house for a rifle. While I was gone the Captain afterwards told me, the head had gradually sunk and risen again even closer to the ship—almost so close as to reach out and touch it. The Captain had a still better view of it.

"It didn't appreciate the dangers of approaching the ship as it

MYSTERIOUS DISAPPEARANCES: THEY NEVER CAME BACK

turned leisurely, sinking at the same time, and swam away in a southwesterly direction, rising to the surface once or twice when the Captain had a shot at it with the rifle. It was seen also by the Quartermaster, the Signalman, and by Lieutenant Lane from his cabin port. The Lieutenant said his attention was drawn to it when it first rose out of the water, making a snorting noise. It is generally considered by those who saw it to be about 48 feet in length. The back of the head was black, the throat and belly white, and the eyes white and set well back. A few others saw it but the crew and ship's company being at breakfast, there were not many people on deck."

In his letter which he sent io *Illustrated London News* with this report, Commander Yonge added more details:

"At the time we'd just come through the Mona Passage between San Domingo and Puerto Rico in the West Indies. The weather was beautiful and fair. I believe now that I must have underestimated the height to which the monster's head rose above water. I do not believe that I should have so distinctly seen it if it had only been five feet. However, I've left it as I originally wrote it down in my journal."

One of the strangest monsters to be reported in the Triangle of the Lost was seen by the crew of an American schooner in 1883. *The New York Times* reported that a creature was at first mistaken for the hull of an overturned boat. When the crew of the schooner came closer, they

MYSTERIOUS DISAPPEARANCES: THEY NEVER CAME BACK

discovered a turtle estimated to measure 60 feet long and 40 feet wide. This "super turtle" sounds like something out of the pages of prehistoric times. If such enormous turtles do inhabit the waters of the Triangle of the Lost, we can only shudder at what may have happened to the occupants of many doomed boats.

Before we dismiss this sighting as the figment of overly active imaginations, we might look at other reports of enormous turtles. In June, 1956, the Liberian registered freighter *Rhapsody* was approaching the coast of Nova Scotia. Crew members aboard that vessel reported seeing a turtle that measured an estimated 45 feet in length. The giant turtle was said to have flippers that were at least 15 feet long. The turtle's enormous head was riding at least 10 feet up out of the water.

In Sumatra, natives have insisted that the "Father-of-All-Turtles" exists and appears occasionally on the shores near their villages. There have been numerous sightings of giant turtles in the Indian Ocean, near Australia, and in the Triangle of the Lost. Such incredible turtles could capsize a small boat with ease. Folk tales handed down in Bermuda also tell of an enormous turtle that was worshipped by the original inhabitants of that island.

Wide World Magazine published an account of the sightings of a sea serpent in the Triangle of the Lost in 1903. The cargo steamer *Tresca* was commanded by Captain W. H. Bartlett when it left Philadelphia on May 28, 1903 and sailed south into the Triangle of the Lost" On the third day of the voyage the second officer of the ship, Joseph Grey, saw a disturbance in the water off the ship's bow. "I took a closer look and discovered there was a shoal of about forty sharks packed tightly together," said Mr. Grey. "They apparently were fleeing some type of danger."

Nearly an hour later the *Tresco's* lookout gave a cry of alarm.

"Wreck ahead!" cried the man in the crow's nest.

The *Tresco* sailed toward what appeared to be a drifting wreck off the ship's port bow. "Keep a sharp eye out for survivors," commanded Captain Bartlett. "There may be some poor souls out there in the sea."

As the ship moved closer, a horrible head rose suddenly up out of the water. According to Second Officer Grey, the tall powerful neck of the monster had the thickness and the strength of cathedral pillars. The sight of the vast creature rising up out of the sea terrified the crew. One frightened sailor fell to his knees on the ship's deck and began to pray. Another cried hysterically and dashed below decks. Others were para-

MYSTERIOUS DISAPPEARANCES: THEY NEVER CAME BACK

lyzed into a shocked sense of immobility.

The bizarre creature remained motionless as it swam towards the ship. Only the beady, reptilian eyes and the long, snakelike tail moved. Second Officer Grey estimated the creature was about 100 feet long, and at least eight feet wide where the body broadened out. Later, in his article in **Wide World Magazine**, Grey described the frightening creature. He wrote:

"There was something unspeakably loathsome about the head, which was five feet long from nose to upper extremity. Such a head I never saw on any denizen of the sea... underneath the jaw there seemed to be a sort of pouch of drooping skin. The nose, like an upturned snout, was somewhat recurved. I can remember no nostrils or blow holes. The lower lip was half rejecting, half pendulous. Presently I noticed something dripping from the ugly lower jaw. Watching, I saw that it was saliva of a dirty drab color. While it displayed no teeth, it did possess very long and formidable molars, like a walrus' tusks. Its eyes were of a dull reddish color and they were elongated vertically. They carried in their depths a somber, baleful glow as if within them was concentrated all the fierce, menacing spirits that raged in the huge bulk behind."

MYSTERIOUS DISAPPEARANCES: THEY NEVER CAME BACK

This massive creature from the depths of the Triangle of the Lost observed the *Tresco* and its crew for several minutes. Then the monster lashed the water into a furious turmoil. The creature's frightening red eyes stared intently at the ship. As threatening as it appeared to the terrified sailors, it came no closer to the ship. At last, the monstrous creature turned and swam away from the ship.

The winter of 1933-34 appears to have been record times for the sighting of sea serpents in the Triangle of the Lost. The Cunard liner *Mauretania* met several of these creatures during a cruise into the West Indies. The first monster was seen on January 30, 1934, by two officers who spotted a jet-black creature about a mile off St. Eustatius Island. They estimated the serpent was at least 65 feet long, six feet wide. The head was raised more than six feet off the surface of the ocean.

On February 6, near the port of La Guaira, a crewman on the *Mauretania* spotted another serpent judged to be about 25 feet long.

The third monster was seen about 600 miles east of Nassau in the Bahama Islands. It was estimated to be 60 feet long, and four large humps capped by a tall fin were seen above the water. Both crewmen and passengers on the giant ocean liner took these sightings seriously. On subsequent voyages the passengers on the *Mauretania* were always on the lookout for sea serpents in the Triangle of the Lost. One afternoon a physician, Dr. R. J. Dodson of New York, approached the ship's captain with an explanation for the unusual frequency of sightings. "What do you do with the garbage from your kitchens?" asked Dr. Dodson.

"We throw the waste into the sea," admitted the captain.

The doctor smiled knowingly. "'I've noticed that sharks seem to be attracted to the food you throw overboard," he said. "It would appear likely that these sea serpents are attracted by this enormous amount of free food. Perhaps sea serpents, like any of God's creatures, large or small, appreciate a free cafeteria."

Danish American Lines' *Amerika* was approaching St. Thomas in the Virgin Islands on October 26, 1934. An Englishman, Mr. George Cooper, was leaning over the side of the ship and gazing into the clear blue ocean waters. His report of what happened next appeared in **Listener Magazine** in 1953:

"The weather was bright and clear and at a distance of about a quarter of a mile, traveling at an opposite course, an elongated mass, 50 to 80 feet in length, broke surface in a flurry of foam and spray. It had a

MYSTERIOUS DISAPPEARANCES: THEY NEVER CAME BACK

long serpentine neck, thrust upwards, and a flattish head, which, however, was flexed and gave it an equine appearance. Behind the neck a series of six or more large, protruding humps appeared. They were chocolate brown in color, moving forward in sinuous motions, giving an illusion of speed which was probably not more than 15 or 20 knots."

Mr. Cooper was excited by the appearance of the unusual maritime monster. He called his wife to the side of the ship and she viewed the creature with several other witnesses. Several of the officers aboard the *Amerika* also confirmed the sighting.

World War II and the necessity for secrecy in the Triangle of the Lost ended sightings of these monsters. In 1948, Ralph Dickens of Ft. Lauderdale, Florida, went sailing into the Triangle of the Lost's bizarre boundaries. Dickens was not expecting to encounter one of the largest creatures in the ocean. After finding a school of fish several miles beyond the shore, Dickens threw out his lines. Suddenly the mass of fish disappeared. Waiting for their return, Dickens leaned back against the side of his boat, ate a sandwich, and drank a cup of coffee.

"Suddenly I had a very strange feeling," Mr. Dickens told newsmen. "It was as if someone were staring at my back. You know the type of feeling when the hair seems to stand up on the back of your neck. I turned around and almost died of shock."

"What was it," asked an interested reporter.

"It was the strangest thing I'd ever seen," answered Mr. Dickens. "It just about scared me out of my sanity. I turned around and looked directly into the face of a giant sea serpent. Its head and neck were raised out of the water to the height of about ten feet. The frightening thing was staring at me with two dull dark eyes. I'll never forget those eyes because they protruded out from a snakelike head like a couple of bumps. The eyes would be five inches across and they just stared directly at me."

The newsman stared at Dickens in near disbelief.

"I know what you're thinking," Ralph Dickens told the reporter. "You weren't out there to see the creature. I'll never forget that head. It was slightly larger than the neck, probably about 36 inches in diameter. The head was green with light brown spots all over the head and neck. The thing stared at me for at least a minute, moving its head slightly from side to side. Then it disappeared beneath the surface. I pulled up anchor as fast as possible and ran full speed right back to shore."

Tim Dinsdale, author of *The Leviathans*, published in England, tells the story of Edward Bryan McCleary who lost four of his friends during a skin diving expedition into the Triangle of the Lost. McCleary, 16, and his four teenage companions had gone skin diving during the afternoon of March 24, 1962, off the coast of Florida. They became lost in the fog five miles out to sea and, as they paddled their way towards shore, they heard a sudden hissing noise in the fog. Everyone on the rubber raft shrank back at the smell of a sickening odor. One boy screamed when the twelve foot pole-like object loomed up out of the fog and started toward their raft.

"The silence was broken once again by something out of the fog," said McCleary. "I can only describe it as a high-pitched whine. We panicked. All five of us put on our fins and went into the water. Patches of brown, crusty slime lay all over the surface of the sea."

Exactly what occurred after that is unclear. McCleary reported there were screams from his friends. He saw a beast with a turtle's head, green eyes, and oval pupils. McCleary escaped by spending the night on the hull of an abandoned ship the young men planned to investigate.

During a discussion with Dr. Ivan T. Sanderson before his death,

MYSTERIOUS DISAPPEARANCES: THEY NEVER CAME BACK

we debated the possibility of sea serpents or some form of super-life in the world's oceans.

"There's probably no limit to the size of creatures in the ocean," said Sanderson. "I expect the limitations occur on form as they get longer. There may be 200-foot creatures that are yet to be discovered in the sea. When we find them they'll probably be very elongated or serpentine in shape. This would be true whether they are seals, whales, other mammals, or even fish."

There have been more than one thousand well-documented cases of sea serpents being sighted throughout the world. A large portion of these sightings have occurred in the deadly waters of the Triangle of the Lost. We cannot dismiss the probability that a lone, small boat could be attacked by such creatures. As the sightings by the terrified crew of the *Tresco* indicated, even the presence of such monsters would frighten an observer into bizarre, possibly psychotic, behavior. Under such strain, people might abandon ship, commit suicide, or even attack each other in a frenzy of shock.

Until a much more detailed investigation is given to the mystery of sea serpents, we can only wonder about their appearance in the Triangle of the Lost.

MYSTERIOUS DISAPPEARANCES: THEY NEVER CAME BACK

CHAPTER TWELVE

HAVE WE ENCOUNTERED UNIDENTIFIED UNDERSEA "FLYING SACUERS?"

Author and UFO reporter Ed Hyde told of an interesting phenomenon that occurred in the Antarctic Ocean. Writing in **Man's Illustrated Magazine**, Hyde reported that "something" startled several observers by smashing through thick layers of ice over the ocean. In **UFOs at 450 Fathoms**, Hyde told of Dr. R. J. Villela, a Brazilian scientist who was with the U.S. Navy during "*Operation Deep Freeze*" at the South Pole. Dr. Villela was shocked into near speechlessness by an "unusual object" that came smashing out of the sea through an estimated 40 feet of ice. The silver-colored "something" soared up and flashed off into the polar sky with amazing speed. Dr. Villela was on an icebreaker in Admiralty Bay when he witnessed this mysterious object. The stunned scientist was walking on deck on a brisk day while the remaining crew members were below due to the extreme cold. Suddenly, Dr. Villela heard an enormous crashing sound beneath the-ice off the ship's bow. Rushing to the edge of the ship, he saw enormous chunks of ice being thrown high in the air. Huge blocks of ice came hurtling down all around the hole in the massive sheet of ice. He reported the water was boiling, that large clouds of steam came from the opening in the ice. The enormous noise brought the officer of the day and a sailor on deck. Seeing the jagged hole in the ice, they caught a glimpse of the silver-colored object as it shot up into the sky. Dr. Villela later reported he was "unnerved by the affair. It was certainly no laughing matter to those of us who observed it."

What Dr. Villela may have observed was an UUFO-underwater unidentified flying object. Since the first sighting of flying saucers by pilot Kenneth Arnold over Mt. Rainier, Washington, on the afternoon of June

MYSTERIOUS DISAPPEARANCES: THEY NEVER CAME BACK

24, 1947, more than fifty per cent of all UFO sightings have been connected with water. Many UFO researchers believe that an alien intelligence has established secret underwater UFO bases on our planet. These researchers claim that a superior race of alien beings have monitored our civilization for several thousands of years. They have remained undetected by building their bases beneath the world's oceans. This concept of a vast underwater civilization is mind-boggling and without any supportive evidence.

Dr. Ivan T. Sanderson, author of several important books on UFOs, suggested in *Invisible Residents* (World Publishing Co., Cleveland, 1970), that just such an underwater civilization has existed on this planet for centuries. Dr. Sanderson explained that this hidden race of beings may possibly have evolved on this planet. He also considered the possibility that they are intelligent entities from another world who have been coming here for a long time. Naturally, if an advanced race of superior beings wished to remain undetected on our planet, they might live on the bottom of our oceans.

The theory for such alien beings indicates their base may be located beneath the waves of the Triangle of the Lost. In the summer of 1963 the U.S. Navy sent several ships to maneuver off the coast of Puerto Rico. Among these vessels was the flagship the *U.S.S. Wasp*, an aircraft carrier. The *Wasp* acted as the commanding ship for "*Operation Detect*" to test and train U.S. Naval personnel in underwater sonar tracking operations. Several submarines also participated in the exercise to provide an object for tracking. The Navy hoped to train advanced sonar crewmen in the use of extremely intricate and highly advanced electronic tracking systems. In addition to the ships and submarines, several airplanes took part in the operation. The planes were equipped with top secret sonar tracking devices which allowed them to fly over the ocean and detect underwater movement of submarines.

The exercise continued without mishap until a sonar operator busted into command headquarters aboard the *Wasp* one night.

"What's up, sailor?" demanded a disgruntled lieutenant commander.

"You've got to come to sonar shack, sir," the sailor blustered out. "Our equipment's gone haywire."

"Get a technician to fix it," ordered the officer.

"We've tried that, sir," explained the technician. "Nothing seems

MYSTERIOUS DISAPPEARANCES: THEY NEVER CAME BACK

to work. We're getting a readout on an object that just can't be correct."

Before the lieutenant commander could make arrangements to leave his post, reports poured into the *Wasp* command post on similar problems on fourteen other ships. The officer rushed to the *Wasp* sonar room and discovered the operators had picked up an underwater object that was apparently driven by a single propeller. Sonar blips indicated the object was moving beneath the waves at a speed of more than 150 knots.

"That's impossible," said the astonished officer. "Nothing goes that fast. I've been around submarines and they can't move that fast!"

As the officer knew, the fastest speed for a submarine traveling under water is around 45 knots, or 51.8 miles per hour. Yet, sophisticated U.S. Navy tracking equipment indicated something was moving at incredible speed through the Triangle of the Lost. During the next two days, Navy technicians maintained an accurate record as the object maneuvered beneath the ocean.

Once, the object submerged to a depth of more than 27,000 feet. This is impossible for an ordinary submarine. The U.S. *Aluminaut* made a dive off the Bahama Islands on November 12, 1957 to a record-breaking 6,250 feet. The *Trieste*, a specially equipped diving craft, descended to 35,800 feet in the Pacific Ocean in 1960. However, nothing like the tiny *Trieste* could move at 150 knots.

U.S. Navy command headquarters at Norfolk, Virginia, was notified of the baffling incident. Admirals conferred quickly and immediately radioed back that no nation in the world had a submarine capable of such high speed maneuvers. The Navy command suggested that the detection and tracking equipment aboard should be carefully checked for the possibility of malfunctions. While one sonar recording machine might give out a mistaken reading, it is doubtful that the equipment aboard fourteen ships would malfunction at the same time. The object eventually vanished in the direction of the Azores Islands. The Navy brass demanded, and then filed away, reports on the incident. No one could account for the origin of the object. Tests indicated the sonar equipment was functioning perfectly. Three years later in 1956, U.S. Navy scientists began to experiment with long range underwater communications systems. They were well aware of the problems of communicating over long distances beneath the water. Several attempts have been made to establish a foolproof system. All have failed. However, as Ed Hyde reported in **Man's Illustrated Magazine,** one scientist evolved a new approach

MYSTERIOUS DISAPPEARANCES: THEY NEVER CAME BACK

to the problem.

Hyde wrote, "... He set up a mile-long antenna to prove his point. The antenna was laid along the continental shelf, which stretches out 100 miles from the east coast of the U.S. before dropping into the very deepest areas of the Atlantic. Far out to sea was a research ship with instruments lowered close to the bottom to pick up signals. Transmissions of signals got under way. What startled the men aboard the research ship was the reception of a signal, and then a repeat of the signal, followed by a strange code which computers are still trying to break."

Hyde reported that what may have occurred, according to subsequent Naval reports, was that in some manner the signals were picked up and mimicked by "something unknown." Then, this unknown "intelligence" decided to begin transmission of its own messages on the same wave length used by the Navy. Hyde reported that scientists tracked the source of these strange signals to the deepest part of the Atlantic Ocean—a point where the depth measured more than 29,000 feet.

The U.S. Navy is not the only organization to encounter trouble in the Triangle of the Lost. On the night of July 6, 1955, the *T. T. Jawenta* sailed through the Triangle. The Norwegian ship was enroute between Venezuela and the Canary Islands. Suddenly, the lookout on the ship reported a bright object moving in a northerly direction across the sky. Captain H. A. Trovik was quickly alerted and he rushed to the bridge. Captain Trovik later prepared a report that was submitted to the Geophysical Institute in Burgen, Norway. In the report chief mate Torgrim Lien stated, "I can say with absolute certainty that this was not an aircraft of any known design. Neither was it a rocket, a meteor or ball lightning."

Lien and several other crewmen described the object as moving at a tremendous rate of speed. It was said to have long tongues of flames spreading out behind it. One crewman added, "The object was visible for approximately one minute. It moved across the sky during that time. Despite this enormous speed and the closeness of its passage over our ship, no one heard any sound. One seaman, Hernandez Ambrosio, has said that it appeared as though the object had come up out of the sea."

Such reports have been coming out of the Triangle of the Lost for many years. In 1887 the *J.P.A.* was captained by C. D. Sweet off Jamaica when "in a fierce storm two objects were sighted in air above the ship, one luminous and the other dark. They fell in the sea with a loud noise." This report comes from the **Monthly Weather Review**, 1897. A similar sighting took place in 1892 when the Panamanian ship, *The Green*, was

MYSTERIOUS DISAPPEARANCES: THEY NEVER CAME BACK

sailing on a calm night on a westerly course past the island of Jamaica. Captain Jonathan Wentworth, a well-respected mariner, reported in his journal that two large, glowing objects suddenly rose up out of the sea beside the ship. Wentworth said that the objects were so brilliant that "the decks of the ship were brighter than I had ever seen them."

He explained that the two objects followed alongside the ship for about five minutes. "Several of my crew members were terrified," said Captain Wentworth. "There was no logical explanation I could give them for this phenomena. I have seen ball lightning and it definitely was not in that category. The glowing balls were about the size of a small house. They followed alongside us, staying a distance of about two hundred yards on each side. After what seemed like an eternity, the intensity of the fiery substance seemed to lessen. They dropped toward the surface of the ocean as they dimmed. Both the crew members and I were particularly grateful when they slipped beneath the waves."

The Diary of Andrew Bloxam was published in 1925 in Honolulu by the Berniece T. Bishop Museum. There is an entry in the book that tells of a similar light being sighted at 3 o'clock on the morning of August 12, 1825 when seaman Bloxam was on a voyage. He reported . . . "About half past 3 o'clock the middle watch on the deck was astonished to find ev-

MYSTERIOUS DISAPPEARANCES: THEY NEVER CAME BACK

erything around them suddenly illuminated. Turning their eyes to the eastward, they beheld a large, round, luminous body rising up about seven degrees from the water to the clouds, and falling again out of sight, then a second time rising and falling. It was the color of a red-hot cannon ball and appeared about the size of the sun. It gave so great a light that a pin might have been picked up on the deck."

The March, 1955 issue of **Fate Magazine** carried a report on the *Groote Beer*—a Dutch ship. Crew mementoes told a strange story of seeing a flat disc-like object rise up out of the ocean. Captain of the vessel was Jan Boshoff and he was called to the deck as soon as the object was sighted. Captain Boshoff observed the flat object through his binoculars. He stated it was grayish in color and turned lighter around the edges as it maneuvered about. Cornelius Kooey, third officer aboard the *Groote Beer*, said the object moved toward the southwest with the setting sun. He measured the object with his sextant at 8:15 p.m. He stated that the object was traveling at an extremely high rate of speed.

On December 13, 1956, a Swedish freighter contacted the harbormaster at La Guaira, Venezuela and announced that cone-shaped devices or objects were falling vertically into the ocean off the coast. "The devices are quite bright and are giving off a strange luminous glare," reported the captain of the ship. "Whenever the objects hit the water we hear explosions. The sea becomes brightly colored where they have dropped."

The captain also announced that the sea became extremely agitated with a "bubbling, boiling motion," when the cone-shaped objects disappeared beneath the waves.

The report was duly recorded as another example of unexplained phenomena in the Triangle of the Lost.

Several years ago, private detective Renfro T. Hays of Memphis, Tennessee, and I did an extensive investigation into the James Earl Ray case. Hays, a top private investigator, at that time was working for the defense attorneys on Ray's case. During our investigation, we encountered many people with strange, even unusual backgrounds. Both Renfro T. Hays and I are convinced that Ray was a pawn in a well-planned paramilitary operation to assassinate Dr. King.

During the investigation, I became acquainted with a Cuban Soldier of Fortune. Known as Raymond Fernandez, the 34-year-old refugee from Fidel Castro's Communist regime in Cuba had originally fought

MYSTERIOUS DISAPPEARANCES: THEY NEVER CAME BACK

with Castro's forces in driving the Batista government from the island.

"Castro would never have gone Communist except for the stupidity of the American state department," Fernandez insisted. "When he took the island, he started executing the monsters who had suppressed the Cuban people for so many years. This is a tradition in Latin America. You don't leave the losers alive to foment trouble for your regime. However, the state department became upset by these executions. They put pressure on Castro. His only alternative was to seek aid from the Russians."

Fernandez became disenchanted with Communist interference in the revolution. With the aid of a boat stolen from a small Cuban port, he left the island and came to Miami as a refugee. "We didn't need the Russians to tell us how to run the country," Fernandez insisted.

Fernandez was one of the soldiers-of-fortune who were financed and trained by the U.S. Central Intelligence Agency to make raids on Castro's Cuban facilities. "We had a regular shuttle route in and out of Cuba in those days," he reported. "The CIA was gearing up for the Bay of Pigs invasion. I'd make a night run into Cuba with a load of guns or explosives for rebel forces recruited by the CIA. On the return trip, I'd bring out refugees who wanted to come to the United States."

During one trip into the Communist waters, Fernandez was the leader of a three-man expedition manning a swift, high-powered Cris-Craft cruiser. "Our engines had been modified and we could really make excellent time," the Cuban stated. "We were running slow that night, however, because it was essential that our cargo of radio transmission equipment reach a rebel leader in Cuba."

The voyage to Cuba was uneventful. The equipment was landed on a small, secluded beach in a well-protected cove. "We were just pulling out to head back to the United States," recalled Raymond Fernandez, "when we were called back to shore. The rebels told us that a fleet of Cuban patrol boats were spotted a few miles down the coast. We took off fast, hoping to outrun their fastest cruisers."

A deadly cat-and-mouse game was triggered when a Cuban patrol boat used radar to lock into the CIA cruiser. "We tried everything to shake him," said Fernandez. "Nothing seemed to work. They were gaining on us and it was only a question of time until we were either captured or sunk."

Deep into the Triangle of the Lost at that time, Fernandez was pi-

MYSTERIOUS DISAPPEARANCES: THEY NEVER CAME BACK

loting his boat and keeping a wary eye on his pursuers. "Now, this is the part that sounds like something out of science-fiction," he reported. "I was looking back at the Cuban patrol boat, trying to gauge when they'd get close enough for a shot. Suddenly, a flicker of light in the sea to my port side caught my eye. I looked in that direction and saw a light beneath the surface of the sea. My attention was drawn to the light, which was getting brighter with each passing second. It went from the intensity of a light bulb to the brilliance of the brightest light I've ever seen within a span of about twenty seconds. It might have been even less than that. You're never sure of time when you're in the middle of a critical situation."

The two other Cubans on the boat piloted by Fernandez saw the light.

"What's that?" one of his companions asked.

"I don't know," Fernandez answered.

The three men watched as the light suddenly moved between the escaping cruiser and the Cuban patrol boat. The waters of the relatively calm ocean began to bubble and boil. The Communist Cuban patrol boat swerved to avoid the turbulent water. Fernandez hit the throttle of his craft, slowing down. The Cuban boat also stopped. Within seconds, Fernandez was shocked to see a silver-colored disc-shaped object rise up from the boiling sea. The ascent was extremely rapid.

"It was enough to almost make me stop drinking," admitted the Cuban adventurer. "The device was exactly like reports I've since read about flying saucers. This was a large disc, perhaps forty feet in diameter. The outer edges of the UFO were glowing bright red and blue when the device came plunging up out of the water. It was also accompanied by two smaller objects that popped up out of the water right behind it."

Fernandez reported the large circular disc rose to a height of about fifty to seventy-five feet above the ocean's surface. "The smaller discs hovered about twenty to thirty feet below the larger ship," he related. "The two miniature discs were about 50 inches in diameter. They separated almost immediately when they came up out of the sea. The little units then moved toward my boat and the Cuban patrol boat. By then, both the Communist boat and my boat started to have trouble. My engines stopped dead. I tried the ignition switch, but there was a complete lack of power. I could hear the patrol boat crew shouting to each other about their engines."

MYSTERIOUS DISAPPEARANCES: THEY NEVER CAME BACK

As their power loss occurred, a large beam of white light poured down from a very large disc hovering overhead.

"There wasn't anything unusual about that light," Fernandez went on. "It was as if someone had turned on a powerful search light that illuminated the entire area. Someone had snapped a switch, turning the night into the brilliance of high noon."

Fernandez kept trying to get his engines started. Having fought with Castro in the mountains of Cuba from the start of the revolution, Fernandez is known as a professional soldier with a calm reaction to any emergency situation. "However, I was getting pretty shaky out there," he admitted. "One of my crew was a kid named Juan Garcia. He was about 22-years-old, a youngster making his first trip. He became agitated and excited, started shouting something about Judgment Day and the end of the world. He fell to the deck of the cruiser and started praying."

Fortunately, Fernandez' other crewman was also an experienced fighter. "He said he was having trouble with getting the engines started," recalled the adventurer. "He started checking everything out. By then, the smaller disc was right above our boat."

MYSTERIOUS DISAPPEARANCES: THEY NEVER CAME BACK

The small disc-shaped object hovered above the boat. It started to blink on and off in a rapid sequence of changing colors. "It was something like orange, blue, green, and white," he related. "The lights changed color every half-second and this continued for perhaps thirty seconds. Then the disc took on a reddish-orange glow and that's when we felt the heat."

The temperature rose suddenly under heat of some unknown source. "Sweat popped out all over my body," explained Fernandez. "This heat was accompanied by a very uncomfortable prickly feeling all over my body. I became nauseous. Juan actually became sick enough to vomit over the side of the boat. Across the way, I could see confusion on the Cuban patrol boat. Men were crying out, running around the boat in a hysterical manner. I assumed they were also feeling the same increase in temperature."

Strangely enough, Raymond Fernandez stated that the metal and other objects aboard his boat did not heat up.

"My hand brushed against the barrel of a small, lightweight machine gun that I always carried with me," he explained. "The metal was actually cool to the touch. Yet my body and the air around the boat was extremely warm."

Fernandez maintained his presence of mind. He continued to try and start his engines. "Suddenly, the small disc above us moved away toward the larger device," he related. "My engine started right up. The man who had been checking for a malfunction screamed with pain. One of the belts on the engine grabbed his finger, carrying his hand around a shaft. He almost lost his hand and, unfortunately, did lose some chunks of skin around two fingers."

Engines running, Fernandez slammed the throttle to full speed and raced away from the scene. "I wanted to get out of there as fast as possible," he admitted. "You'll see a lot of strange things in war, but that was the wildest experience I've ever had. As we moved away toward Florida, I saw the second small disc move away from the Cuban patrol boat. The brilliant light dimmed and the only light came from the stars and a pale moon. The Cubans got their engines running. They turned around and headed back to the island. Like me, I don't expect they wanted to take any chances."

Fernandez reported that his young companion gradually regained his composure during the voyage back to Florida. "Juan was really out

MYSTERIOUS DISAPPEARANCES: THEY NEVER CAME BACK

of it for a while," he stated. "It was a bad experience for a young man. Hell, that was his first trip in and out of Cuba. It was a tough run with plenty of danger. To have something like that happen caused him to go into temporary shock."

On their return to Florida, Raymond Fernandez, Juan, and the third member of the crew were debriefed extensively by members of the Central Intelligence Agency. "I kept insisting they tell me the truth," said the soldier-of-fortune. "I had assumed this was some sort of secret weapon built and operated by the United States. We were in danger of being killed or captured when the saucer came popping up out of the ocean. The CIA agent who debriefed me refused to say anything. He did keep going over my story and kept asking me if we'd been drinking."

The following afternoon, Fernandez was asked to repeat his story. "This was a new man," he stated. "Probably from another part of the company, which is what he called the C.I.A. He interrogated each of us separately for several hours. He was extremely interested in the trouble I'd had with my engines. He never gave any indication that this might have been a secret weapon for the U.S."

Another strange occurrence related to the third man's injured hand. "Twenty-four hours after we'd left Cuba and had this experience, his hand was completely healed," said Fernandez. "It was almost like a miracle. I'd never seen anything heal that rapidly. When the agent who directed us heard about this, the guy was flown off somewhere for medical tests. I never saw him again. His name was Gomez. I never did know his first name. And Gomez might have been a name he was using instead of his real one."

Fernandez and the second man, Juan, remained in the C.I.A. encampment. "Juan seemed to be the one who was troubled the most by the experience," said Fernandez. "He'd had trouble coping with things on the boat. On the way back, he complained of a severe headache. By noon on the following day, he'd broken out in a horrible red rash. It was as if he had hives from eating too many strawberries or something like that. His temperature rose to about 102 degrees at the same time. Juan was put in sick bay for observation." The rash disappeared after a few hours.

Like everything else in life, the story told by Raymond Fernandez is either true or false. There was no reason at that time, or since, for the man to make up such a story. He was not involved in the assassination of Dr. Martin Luther King, was not a suspect in the case. Renfro T. Hays and

MYSTERIOUS DISAPPEARANCES: THEY NEVER CAME BACK

I encountered him only by accident during our investigation.

Some of the questions asked after the incident related included: Did you hear of other experiences like this happening at that time?

Fernandez: "I heard a bit about something like this happening a few nights before the invasion of the Bay of pigs. A man was accidentally lost overboard during a running gun battle with a Cuban patrol boat. There were patrol boats all over the place, according to the story. The leader of the group made one run back to try and find the man, decided it was too dark to save him. The boat turned toward Florida when a greenish-like fog suddenly materialized behind them. They made a quick run back to this luminous fog, found the man in the water was enveloped by the mysterious vapor.

"I can't vouch for the truth of these reports. There's always all sorts of rumors floating around a camp just before an invasion. Someone could have made this up as an interesting story to tell their friends."

Did you hear any more about the C.I.A. investigation of the incident?

Fernandez: "Only that they were darn interested in my report. Right after that orders went out to inform your agent-in-charge of anything unusual that happened during a run. Naturally, we were always debriefed after a trip. I found it odd that they would make a special request like this. We discussed it among ourselves and decided that some people might have an incident like mine happen, then not report it for fear of being ridiculed."

Were you interested in flying saucers or UFOs prior to this?

Fernandez: "Absolutely not! I thought they were something that might be around, but I hadn't seen one so I never gave them any thought. I was more interested in the revolution and freeing Cuba from Batista's rule. I operated underground until Castro took to the mountains. I didn't have much time to think of anything other than avoiding Batista's secret police and a firing squad."

Had you heard of the Bermuda Triangle or The Triangle of the Lost at that time?

Fernandez: "I hadn't realized that either of these areas existed until I started reading up on UFOs."

What do you think happened out there?

MYSTERIOUS DISAPPEARANCES: THEY NEVER CAME BACK

Fernandez: "After the Bay of Pigs, I settled down. I've taken time to read everything on flying saucers, the Bermuda Triangle, and other facets of the mystery. I think that a flying saucer came up out of the sea, accompanied by two smaller discs that were surveillance units. Why they came up at that time I don't know. I'd give a couple of years off my life for that answer."

You've been checking on UFOs for some time?

"The phenomena is about the same. There's reports of UFOs being accompanied by bright lights that beam down. They often produce heat and high temperatures. The uncomfortable prickly feeling we experienced is also associated with flying saucers. Beyond that, it's anyone's guess. At no time did we see anything like a pilot or any kind of person. For all I know, these devices could have been operated by remote control."

Was the disc solid in appearance?

Fernandez: "Christ, yes! A silver-grayish colored metal. There was nothing you could see after that searchlight was turned on. It was like looking into a big bulb. I didn't even try to do it. But the thing that came roaring up out of the ocean was definitely solid, made out of some kind of metal."

Have you had any loss of time, received any mental messages or anything like that? Some people who see a UFO have these experiences.

Fernandez: "Nothing like that. The only change in my life was that I quit soldiering and fighting wars. I was lucky to get out of the Bay of Pigs alive. I decided to find excitement in some other way. I decided shortly after the invasion that it really didn't matter who ran Cuba. One regime would be about as bad as another for the ordinary person. However, Juan did have a lot of dreams right after the incident. He was so shaken up that he couldn't go on the invasion."

Do you think there's an intelligence behind these UFOs?

Fernandez: "Absolutely. I don't know if this is an alien form of life from another planet. I've done some reading on the subject and travel through outer space seems almost impossible due to the distances involved. But you never know what a highly advanced bunch of people can do. Give me a machine gun and a trip back in time for a few hundred years and I could rule the world.

"I've also given thought to the theory that some sort of intelligence

MYSTERIOUS DISAPPEARANCES: THEY NEVER CAME BACK

might have lived side-by-side with us right here on this planet for thousands of years. There's a real possibility of that because we've had legends of Gods rising up out of the sea and that sort of thing. I never used to think about such things, but I occasionally get to chewing on it now."

Did the C.I.A. agents ever mention anything to you?

Fernandez: "The agent I reported to at that time was changed to another guy. I didn't particularly care for the replacement. But he was a bit more talkative than my original contact. The new man told me that a section of the agency is devoted to checking out UFO reports. Not only here but all over the world. He said they have a big computer where reports are filed. They translate foreign reports. The idea is to try and find some pattern in the sightings."

Have they discovered a pattern?

Fernandez: "Until then there was nothing that made sense. We were talking in a bar and it was just a brief conversation."

Did you ask him about the Triangle?

Fernandez: "I didn't know about it at that time."

Whatever happened to him?

Fernandez: "He's living here in Miami. I'll try and find him if you'd like to talk with him."

Once again, we are faced with an enigma concerning this report of an underwater UFO in the Triangle of the Lost. There are many questions and very few answers. Why would an unknown intelligence, whether from another planet or from earth, decide to interrupt a running battle between a Castro patrol boat and a crew employed by the Central Intelligence Agency?

Later, I did verify the incident with Juan. His report was taken when Raymond Fernandez was not present. Juan's accounting of the incident was identical to that given by Fernandez, except he felt the UFO had interceded for some vague, unknown reason. Recently, I also discovered that Raymond Fernandez was telling the truth when he mentioned the computer used by the Central Intelligence Agency to put UFO data in a memory bank. Such a computer does exist at the C.I.A.'s headquarters in Langley, Virginia, and on several occasions I have obtained clandestine printouts from this memory bank. At the present time, the C.I.A. has yet to find a distinct pattern in UFO reports from around the world.

MYSTERIOUS DISAPPEARANCES: THEY NEVER CAME BACK

CHAPTER THIRTEEN

DOES A MYSTERIOUS CITY EXIST ON THE OCEAN FLOOR?

Juan Garcia was a short, thin man with sloping shoulders, a wiry body, and ears that protruded abruptly from his head. A mass of dark curly hair, carefully combed and trimmed short, capped his long forehead. He was about 33 years old and he was nervous when he entered our motel room. His expensive suit, matching shirt and a carefully knotted tie, gave Juan Garcia the look of a stockbroker. He had the alert darting eyes of a man used to living on the easy side of a dollar.

Renfro T. Hays made the introductions. Garcia nodded quietly and dropped onto a couch in the suite of the Miami Beach hotel.

"Do you mind if we tape this?" Renfro drawled. "It'll save Warren the trouble of taking notes."

Garcia looked startled. "I guess it's all right," he agreed with a reluctant glance. "It's just that I don't like to talk about it. People will think I'm flipping out or something."

Renfro set up the tape recorder on a cocktail table. He poured fresh drinks and our interview with Juan Garcia started. Without being asked, the Cuban refugee went into the details of the run with Fernandez into Cuba. When he came to the part where the UFO appeared, Garcia's precise English lapsed into a thick, almost indistinguishable mixture of Spanish and English. He rose from his chair and, still talking, paced the motel room.

"I hear the company agents were interested in your report," drawled Renfro in his mid-south accent.

MYSTERIOUS DISAPPEARANCES: THEY NEVER CAME BACK

"They wanted me to fly to Washington and check into the Naval hospital at Bethesda, Maryland," Garcia said.

"The day after that happened out there I got a rash. My temperature rose suddenly. The doctors couldn't find out any reason for it. My agent thought the company should check me to be sure I hadn't got radioactive poisoning or something like that."

"Did you go?" I asked,

Garcia shook his head. "Nope. I'd come in for the invasion. I didn't want to be someone's guinea pig in a hospital when we liberated Cuba. As things turned out, I was left behind because they thought I was too nervous."

Garcia explained that his headaches were mind-splitting, that they came with tremendous pain. "The only thing I could do was close my eyes, lay down in a dark room and pray," he went on. "Nothing helped except that. My doctors even tried codeine pain pills. Those things are dynamite. They didn't work. Whenever I laid down I'd drift off into a sleep and that's when I'd get the dream. It was always the same, like watching a movie over and over again. I started doubting my sanity, thinking something might have happened to my mind out there."

Garcia took another martini, gulped the drink quickly and continued. "I think there's a message in the dream. I've read a bit later about UFO contactees and their experiences. A lot of them have headaches just like mine after being around a UFO. A rash can develop after they've been near a flying saucer."

"That's true," I agreed. I told him of my investigation of a contactee in Nebraska, a young patrolman who was placed under hypnosis and blurted out details of a startling encounter with beings from other planets. The policeman had first been hypnotized by the controversial Condon Committee at the University of Colorado, then subsequently put into a trance by Loring G. Williams, a New England hypnotist. The Nebraska contactee had complained of severe headaches and a rash had popped up on the side of his neck after the experience.

"He was lucky," commented Juan Garcia. "My rash was all over my body."

He went on to tell the details of his dream. The dream opened with a picture of the C.I.A. cruiser pulling away from the UFO in the Triangle of the Lost. Garcia could see himself in the exact position he had occu-

MYSTERIOUS DISAPPEARANCES: THEY NEVER CAME BACK

pied on the deck, kneeling on the side of the boat, eyes closed. He had been praying for deliverance from Judgment Day. "I really thought the end of the world was coming when that UFO was out there," Garcia said solemnly.

The dream then focused on the large, hovering UFO. The craft hung above the scene momentarily; then a hatch opened. The two smaller discs entered the larger craft. The hatch closed with a sliding motion and the large disc dropped slowly to the surface of the sea. It descended into the water and drifted slowly toward the bottom.

"The terrifying part of this is that I believe the dream is a picture of reality out there," was Garcia's comment. "As the UFO—maybe I should call it a flying saucer—neared bottom it straightened out and traveled just above the bottom of the ocean floor for quite a distance. It slowed down when it approached what looked like a mountain on the sea floor. Part of the mountain opened up and the device went into some sort of tunnel. In the dream, I followed the UFO right into the middle of this undersea mountain."

The mountain was actually a camouflaged undersea UFO base. "Inside was an entire city," said Garcia. "Not a city as we might expect, but more like a well-run military installation. The flying saucer came out of the tunnel into a large room. This was sort of like a large aircraft hangar. There were several other disc-shaped objects there. They varied in size from the small objects, which I seemed to know were a surveillance craft, to the large oval discs that had come up out of the sea. Inside the hangar were a couple of people working on the saucers. They wore coveralls, although there didn't appear to be any zippers or buttons or belts on the garments."

Garcia explained that his dream focused on the storage area for several minutes. "Of course, in a dream you don't really have a concept of time," he smiled forlornly. "Anyway, the big disc hovered over a platform for a second, then some legs shot out and it seemed as if the craft sort of rested on this concrete-like platform. A hatch opened and two men stepped out. They were short, about my height, and they had thin bodies. Their faces were slightly different than ours, but not enough to be noticed. It could have been the light in the hangar, but they seemed to have an Oriental or Indian color to their skin. They left the ship, walked over to the mechanics and there was a discussion about something or another. I was there, but yet I couldn't hear what they said."

The two UFOnauts left the hangar and entered another part of the

MYSTERIOUS DISAPPEARANCES: THEY NEVER CAME BACK

undersea facility. "This was a long corridor that led to another room," Garcia explained. "Sort of like a mission control operation with computers and lots of unusual machines. This was a debriefing room. They didn't debrief verbally. They took off their helmets and placed a gadget over their head. The gadget had electrodes that appeared to spark a little when they struck their foreheads. The men didn't show any pain from this. They kept the gadgets on their head for perhaps a minute, maybe less. Then, the computers started up. I've thought a lot about this and, I think, they were debriefing by reading their minds. That would be an incredible device! An agent or soldier wouldn't be able to withhold information about an operation. The computers would just go into his mind and pull everything out of it."

In the dream, Garcia left the two UFOnauts in the control room and followed a man with a long pair of white coveralls down the corridor. "He didn't look like the other two men," explained the Cuban. "He looked like your average American or Englishman. The only difference was that he walked a bit too precisely, like a soldier. He went into a room that looked something like a lounge—you know, a place where people gather to talk, drink coffee, and rest. There were several people there. Both men and women. I saw a couple of people with long hair. They also wore those coveralls, although they were of different colors. They seemed to get along with each other on an equal basis. I feel some of those people were originally there, that some were prisoners or captives from our surface world. Naturally, I can't swear to this. It's more

MYSTERIOUS DISAPPEARANCES: THEY NEVER CAME BACK

like a feeling—something you know intuitively rather than knowledge that you gain through actual fact."

In his dream about the undersea city, Garcia said he was envisioning the installation when a horn started blowing. "This would be like the emergency horns in a military operation. You know—honk, honk, honk—to indicate that everyone should assume their prearranged battle stations. I seemed about to gain some more information, but everyone started running toward the hangar area. That's where the dream always ended. I've tried everything, including meditation but I can't get any more."

I asked: "Do you that this was a dream or a message planted there by the people in the UFO?"

Garcia frowned slightly and hesitated before he replied. "I know it was a message."

"Why are you so sure?" asked Renfro.

"I just know," Garcia said impatiently. "I know this sounds crazy and maybe I should just leave and go home. Maybe you don't believe me. Maybe you think I'm some kind of crazy nut. But I really believe that dream was somehow put into my mind when we were out there on the ocean."

Renfro shook his head in despair. "It certainly isn't evidence that would stand up in court."

Garcia faltered. "I'm not planning to go to court."

After the use of hypnotism on the Nebraska patrolman, Loring G. Williams had shown the patrolman and myself how to utilize self-hypnosis. That experience triggered my interest in the subject. Over the next few months I studied this often maligned subject, worked with a professor from the University of Iowa on hypnotic experiments, and learned to become a fair hypnotist. I'm able to place a willing subject into a fairly deep trance.

"Would you object to being hypnotized?" I asked Garcia.

"I'm not sure," he said nervously. He eyed me doubtfully. "Warren's a good hypnotist," Renfro boasted. "He's studied the subject. There's no harm in trying. It might open up your mind."

Garcia expelled a deep sigh. "Could you find out some answers?"

"Maybe," I replied. "Assuming there's something there."

MYSTERIOUS DISAPPEARANCES: THEY NEVER CAME BACK

Renfro snapped a fresh tape on the machine. Garcia relaxed and, after two false tries, he entered a light trance. Gradually, I was able to induce a really deep trance.

I utilized a hypnotic "override" with Garcia's fingers, suggesting that if he lied his middle finger on his left hand would rise up and begin to tap his knee. With the Cuban in a trance, Renfro snapped on the tape recorder, and we questioned Garcia about his dream. A portion of that transcript includes: Have you had this dream more than once?

Garcia: (nods head affirmatively). Y-yes.

When did it start?

Garcia: Right after we went to Cuba that night.

Is this just a dream?

Garcia: (Shakes head in a negative motion). It is more than that.

Would you explain that?

Garcia: I—I—I'm told this is a message from them.

Who are they?

Garcia: The people in the flying saucer.

Did they put this dream in your subconscious mind?

Garcia: Yes.

Why would they do this?

Garcia: They want us to know that they are friendly to us. They are our friends and they don't intend to harm us.

How do you know this?

Garcia: They told me through my mind.

Are they from another planet?

Garcia: Some of them are.

Where are the rest from?

Garcia: They are like us.

You mean people like you, me and Renfro?

Garcia: Uh-hum. But they are not like us.

MYSTERIOUS DISAPPEARANCES: THEY NEVER CAME BACK

Why aren't they like us?

Garcia: They are with the other ones down below.

Does that change people to be different than us?

Garcia: They have always been the Protected Ones.

Could you explain that?

Garcia: They have always been a part of the others. Their fathers are from the Original Ones.

How could this be?

Garcia: They have been in our world for a very long time. It is time for the new race to begin. The old order is going away, the new order is coming. The new race is necessary to save mankind.

Gradually, we drew out an incredible story of the selection of mothers to bear children that would be part alien intelligence, part human. Agents of the UFO intelligence moved through the surface world starting in 1929. Certain women were carefully selected for their health, genes, and strength. At no time, according to Garcia, did these women know that their lovers or husbands were members of the UFO group. After the children were born, starting in late 1929, they were watched carefully by the UFO intelligence. While they were allowed to live as if they were normal homo sapiens, they were the "Protected Ones." The Protected Ones were allowed to have the usual trials and tribulations of a normal life. However, they were given "protection" by the UFO group.

How was this protection given?

Garcia: Through the gift of advanced intuition. Fatal accidents, deadly situations that threatened their lives were guarded against by the original ones. A scientist might call it the projection of a field of energy—a sort of angel or guiding spirit is always with the Protected Ones.

Does a Protected One know they are being guarded?

Garcia: I am being told that they never know this until the time of decision arrives.

What is the time of decision?

Garcia: When they are offered the chance to join the original ones.

How does this offer take place?

Garcia: Through a series of tests. Some are never asked.

MYSTERIOUS DISAPPEARANCES: THEY NEVER CAME BACK

Why aren't the others asked?

Garcia: They are needed in the world to raise children. Protected Ones are attracted to mates who are also from mothers impregnated by the UFO people. They are allowed to live in our society and conceive children that are true members of the new race.

Are these children of the Protected parents given this protection?

Garcia: I don't know. That information has not been given to me.

What is the plan for these children?

Garcia: They will assume leadership in the world.

You mean political leadership?

Garcia: That, too. But there are other types of leadership that are equally important. I am told they must devise a better way of doing things. They are to develop a new system of economics that will be fair and equitable to all members of society. The new order is to come in the future. Leaders will be needed in all areas of life. Children of the Protected Ones have the intelligence and motivation to bring about these changes.

What about the Protected Ones themselves?

Garcia: Their time started when they were born. They are responsible for the many changes that have taken place in our world.

Who are the original ones?

Garcia: They were the first ones here.

I mean where do they come from?

Garcia: I don't know.

What do they do in their city beneath the sea?

Garcia: (speaking in a halting voice). That is a base for one of their operations. There are bases in other parts of the world.

What is the purpose of these bases?

Garcia: To allow them to handle their work without being found out.

What is their work?

Garcia: To change our... I am being given a word-g-ggenet . . .

MYSTERIOUS DISAPPEARANCES: THEY NEVER CAME BACK

genetic structure so that a new race may evolve on this planet.

Why is that so important?

Garcia: It is part of the plan.

What plan?

Garcia: The plan they have for us.

Can you be more specific?

Garcia: Because of many factors there is a need for the new race. They saw this many years ago in 1929. They started then to slowly change the races of their world. As the old ones—those with the genetic structure of the dying race—pass away, the power will go to the Protected Ones and their children. This is evolution for the good of the universe,

It is for the good of humanity?

Garcia: We have no choice in the operation. The Original Ones are doing it. We cannot prevent their plan from taking place. Their Protected Ones and their children are now starting to take control of the world. The old ones are being pushed out of power. Members of the new race will succeed them. There is a changing of the guard. The old guard has not handled things in a desirable manner.

Are you a Protected One?

Garcia: I am being told that I am not. There was a Protected One on the boat that night. That was the reason why the UFO appeared on the scene. It was there to protect the life of one of their own.

Is Raymond Fernandez a Protected One?

Garcia: I don't know. One of the other two men must have been protected.

What about Renfro and me?

Garcia: I don't know.

Have you ever heard of the Bermuda Triangle or the Devil's Triangle?

Garcia: No.

Would this undersea city be connected with the disappearance of people who travel in the Caribbean sea?

Garcia: I am being told now that a few of these disappearing people

MYSTERIOUS DISAPPEARANCES: THEY NEVER CAME BACK

have been brought to the city. They were some of the people I saw in my dream. They went there willingly and not by force.

Why were they taken to the city?

Garcia: It is sometimes necessary for an analysis to be made. Humans from the old race are taken there. So are some of the Protected Ones and their selected children.

What sort of an analysis?

Garcia: They need to study people to see if their plan is working.

Are those people ever allowed to leave?

Garcia: No. For purposes of security, they are not allowed to leave. They do not want to return to the surface. They become a part of the group and they work to help bring the new race about.

You mean they're brainwashed?

Garcia: I'm being told they are happy there.

Is there a spirit or an angel in this room now?

Garcia: I don't know.

MYSTERIOUS DISAPPEARANCES: THEY NEVER CAME BACK

Is this underground city connected with the lost civilization of Atlantis?

Garcia: There is a link. I am not certain what it is. All things are the same. All is a part of the whole.

What does that mean?

Garcia: That the answer is already known but is being ignored.

Can you be a little more specific?

Garcia: No.

What is your name?

Garcia: Juan Garcia.

What do you do for a living?

Garcia: (Index finger raises and starts to tap his knee) I-I-I am an insurance salesman.

Juan Garcia came out of his hypnotic trance quickly, rubbed his eyes.

"Do you know what you said?" I inquired.

"I know most of it," he said, a sleepy look on his face. "I sure as hell don't understand it."

"Do you think you were used?"

Garcia looked grim. "I think we're all being used. That stuff about a new race and change in the ruling group is really frightening."

Renfro drawled, "The way things are going maybe we need a change."

"There's a point I'd like to clear up," I went on. "When you said you were an insurance salesman, your finger indicated you were lying. That was the only time when your finger moved throughout the entire session. Are you a salesman?"

Garcia looked worried. "'No. That's just what I tell everyone."

I asked: "Care to clear that up?"

The Cuban's face was grave. "I do a little of this and that."

Renfro snapped off the tape recorder.

MYSTERIOUS DISAPPEARANCES: THEY NEVER CAME BACK

"I do some smuggling," said Garcia with a bleak look.

"I've got some pipelines into Cuba. I go in by plane or boat and bring back people who want to get out. It's a dangerous business but the pay is right."

"What do you think about running a boat through the Triangle now?"

"I don't think these people would hurt me," said Garcia. "They saved my life once. I'll go in anytime I need to and I'm only worrying about Mother Nature."

During the next few days, Juan Garcia submitted to several additional hypnotic sessions. There was other data gained from these sessions. The most interesting segment of the transcript has been edited and reproduced above. Many times on the tapes the Cuban lapsed into broken English. For the sake of clarity, this was changed to words he would have used if his English were better. While a few words were changed, the meaning of his statements have not been changed.

What can we make of such a transcript?

First, although a hypnotist can use an "induction override" such as fingers rising, or a pendulum, we can never be certain that a subject isn't lying. However, there was no reason for either Raymond Fernandez or Juan Garcia to lie about their experiences. At no time was money or publicity offered them. Their experiences were taped without payment. Nothing was said about publishing their statements.

The significant item in Garcia's statements under hypnosis is the use of the phrase "I am being told . " ." or "I am told . . ." I have been investigating UFOs and contactees for several years. While you can't ever become an expert in such a controversial subject, there are patterns that an experienced investigator learns to detect. One of these patterns is "I am told" stated during a hypnotic session. "It's almost as if they're being monitored," a police chief said after witnessing hypnotic induction of a subject.

If we accept Garcia's statements as fact, then we have an underground city beneath the Triangle of the Lost. It is inhabited by an apparently advanced race of people who are embarked on a massive genetic change within our society. Garcia indicated that these changes include all races, all parts of the world.

Private Investigator Renfro T. Hays expressed admiration for such

MYSTERIOUS DISAPPEARANCES: THEY NEVER CAME BACK

an undertaking. "That's one of the most subtle plans I've ever heard," he drawled. "Let's say there's an alien group like Garcia claims. Or even a group that has been here for a long time. Instead of revealing themselves, they remain hidden. They change the world by changing the people in it. And if they're diabolical, they use agents in high places to make sure their people are put in positions of power. Within a generation or two, these mutants—or should we say Protected Ones—rule the world. You've got to admire a plan like that. There's a real intelligence behind it. Even an old political boss like Boss Crump in Memphis would have had to work hard to come up with something like that."

Are we being replaced by a new race? Is there a concealed city beneath the waves of the Triangle of the Lost? We can only speculate on these possibilities and wonder about Juan Garcia's statement that "the answer is already known and is being ignored."

Since our original meeting, I have kept in touch with Juan Garcia from time to time. A shadowy figure in an unusual business, he moves between Tampa, Miami, and New Orleans. He has not shown any interest in learning more about UFOs since our taped sessions.

"I know why they're here," he laughed during a recent phone conversation. "I don't have the time these days to read books. Their plan is steamrolling and they'll be in charge in a few years."

MYSTERIOUS DISAPPEARANCES: THEY NEVER CAME BACK

CHAPTER FOURTEEN

BIZARRE GIANTS IN THE TRIANGLE

Juan Garcia's dream of the underseas city included the vision of a race of giant inhabitants. These creatures allegedly guard the portals of the facility. Before we dismiss giants as a figment of Garcia's imagination, we might check reports of behemoth beings in and around the Triangle of the Lost. Early mariners in the Triangle reported sighting such beings, both on land and sea. There are even current reports of giants inhabiting the jungles of Central and South America.

As an example, giants may be living in the boondocks of the South American jungles if we can believe the recent reports from that region. *The London Daily Mirror*, in a dispatch from Rio de Janeiro in 1966, told of a civilized tribe of the Caiapo nation of natives that were being harassed by a band of marauding giants. Several hunters and Indian villagers had been killed by these raiders.

A group of Brazilian Air Force Cadets were on a survival training mission in the dense jungles when they heard of the giants. The cadets tried unsuccessfully to make contact with the seven and one-half foot giants, who prowl the Xingu region of the Matto Grasso. "We captured a young boy during a skirmish with the giants," reported a chief of the peaceful Calapalos-Caiapo tribe. "He grew to be almost eight feet tall."

"Where is he now?" asked a cadet.

The chief shrugged. "He became so huge and strong that he frightened the villagers. When he became rebellious he was sentenced to death and executed."

Traditions affirming the existence of giants can be found all over

MYSTERIOUS DISAPPEARANCES: THEY NEVER CAME BACK

South America and in Mexico. In the books of Ischtlil-Tschotschitl, who was an Aztec king, we can read:

". . There is a general agreement that the giant Kinames were the first inhabitants of our country. They were horrible monsters. They had the habits of ugly vices. They terrorized all of the people" Fate marked them down at last. They were slain by the angry gods. All nature trembled. The seas rose up. The mountains became volcanoes..."

A similar version can also be found in the *Saxo Grammaticus*.

". . . Ages ago there existed three types of men. There were those of great stature and immense height. They were called the giants. Next, there were those of high spirit who had the ability to predict; they had the art of prophecy. Last was the ordinary man. The common man lost the arts of the earlier races—the power to change the body and deceive the eyes of men. Yet, they conquered the older races. They exterminated the giants."

When the rapacious, gold-hungry Spanish Conquistadores waded through the surf and onto the shores of the New World, they were greeted with stories from the natives about a race of giants who plundered villages, raped captive women to death, and ambushed men and small children for their cannibal's feasts. These legends have endured to this day as part of the Incan folk tradition. Several were preserved in the writings of Incan Garcilasso de la Vega, a paradoxical native adventurer. A fiery Incan patriot, a young man who led a bloody rebellion against the Spanish invaders, a rebel who escaped death from the Spaniard's Toledo steel swords, Garcilasso was also a notable scholar who appreciated good books, rare wines, fine art, and shapely women.

An ill-planned night raid against a Spanish outpost was the start of his adventures. Garcilasso and his native rebels were overwhelmed by the Spaniards. They were thrown into a prison stockade to await judgment from a tribunal of Conquistadores and priests. Garcilasso duped a sleepy-eyed guard and engineered the escape of his followers. Trying to be certain that all of his men had reached safety, Garcilasso was nabbed by a detachment of soldiers. He was dragged before a sour-faced tribunal.

"I pay respect to your fighting ability," remarked a thin faced captain of the Conquistadores. "If all of your people were such furious fighters, we would have been driven back into the sea."

"Why do you fight us?" inquired a balding priest. "We bring you

MYSTERIOUS DISAPPEARANCES: THEY NEVER CAME BACK

the true word of God."

"It is not my God," Garcilasso replied.

"Shall we torture him unto death?" asked the captain.

"Wait! Look at his body," said the priest. "Notice the sullen look on his face. He is a real prize. We must follow orders and send a specimen of these people to the king in Seville. His majesty wants an Incan at his court. This man is intelligent; he is quick-witted. He would be a marvelous present."

"Would you like to go to Spain?" asked the captain.

"It is better than death." Garcilasso was a realist.

Upon his arrival in Spain, the Incan was given a Spanish name. Despite his primitive background, he was quickly acquiring a knowledge of the Spanish language. A Jesuit priest taught Latin to the captive native. Garcilasso skimmed through the elementary manuscripts and accepted the church to obtain an advanced education.

A monumental scholar, Garcilasso wrote the formidable **Commentarios Realesde los Incas**, a five volume history of his people. The book contained an honest description of the religion and rituals of the Incans. Patriotism and sorrow for his people still burned in Garcilasso's mind; he included passages in his books condemning the brutality of the Spanish conquerors. In 1602, the Spanish king and the church consigned the books to the bonfire. Every available copy was collected and publicly burned.

Garcilasso's books were available only to scholars, until 1942 when they were reprinted by a Brazilian publisher. In Chapter IX, Book Nine, Volume Two, a passage is headlined **Of The Giants Who Were In The Manta Region and Their Death**. A modernized, free translation reads:

.. On the northern coast of Peru, in the Manta region, there lived people who worshipped a huge emerald. This fiery, glistening gem was larger than an ostrich egg. It was placed on a sacred altar and the people of that region brought many other emeralds and precious stones as gifts to their goddess of the green gem.

"Many centuries ago, this land was invaded by an army of giants who arrived there from the sea. These giant men were strange to behold: their eyes were very large, and their hair was worn long. They were beardless and their skin was light. A few of the giants wore animal

MYSTERIOUS DISAPPEARANCES: THEY NEVER CAME BACK

skins for clothing; others walked the land without clothes as they had not brought any women with them.

"They built a settlement near the sea, at a spot along the desert land of the Manta region. Water is scarce here, so they dug enormous wells that were slashed deep into the earth to obtain cool, sweet water. These wells were lined with rocks and were built to last for centuries.

"The giants were unable to kill enough wild game to feed their enormous appetites. They started to raid the native villages in that land. These giants stood almost twenty feet tall and their raids on the villages struck terror in the heart of every man. Men and children who were captured or killed were taken to the giant's village, where they became part of a cannibal's feast. The women were carried back to the giant's settlement, where they were attacked. Most of the women ruptured from this abuse and none survived the terrible ordeal.

"In a few years, the giants were without women and they became degenerates. They committed many unnatural acts for their self-gratification and their actions were an abomination to everyone.

"One afternoon an angel appeared in the skies over the village of the giants.

"The angel attacked them with a flaming sword. Only a few of these giant men escaped the fury and many were consumed in the fire. When

MYSTERIOUS DISAPPEARANCES: THEY NEVER CAME BACK

the angel departed, there were only a few bones to show that the giants had ever existed."

What can we conclude from this remarkable account of twenty-foot giants? The legend has all the elements of a sensational science fiction movie: a primitive cult of emerald worshippers; bands of demonic giants who raid native villages, and flaming retribution from the skies. Is it possible that the angel was a spaceman from another world or dimension? Did he witness the terrible deeds of the giants and decide to eliminate their race? Did a band of benevolent giants survive to build a secret city beneath the Triangle of the Lost?

If Garcilasso's giants did exist, then there should be records in the Spanish archives of their reality. The Conquistadores looted the land and shipped galleons of gold to a greedy king in Spain. They also searched for curiosities, oddities, and unusual specimens of life that might amuse the man on the throne. Giant bones would have been a natural gift to the king and his court.

When we turned to the records maintained by Bernal Diaz del Castillo, we learn that Captain Cortez shipped the thigh bone of a giant to the monarch. He stated:

". . They (the natives) reported that their ancestors " told of giants with huge bones who lived there in times past. Because the giants were an evil people with bad habits, they were killed off. So that we could see how tall these giants were, the natives brought us the leg bone of one. It was very thick and the height of an ordinary man would reach only from the hip to the knee. We were amazed at seeing these bones and felt certain there must have been giants in this country. Our Captain Cortez said to us that it might be well to send the bone to Castille so that his majesty could see it, so we sent it with one of the first agents who returned to Spain . . ."

A lust for gold brought the King's conquistadores pouring into the New World. They were ignorant, uneducated men with few scholarly intentions. Treacherous, wily old Francisco Pizarro, the ambitious leader of this rapacious horde, was typical of the adventurers who imposed the King's rule in the New World. Pizarro had been a swine herder on a Spanish farm before he threw down his shepherd's staff, washed his face, and ventured out into the world in search for riches. The natives could have easily duped such men with the bleached bones from some large jungle animal; their motive could have been a small reward. We need considerably more evidence to back up the claim of twenty-foot giants, prefer-

MYSTERIOUS DISAPPEARANCES: THEY NEVER CAME BACK

ably a complete skeleton.

And just such evidence mouldered in a mountainous tomb near Cuzco, Peru. Don Antonio de Mendoza was the viceroy of Peru in A.D. 1560 and his staff heard the whispered stories of a "sacred tomb" in the mountains. ". . . This underground vault was a sacred place and the location was carefully guarded by the native priests," wrote Cieza de Leon, the viceroy's secretary. "It was said that the powdered remains of giant bones was capable of curing many diseases. We finally located the site of this tomb. It contained several skeletons of huge men. There were many objects and curiosities contained in the place . . . the remains were shipped to the king for his interest." Later, reports indicated the Spanish king forwarded the giant's skeletons and many of the artifacts to the Pope in Rome.

The discovery of more giant skeletons was reported in 1928. Workmen were blasting a tunnel for the Central Railroad in Ecuador when a dynamite blast ripped open a wall of a cave. The workers explored the area and discovered coffins containing the skeletons of several eight-foot giants. The bones were forwarded to a university and then disappeared.

Spanish records report many similar discoveries as the conquistadores pushed into the unexplored New World. Many occult authorities believe that giants ruled Mexico, Bermuda and the Caribbean Islands during some dim age in the past. Diego de Ordaz led a detachment of soldiers into searching for the legendary seven cities of gold. He stumbled onto more evidence of giants. The story was told by Peter Matyr de Anghie in his ***Historia de las Indias***:

". . . de Ordaz found a sanctuary near a volcanic mountain and inside the temple was the thigh bone of a giant, which had been cut and half-gnawed away with age. This bone was carried to Vittoria to be sent to Rome for the Pope . . . This bone, which has been preserved, measured from the hip to the knee-cap (patella) about five cubits. (Note: this would be approximately eight and one-half feet!) It has a width in proportion. Men sent into the mountains of the south by Cortez . . . brought back several ribs which they removed from the skeletons of giant men."

In 1936, a Senor de Valda excavated an ancient grave mound near Tepic, Mexico. He found seven skeletons of nine-foot men and women buried under thin tablets of blue-gray slate. This mound also contained fragments of unglazed pottery, painted bowls, and additional objects to indicate the beings maintained a primitive culture during their lives.

MYSTERIOUS DISAPPEARANCES: THEY NEVER CAME BACK

The enigma of the "giants of Patagonia" has puzzled researchers for several centuries. In June, 1520, Ferdinand Magellan anchored his fleet off the coast of what is now the southern most tip of South America. The fleet anchored at Port San Julian, sending a party ashore to replenish their water supply. The sailors were astonished to see a giant walking along the beach. "...Our heads barely came to his waist," wrote Pigafetta, a historian on Magellan's staff. " . . . his voice was like that of a bull."

In 1578, Sir Francis Drake stopped at Port San Julian to fill the water casks of his ships and, when the crewmen landed on shore, a howling horde of giants roared out of the jungle. Drake said the men were up to "seven and one-half to eight feet tall," and "people of large stature." Two of Drake's sailors were killed in the furious battle.

This race of giant natives quickly gained a reputation for treachery. In 1598, explorer Sebald de Weert reported natives of "ten foot in stature" in Patagonia. Anthony Knyvet said he saw no living giants, but measured several dead bodies that were up to ten feet in height. In 1764, Commodore Bryan anchored his *Dolphin* in Magellan Strait and had a peaceful meeting with the giants. Hundreds of natives crowded onto the beach as Commodore Bryan warily approached their chieftain.

"He was of gigantic stature, and seemed to realize the tales of monsters in human shapes: he had the skin of some wild beast thrown over his shoulder," Commodore Bryan reported. ". . . I did not measure him, but by the proportion of his stature to my own, it could not be much less than seven feet. When this frightful Colossus came up, we muttered somewhat to each other as a salutation, and then I walked with him towards his companions . . ."

The ***Annual Register of 1768*** contained the report of an officer on Bryan's staff. ". . . some of them are certainly nine feet tall, if they do not exceed it. The commodore, who is very near six feet, could just reach the top of one of their heads, which he attempted on tiptoes, and there were several taller than him on whom the experiment was tried . . . there was hardly a man less than eight feet tall.

". . . the women are from seven and one-half to eight feet in stature. . ." For some unknown reason, the Patagonian giants suddenly vanished. Sir John Marborough explored the Patagonian coast for several months. He was disappointed in not finding a single giant. "They do not exist," he reported. "Such giants are nothing more than the imaginative tales of sailors." Reluctantly, the world dismissed the giants until an ar-

MYSTERIOUS DISAPPEARANCES: THEY NEVER CAME BACK

ticle was printed in *Chamber's Journal* in 1853 and subsequently reprinted in *Littell's Living Age* magazine, No. 478, July 16, 1853" Headlined *"Adventures With the Giants,"* the article reports the harrowing experiences of a sailor, John Bourne, who was a mate on the American schooner, *John Allyne*, bound for California. The *John Allyne* left New Bedford, Massachusetts, sailing toward the western gold fields on February 13, 1849, with supplies and passengers, he ship took longer than planned to sail through the Triangle of the Lost. Needing fresh provisions, the captain of the ship anchored at the Strait of Magellan and ordered John Bourne and several other crewmen to go ashore in a small boat.

When the boat drew near the shore, a crowd of huge barbarians came down to the beach and greeted them in broken Spanish, the report stated. "The natives pretended to be friendly and urged them to land, promising them plenty of beef, fowl and eggs in barter. But no sooner had the boat touched the shore than the natives crowded into it; and Mr. Bourne found himself and his men to be prisoners."

The giants demanded ransom for the return of the sailors. Tobacco, rum, bread, flour, and other articles were brought to the beach by the ship's captain. The giant natives released all of the sailors except Bourne; he was held for additional ransom.

"The boats returned to the ship. They were to return the next day," the account said. "During the night a violent gale arose and the *John Allyne* was driven from her anchorage. Nothing more was seen of her from the shore."

Abandoned as a captive of the giant natives, John Bourne was in serious danger. More than one giant wanted to kill their prisoner; but others demanded his services as a slave. Bourne described the giants in this manner:

"... In person, they are large; at first sight, they appear absolutely gigantic. They are taller than any other race I have seen, though it is impossible to give any accurate description. The only accurate measurement I had was my own height, which is about five feet, ten inches. I could stand very easily under the arm of many of them. All of the men were at least a head taller than myself. Their average height is at least six and one-half feet; and there were specimens that were at least seven feet tall. They have broad shoulders, full and well-developed chests, frames muscular and well-proportioned ... They exhibited enormous strength when they were sufficiently aroused from their constitutional

MYSTERIOUS DISAPPEARANCES: THEY NEVER CAME BACK

laziness... They have large heads, high cheekbones like the North American Indians, whom they also resemble in their complexion, although it is a shade or two darker. Their foreheads are broad, but low, and their hair covering reaches almost to the eyes... Their teeth are really beautiful—about the only attractive and enviable feature of their persons. They have deep, heavy voices, and speak in a guttural tone- the worst guttural talk I have ever heard—with a muttering, as if their mouth was filled with hot pudding. Their countenances are generally stupid; but on closer examination, there is a gleam of low cunning that flashes through this dull mask, and is increasingly discernible on acquaintance with them.

"... They are almost as imitative as monkeys, and are all great liars; falsehood is universal and inveterate with men, women, and children. To these traits should be added a thorough-paced treachery, and, what might seem inconsistent with their other qualities, a large share of vanity, and an immoderate love of praise. They are excessively filthy in their personal habits. They never wash themselves; hands and faces are covered with a thick deposit of dirt."

Mr. Bourne was dragged along on the nomadic wanderings of the tribe as a slave in the chieftain's household. The only form of worship he witnessed was a ritualistic ceremony where the giants smoked a narcotic weed, grunting and rolling during the early stages, and ending up with a howling roar of guttural screams. After several months of captivity, the first mate was taken to the mouth of the Santa Cruz river, where the stream empties into the Atlantic ocean. A settlement of Englishmen were collecting guano on Sea-Lion Island. The giants traded their captive to the white men in return for goods. After several weeks, Bourne boarded an American whale ship and returned to the United States.

There are scores of additional cases in the annals of giantism. There is a vast mountain of evidence to indicate that an ancient race of gigantic men and women once lived in Europe, Asia, Africa, South and North America. Their remains have been found even in the remote desolation of the polar regions. This documentation certainly lends credence to the words of Genesis that giants were on the earth during the days of old.

Who were the giants? How did they originate? We can only theorize on several possibilities.

"Giants will remain a mystery until we have successfully developed more knowledge about the origin of man," said John T. Battle, an English giant hunter who checks out reports around the world. "After

MYSTERIOUS DISAPPEARANCES: THEY NEVER CAME BACK

spending half a century in chasing down the remains and reports of these creatures, I have naturally theorized on how or where they might have originated."

His theories include:

Giants were the descendants of the "Sons of God": "There are powerful truths in the Bible," Battle remarked. "Our earth may have been visited by an army of astronauts sometime in the remote past. These astronauts may have been men of tall stature. They may have been from other worlds in our universe, or from another dimension.

Genesis said they bred with our earth women and their offspring were giants. The astronauts may have returned to their worlds. Or they may have been the victims of time and simply died.

"Their descendants may have multiplied and, in time, this interbreeding would have created genetic defects. The racial strain may have degenerated. The giants may have hunted for their own kind and spread out over the earth."

The giants were the first race: "The occultists have explored the possibility that 'Adam' is the collective name for the first race on earth," Battle reported. "They were a red-skinned race, living in the golden age of Eden until they warred with each other or with the Gods. Or, they may have been wiped out by some catastrophe. The occultists often speak of a collision with the moon in ages past. Or the flood mentioned in the Bible may have drowned this first race. Only a small number might have survived."

John Battle believes that myths and legends are the oral account of mankind's racial memories. "The Chinese have developed a legend concerning root races," he explained. "They believed giants were members of the Fourth Root Race. Their legends say the giants lived during the epoch of Atlantis" This would mean that the giants of old are now buried in the land beneath our seas.

"While this theory may seem to be quite far-out, I believe that UFOs, angels, demons, psychic phenomena, giants, and the whole ball of occultism may actually originate from the same source."

Giants are the "Sky People":

The Incas have legends of giants descending from the clouds and having sexual intercourse with Incan women. "There are similar myths in almost every culture," Battle remarked. "These stories create a pro-

MYSTERIOUS DISAPPEARANCES: THEY NEVER CAME BACK

found case for visitations from other planets" Greek mythology relates that gods and goddesses descended from the skies and lived with mortals. The North American Indians have tales of white beings who came down out of the skies and helped them during times of crisis."

Ancient legends report that beings from the skies landed on earth. These people were of exceptional stature, marvelous beauty and were gifted with transcendent wisdom. "The myths say these things landed at what would be termed a holy mountain," continued Battle. "They called chosen leaders to these places—Mount Olympus in Greece would be an example—and mysteries and prophesies were explained to the chosen earth-men. Some of these celestial visitors visited our cities, became teachers, and had more than one bedroom adventure with the daughters of the earth."

Giants were the product of cosmic rays: W. R. Drake related this possibility in his book, ***God or Spacemen***, published in 1964 by The Amherst Press, Amherst, Wisconsin. He wrote:

". . . Earth was probably much nearer the Sun and basked in tropical climate with luxuriant vegetation, a veritable Eden. Hundreds of thousands, possibly millions of years ago, the then-Moon, a predecessor of our present satellite, loomed close to Earth; its powerful gravitational attraction allied with more potent cosmic rays, produced giantism not only on the prehistoric animals but on Man himself. Adam is recognized as the collective name for the first, a red skinned race, who were believed to be giants living in a golden age in Eden until war with the gods, followed by catastrophes such as collision by the Moon, smashed civilizations to barbarism. Gigantic monoliths with still discernible features of profound intelligence abound in America, Europe, Polynesia, and Tiahuanco in the Andes, inscrutable witnesses from the mysterious past. With the destruction of the moon the stature of mankind diminished but some giant races took ages to die out . . ."

Recently, one hundred and forty-seven scientists gathered in Paris, France at a "stones and bones" Congress sponsored by the United National Economic and Social Council, (UNESCO). The assembly included anthropologists, prehistorians, geologists, glaciologists, and paleontologists from thirty-five countries. They were given the riddle of "Who is man and where did he cone from?"

There were general agreements that homo sapiens was much older than his textbook age. Recent findings indicate man has been on earth for at least 100,000 years, possibly longer. "The only certainty about the

MYSTERIOUS DISAPPEARANCES: THEY NEVER CAME BACK

origin of man is that they are uncertain," the symposium concluded.

Possibly, in assigning giants to the category of an "impossibility," we have dismissed evidence of past visits of extraterrestrials to our planet.

MYSTERIOUS DISAPPEARANCES: THEY NEVER CAME BACK

CHAPTER FIFTEEN
SHAMBALLAH: LAND OF THE SMOKY GODS
...UNDERSEA CITIES!

. . . Subterranean tunnels that run beneath the oceans and link the continents! . . . Hidden entrances to an underground kingdom! These and other beliefs are included in a bizarre theory known as The Hollow Earth mystery. Perhaps, in some manner, the mysterious disappearances within the Triangle of the Lost are connected with the occult belief that our planet is hollow, that a vast civilization exists under the surface. Some researchers have advanced just such a notion. They speculate that the interior of our planet is filled with undiscovered lands, subterranean cities, and unknown races of people.

"We feel there is considerable evidence throughout history to indicate such a civilization is possible," reported Albert McDonald, president of the Hollow Earth Society, an English group that recently disbanded. "We believe this is the origination point for flying saucers. You asked about the Triangle of the Lost? Our research indicates there is something—a submerged continent, an undersea city, a vast installation of alien intelligence—under the sea in the Triangle. This may be a spot where entrance can be gained into the subterranean world. Naturally, only a chosen few would be allowed to enter this underground paradise."

Until recently, the world's occultists simply dismissed the hollow earth theory as the misguided rantings of ignorant cultists. However, over the past few years, sightings of Unidentified Flying Objects and the antics of their occupants has mystified both official and civilian investigators. Several civilian UFO organizations established strict guidelines

MYSTERIOUS DISAPPEARANCES: THEY NEVER CAME BACK

concerning this space age mystery. They clung to the belief that UFOs originated from another planet in outer space. Accounts of UFO occupants or pilots were summarily dismissed as unbelievable.

Despite criticism for their views, a small group of UFO researchers accepted an open-minded, admittedly sometimes far-out approach to the origin of UFOs. These "far-out" hypotheses included the possibility that UFOs and their occupants were from other dimensions—or from inside the hollow earth. ". . . It is no good trying to evaluate the flying saucers and their occupants on the basis of present knowledge," wrote the noted UFO authority and author, Brinsley le Pour Trench in **Operation Earth**, (Neville Spearman, Ltd", 112 Whitefield St., London, W1; 1969.)

". . . The people who ride in flying saucers, whether they are the real sky people, or those who have their habitat nearer to us, have certain abilities that most of us are not capable of using at the present time.

". . So, then, that is this 'way-out' extension to the theory of flying saucers emanating from an invisible area surrounding the planet . . . it is that the center of the earth is hollow and that to some extent the planet is shaped like a doughnut with vast openings at the polar regions, and that an underground race lives in the interior."

Mr. Trench listed some of the books and pamphlets that have been published to support the hollow earth theory. He felt the hypothesis was not entirely acceptable. "However, we are dealing with a fantastic subject (UFOs) and nothing is impossible," Mr. Trench admitted. "Just improbable."

"Well, saucers from inside the earth would certainly fit the fantastic," he concluded.

Albert McDonald's *Hollow Earth Society* also points to ancient manuscripts and other writings to document their case for a hollow earth. They claim that throughout history, humanity has produced reports of men who entered the subterranean world and then returned. "Solve the Hollow Earth mystery and you'll find it is linked to the Triangle of the Lost and other areas where people disappear," McDonald claimed.

"A few people have managed to return to the surface world," McDonald reported. "We feel that most prefer to remain inside this paradise inside our planet. When someone did return with stories of this subterranean civilization, no one bothered to check out their stories. These survivors of the fantastic voyage were ridiculed, harassed, and frequently

MYSTERIOUS DISAPPEARANCES: THEY NEVER CAME BACK

placed in the lunatic ward of an insane asylum. This is what happened to Olaf Jansen."

Jansen's story came to the world's attention when the old Scandinavian sailor lay back on the wide bed in his cluttered room in a third floor of a Los Angeles hotel. He was dying and the sour aroma of his illness mingled with the dark odors of human misery in the cheap, skid-row hotel. His only friend was a young, unpublished writer, who sat solemnly in a battered, dirt-covered chair near the death bed.

The old man feebly raised his gray head from a stained pillow. He leaned his weight on a bony arm. A feverish flicker of fear glinted in his eyes. "Sometimes death takes a long time to reach a man," he rasped.

"Take it easy, Olaf," whispered the young writer. "The doctor will be here in a few minutes."

"Forget the doctors. There ain't no cure for old age," Olaf Jansen said, hoarsely. "But there is still time to tell you about the giants. Maybe you can go there someday."

"Where's that?" asked Willis George Emerson, the young writer.

"The land where the giants live," said the old sailor. "The world that exists inside the earth."

As Olaf Jansen waited for death, he told of a strange world inhabited by giants and other supposedly mythical creatures. Jansen stated that he and his father had entered the hollow earth through a northern opening. They had sailed the seas in a tiny fishing boat and, when a strong wind enveloped their ship, they decided to test the tales and myths of their ancestors. Ever since the Scandinavians had sailed out of their fiords in their long warships and fishing vessels, seamen had talked seriously about "that land beyond the north wind."

Olaf Jansen claimed that he and his father had sailed into this bizarre world. "The giants were friendly and we lived there for two years," he related. "There were many marvelous wonders inside the earth."

The dying sailor told of how he was dwarfed by his amiable hosts, a race of giants.

"The giants are not just things in fairy tales," he rasped. "They live down there. Like it said in the Bible, they live for five or eight hundred years before they die. They taught us their language."

"What kind of world is it?" asked the incredulous writer.

MYSTERIOUS DISAPPEARANCES: THEY NEVER CAME BACK

"They're much more advanced in doing things," Jansen said. He explained that the people inside the earth possessed a mysterious power that was greater than electricity. This power source enabled them to operate aircraft by drawing fuel from the atmosphere. The giants in the earth's interior were warmed by a single sun, less brilliant than our solar star. This interior sun was dim and they called it the "Smoky One or the Smoky God," Jansen said.

"How did you get out?"

"We got homesick after a couple of years," answered Olaf Jansen. "Even paradise can be dull if you don't have friends and relatives with you. The giants allowed us to sail toward home. On the return trip, our little boat was dashed about by giant waves on their ocean. Our compass was lost overboard. We didn't know the directions and we couldn't steer by the stars, We drifted for a long time and then we were pulled into the south opening at the South Pole."

Back on the surface world, the two sailors steered northward toward their home. Tragedy struck when an iceberg slammed into the fishing boat. Olaf Jansen's father was apparently killed in the accident. The young sailor was tossed from the deck and out into the frigid waters of the ocean.

"The luck of Leif Erickson was with me," claimed the old sailor. "I was rescued by a vessel that had just passed us. They returned me to my home in Norway."

"But didn't you tell someone of your adventure?" asked the writer. "The world would be excited over such a discovery."

"That was my biggest mistake in life. I did tell them," replied the old man in a low, bitter tone. "I started talking about the inner land when I was on the ship. They thought I was crazy. I kept telling them I was not making up stories. When the ship docked in Norway, I was taken off and placed in a mental hospital for the insane. I spent the next twenty-four years of my life in a lunatic's ward!"

Jansen claimed that he entered the asylum as a strong, spirited youth. He left as an embittered, broken, middle aged man.

"I have a manuscript of my adventures," he said. "When I was in the inner land, I drew some maps of the place. I kept them with me during those twenty-four years in the mental hospital. When I got out, I swore to never show them to anyone again or tell about that place. I wanted to

MYSTERIOUS DISAPPEARANCES: THEY NEVER CAME BACK

stay free. The way to do that was to keep my mouth shut."

After his release from the asylum, Olaf Jansen worked as a seaman on fishing boats and saved his pay. He immigrated to the United States, settled for a few years in a small town in Illinois, and eventually moved to California.

"I came to California because it is the one place on earth that looks like the paradise inside the earth," the dying man claimed.

Before his death, the old sailor provided further details concerning his adventures in the land of the giants. As Willis George Emerson, the writer, had befriended the elderly man, he was heir to the manuscript and maps. Emerson published his original edition of ***The Smoky God*** in 1908. The book was reprinted in 1965 by Palmer Publications, Amherst, Wisconsin.

Like everything else in life, this strange deathbed story is either true or false. The approach of death is a solemn moment for all men. A madness to confess seizes the minds of many dying people. They have a compulsion to blurt out their sins and secrets, to cleanse their soul before meeting our Creator. Olaf Jansen's unusual story is bizarre and seemingly fantastic. It is totally unsupported by factual documentation. Maps and manuscripts can also be created out of a writer's imagination, yet Willis George Emerson always maintained that Olaf Jansen was a real man, not a figure conjured up from his writer's mind. Those who believe in the hollow earth feel that a dying man would not spend his last moments of life in spinning imaginative lies.

According to Buddhist doctrine, Agharta is a subterranean land located deep within the center of our planet. The Buddhists believe there are millions of people living in this underworld paradise. Their daily lives and ultimate destiny is directed by a wise, all-powerful ruler known as Rigden jyepo—The King of the World. Rigden-jyepo reigns in Shamballah, the capital city of Agharta, one of the most beautiful cities in the universe.

"From his palace in Shamballah, Rigden-jyepo also directs many of the activities of homo sapiens on the surface world," reported Gunther Rosenberg. His European Occult Research Society has conducted widespread research into the legends of the Far East. "The King of the World is allegedly in close communication with the Dalai Lama, spiritual leader of Tibet. These messages from the underworld are carried by emissaries, a corps of subterranean monks who have been trained as secret cou-

MYSTERIOUS DISAPPEARANCES: THEY NEVER CAME BACK

riers from Agharta. They are supposed to travel to and from Agharta through a vast network of underground tunnels. These secret tunnels are supposed to be connected to many of the ancient Tibetan monasteries and, of course, the surface entrance is carefully guarded by monks selected by the Dalai Lama. These Tibetan tunnels are just part of a honeycomb of tunnels linking many parts of the world."

Nicholas Roerich (1874-1947), was a noted Russian artist, explorer, and philosopher. A talented individual with mystical inclinations, Roerich also had a lengthy association with the Moscow Art Theater and the Doaghilev Ballet Company. In the 1920's, Roerich spent five years exploring the Himalayan mountains, Tibet, and the isolated regions of Asia.

"Roerich's artistic accomplishments almost obscure his scientific achievements," explained Gunther Rosenberg. "He is listed in the encyclopedia as an archeologist. Roerich became convinced that Lhasa, the Tibetan capital, was connected to Shamballah by a network of tunnels. He said these same tunnels connected to the Great Pyramid at Giza, where there is a mysterious subterranean chamber. He felt the old pharaohs of Egypt were in contact with the super gods of the underworld, through emissaries from Shamballah."

Buddhist scripture claims Agharta was founded many millions of years ago, far back in the dim era of prehistory. "A great holy man was warned by the gods of an impending disaster," explained Gunther Rosenberg. "He led his people down through the tunnels and into the inner lands. This has elements of the Biblical story of Noah, along with a touch of the catastrophe that allegedly destroyed Atlantis."

Why and when do the representatives of Agharta come to the surface world?

"Buddhist tradition claims these visitations occur during times of great turmoil," continued Gunther Rosenberg. "UFOs, or flying saucers, appeared shortly after the nuclear explosions during World War II that heralded man's entrance into the atomic age. Some people believe that man's knowledge of atomic energy is a threat to this entire planet. Hence, they feel these god-like supermen from the hollow earth are maintaining a close watch over surface activities."

In his out-of-print book, **Shamballah** (Frederick Stokes & Company; New York; 1930) Nicholas Roerich wrote of his experiences in Tibet. In the opening chapter, *"Shamballah, The Resplendent,"* the Russian archeologist told of his conversation with a High Lama in Tibet in his

MYSTERIOUS DISAPPEARANCES: THEY NEVER CAME BACK

visit to that land in 1928."

"Lama, tell me of Shamballah," Roerich said.

"But you westerners know nothing of Shamballah," the lama answered. "You wish to know nothing. Probably you ask out of curiosity; and you pronounce the sacred word in vain."

"Lama, I don't ask about Shamballah aimlessly," Roerich replied. "Everywhere, people know of this great symbol under different names. Our scientists seek each new spark containing this remarkable realm. Csoma de Koros knew of Shamballah, when he made his prolonged visits to the Buddhist monasteries. Grunwendel translated the book of the famous Tashi Lama, pal-den-ye-she, about the *'Way To Shamballah.'* We sense how, under these sweet symbols, a great truth is concealed . . ."

The lama stared intently at Nicholas Roerich for a moment, looking at the Russian scientist with unblinking, piercing eyes. Roerich and the lama were alone in a long room in the monastery. The lama broke the silence of the darkened room by clapping his hands. A monk appeared with tea in two porcelain cups on a gold tray. As they sipped the bitter liquid, the lama explained that Shamballah was simply an enormous celestial kingdom, akin to the heavenly kingdom of the Christian religion.

Roerich was not content with this explanation. He placed a portfolio of notes on a rug between them. "Lama, I have heard of the reality of this indescribable place—an earthly Shamballah. I've been told that some high lamas have visited Shamballah. I've heard of the Buryat Lama and how he was taken through a narrow, secret passageway. So, please don't tell me of only the heavenly Shamballah because I know that a real one exists on earth. I and you both know that these earthly and heavenly Shamballah are linked together, with the two worlds unified."

The lama meditated for several minutes. The only sound in the room was the gentle tinkle of distant prayer bells.

"He is there in Shamballah," the old Tibetan holy man said. "Vigilant, indefatigable, and with his magical mirror he can tune in on all the events on this planet. He is Rigden-jyepo and his might is such that distance does not exist for him. He has been known to bring instantaneous aid to those he considers worthy. His riches are there to assist the needy. He is so powerful that he may change the karma of humans."

After a description of the supernatural power of the King of the

MYSTERIOUS DISAPPEARANCES: THEY NEVER CAME BACK

World, the lama added: "Uncountable are the inhabitants of that marvelous land! There are many new forces and achievements being prepared for those of us on the surface world.."

"Lama, the Vedanta says that very soon a new energy will be given to humanity," Roerich said. (Note: This interview took place only a few years before the discovery of atomic energy.)

"There are numerous things being prepared under predestiny," replied the lama. "Through our Holy Books we become acquainted with the teachings of the Blessed One. We have heard of this new energy. We have heard about the inhabitants of distant stars. We have also heard of the flying steel birds . . . and of those serpents that devour space with fire and smoke."

Roerich informed the lama of an experience when he traveled in the deserts of Asia. "Lama, a huge black vulture flew close to our camp when we remained near Ulan-Davan," the Russian said. "The vulture crossed the direction of something shining and beautiful, which flew over our camp and glistened in the rays of the sun."

"Did you smell an unusual fragrance at that time?" the lama inquired eagerly.

"We were in a large desert and several days' march away from the nearest settlement," said Roerich. "Yet, we became aware of a strange, exquisite perfume. I've never smelt such lovely perfume."

"You are watched over by Shamballah," declared the Tibetan. "The protecting forces of Shamballah have guarded in the Radiant Form of Matter. This force is always close to the Chosen Ones—although, they may not be aware of its existence. On occasion, this force is manifested for directing you. Whatever direction the sphere may have moved, you

MYSTERIOUS DISAPPEARANCES: THEY NEVER CAME BACK

should follow in that same direction. You have also mentioned the sacred calls—Kalagiva! When an individual hears this call, he knows that the route to Shamballah is open for him!"

The lama informed his Russian visitor that anyone who hears the cry of Kalagiva is henceforth given assistance by the Blessed Rigden-jyepo-The King of the World. "You must know the way in which help is given," he advised, "because people can often repel the help which is given."

Roerich was also interested in how the secret of Shamballah was guarded. He asked, "Does Shamballah have many messengers throughout the world? How are the secrets entrusted to them protected?"

"There is a great Keeper of the Mysteries'" explained the lama. "He watches closely over those who have been given important missions and secret work. If a sudden evil should threaten the couriers, they are given immediate assistance. The entrusted treasure must forever be guarded. Forty years ago, a man who lived in the Mongolian Gobi desert was entrusted with a secret treasure. When he felt he was about to die of old age, he tried to find a worthy soul to give the secret to before death claimed him. He was unable to find anyone in a state of worthiness. But the Great Keeper of the mysteries was ever vigilant and he reached the sick man, revived his spirits, and permitted him to find a purified individual to entrust the treasure."

"Why didn't the keeper of the mysteries take the treasure with him?"

The lama sighed and closed his eyes for a moment. "Karma has its special ways and even the renowned Keeper of the Mysteries does not wish to touch the threads of Karma. A single Karmic thread that is broken can result in tremendous harm and danger."

Roerich told of his travels in Tourfan and Turkestan, where he was shown long caves with secret passages and long, unexplored tunnels.

"Can a person follow these caves to reach the Ashrams of Shamballah?" he inquired, "We were informed that on occasion people—strangers to those regions—came out of those caves. These strange beings went into the cities and purchased supplies with ancient, strange coins of an unknown mintage."

"Verily, verily," chanted the lama. "People from Shamballah do sometimes visit the surface world. These visits are to meet with the earthly

MYSTERIOUS DISAPPEARANCES: THEY NEVER CAME BACK

co-workers of the powerful Rigden-jyepo. They may also visit to send forth remarkable gifts and precious relics. Even Rigden-jyepo has been known to appear in human form in the monasteries. These visits are pre-destined and he makes his prophecies for the future."

The lama related that when the King of the World appears before surface men, his visit heralds the approach of a great epoch in human events. "Many events are now being manifested," the Tibetan continued. "The cosmic fire once again nears the earth. The planets are in a position to create a new dawning for mankind. But there will be many cataclysms that will happen before the new era arrives. Mankind must again be tested to discover if the spirit has progressed sufficiently. Even now, the subterranean fire seeks to unite with the celestial elements of Akasha. The good forces must combine their power throughout the world else the greatest catastrophes are destined to occur in the word."

If Shamballah exists as a reality on or within the earth, why has not some adventurous explorer discovered a route to this fabled city? Roerich was puzzled by this same enigma and he mentioned that most heights have been explored, most valleys mapped, marked, and surveyed. "Why hasn't someone found a route to Shamballah?" he inquired.

"There is gold within the earth and diamonds and rubies in the mountains," said the lama. "People are eager to possess these precious gifts and many people attempt to find them. To date, people have not discovered all things on this earth. So, let no man try to reach Shamballah without being called. You have heard the stories of poisoned streams which have deadly gasses emitting from their vaporous surface. Have you ever perceived how animals and humans tremble when they reach certain localities? Many people have tried to reach Shamballah—people who have been uncalled. Some of these people have vanished forever. A few have found the holy place, which indicated their Karma was ready."

"Few people can understand the thoughts of people," continued

MYSTERIOUS DISAPPEARANCES: THEY NEVER CAME BACK

the lama. "And those who can do so are silent!"

Have you ever met strangers during your travels, simply dressed strangers, who walk quietly through the heat or cold toward some unknown goal? Never believe that because their garment is simple any stranger is insignificant. It is an impossibility for man to determine from which direction a powerful presence may approach."

"Tell me about the three monasteries near Lhassa—Sera, Depung, and Ganden."

The lama leaned back against his ornate chair. His yellowed, wrinkled skin stretched like aged parchment into a thin smile. "There are many holy monks in each monastery," he said.

Roerich shook his head. "I'm sure each monastery has holy men. Are there hidden tunnels under the Potala monastery? Can you tell me if there is a subterranean lake beneath one of these chief temples?"

The aged Tibetan smiled indulgently at his visitor. "You are aware of so many things that I wonder if you have not come from Lhassa," he remarked. "If you have seen the subterranean lake you are either a very great lama, or a servant trained to guide holy men there by torchlight."

"Neither," Roerich replied, "but I have heard of these wondrous places. Lama, have you met the Azaras?"

"You are familiar with many events. You must be a very successful man in your country," the lama said, following a moment's meditation. "To know so much about Shamballah is to have bathed in the stream of purification. Many of our people during their lives have met the Azaras and the snow people who serve them. Only in recent times have the Azaras quit coming into our cities. They are said to be settled now somewhere in the mountains. They are very tall, very erect, people with long hair and beards. Outwardly, they appear to look like a Hindu. The Azaras are the holy people who hold the secrets of Shamballah. Once, when I was walking in the mountains, I saw one of these chosen people. When I tried to run toward him, he turned beyond a rock and simply vanished. Yet I found no cave or cavern where he might have hidden. Even the snow people do not appear in these times."

It was the lama's turn to question his visitor. "Do you in the western world know of the magic stick which reveals the subterranean treasures of the earth?" he inquired.

"We have heard many stories of the unusual moving stick," said

MYSTERIOUS DISAPPEARANCES: THEY NEVER CAME BACK

Roerich. "I understand that this magical scepter enables a man to find lost mines, underground springs, and water."

"Who is the most important element in these experiments? The man or the stick?"

Roerich pursed his lips as he reflected on the question. "The stick has no life, but man is brimming with vibration and magnetic power," he replied. "The stick is like a pen in the hand of a man."

"All things are concentrated in the human body," related the lama. "The key is the knowledge of how to use it, not how to abuse it. Do you westerners know of the Great Stone? The stone which possesses magic powers? Do you know that this stone came from another planet? Do you know who possessed this fabulous treasure?"

Roerich said he had heard legends of such stones. "These stories go back to the time of the Druids. They tell of a great natural energy contained in this stone."

"Do you have a name for the stone?"

"Lapis Exilis is the name of the stone." Nicholas Roerich twisted in his chair. "Have you talked with many Christian missionaries, lama?"

The old man gathered his robe around his thin body, seeking to keep away the evening chill. "Your missionaries have visited our temples in centuries past," he said quietly. "Those who have visited Lhassa told us of many marvelous tales. We knew some of these stories because some of the books of your religions are sealed in our libraries. We may know more about your religions than you realize. We have seen many missionaries in the past few years—they speak of one Christ, but they speak ill of one another. Does western man think that we are ignorant? We know that the rites practiced by one sect of Christians are not recognized by other Christians. Therefore, your priests must have many Christs."

In another chapter at Shamballah entitled *"Subterranean Dwellers,"* author Roerich informed his readers of the world-wide belief in the hollow earth and underground kingdoms. "The subject of great migrations is the most fascinating in the history of humanity," he wrote. "What spirit was it that thus moved whole nations and innumerable tribes? What cataclysm drove the hordes from their familiar steppes? What new happiness and privileges did they anticipate in the blue mists of the desert?"

Roerich told of noticing similar carvings on rocks in the Himalayan Mountains of Asia, in Mongolia, Siberia, and "finally the same creative

MYSTERIOUS DISAPPEARANCES: THEY NEVER CAME BACK

psychology in the halristningars of Sweden and Norway." He mentioned that he had discovered these same ancient patterns carved into the stones of early Romanesque ruins.

A paradoxical man, Roerich was a trained archeologist who felt there was an underlying truth in folk tales and old legends. He wrote:

". . . Among the innumerable legends and fairy tales of various countries may be found the tales of lost tribes or subterranean dwellers. In wide and diverse directions, people are speaking of identical facts. But in correlating them you can readily see that these are just chapters from the one story. At first it seems impossible that there should exist any connection between these distorted whispers under the light of the desert bonfires. But afterward you begin to grasp a peculiar coincidence in these manifold legends by people who are even ignorant of each other's names.

"You recognize the same relationship in the folklores of Tibet, Mongolia, China, Turkestan, Kashmir, Persia, Altia, Siberia, and Ural. Caucasia, the Russian steppes, Lithuania, Poland, Hungary, France, Germany; from the highest mountains to the deepest oceans . . . They tell how a holy tribe was persecuted by tyrant and how the people, not willing to submit to cruelty, closed themselves into subterranean mountains. They even ask you if you want to see the entrance of the cave through which the saintly persecuted folk fled."

During his travels through the most unexplored areas of the Himalayan mountains, Roerich discovered many mysterious structures. Guides had been sent ahead one evening to set up a camp. When Roerich and his heavily-laden porters arrived at the encampment, it was built around a flat area some sixteen-thousand feet high in the mountains. The camp site was near a stone ruin, described as similar to the Druid ruins at Stonehenge or Carnac. The stone ruins were composed of the giant, long stones so familiar to archeologists who have studied the vast ruins of ancient races. The Tibetan guides had no knowledge of who might have constructed the unusual rock structure. They simply said the site was sacred, a holy place where no one was allowed to excavate.

One of the most amazing, most controversial women in the annals of the occult is Madame Blavatsky, who is credited with founding Theosophical Society. She claimed to be a magician, wizard, occultist, prophet, and a pupil of the "Masters of Wisdom." Born Helen Petrovna Hahn in a small village in the Russian Ukraine on July 31, 1831, she claimed to be ten years old when the mysterious "Masters', began to talk with her. At the age of ten, the young girl told her aunt: ". . . There has always existed wise men who have all the knowledge of the world. They have total command over the forces of nature and they make themselves known only to those persons who are deemed worthy of knowing and seeing them. A person must also believe in them before you see them."

At age seventeen, a marriage was arranged between the young girl and General Blavatsky, a commander of the czar's armies. She lived with the aged military man less than three weeks. She left to travel the world for three decades. "Love is a nightmare—a vile dream," she recorded in her diary, "Woman finds her true happiness in acquiring supernatural powers."

Her years of travel are veiled in mystery. Her Theosophical followers believe the fabulous occultist leader traveled in virtually every country of the world. She is supposed to have gone to Egypt, where she held a midnight seance in the Queen's Chamber of the Great Pyramid at Giza, Egypt. She performed rites and chanted incantations to raise the ancient spirits of long-dead Egyptian priests. Later, she was in India where she became engrossed with the magical performances of the Asian wizards.

Finally, clad in the garments of a man, she is supposed to have visited several of the monasteries of Tibet. In 1874, she founded the Theosophy Society. This group was founded to "lead men to their true spiritual nature."

Madame Blavatsky's greatest literary work is *The Secret Doctrine*, one of the most remarkable occult books ever published. In *The Secret Doctrine* she told of ancient, subterranean tunnels, underground cities, and hidden depositories of ancient literature. The book was published shortly before her death on July 8, 1891. Selections related to the hollow earth mystery include:

". . . Moreover in all of the large and wealthy Lamaseries, there are subterranean crypts and cave-libraries, cut in the rock, where the Gonpa and the Ihakhang are situated in the mountains. Beyond the western Tsaydam, in the solitary passes of Kuen-len, there are several such hiding places. Along the ridge of Altyn-tag, whose soil no European foot has ever trodden so far, there exists a certain hamlet, lost in a deep gorge. It is a small cluster of houses, a hamlet rather than a monastery, with a poor-looking temple in it, and one old lama, a hermit, living near to watch it. Pilgrims say that the subterranean galleries and halls under it contain a collection of books, the number of which, according to the accounts

MYSTERIOUS DISAPPEARANCES: THEY NEVER CAME BACK

given, is too large to find room even in the British Museum.

"According to the same tradition the now desolate regions of the waterless land of Tamin—a virtual wilderness in the heart of Turkestan—were in days of old covered with flourishing and wealthy cities. At present, a few verdant oases only relieve its dread solitude. One such, carpeting the sepulchre of a vast city buried under the sandy soil of the desert, belongs to no one, but is often visited by Mongolians and Buddhists. The tradition also speaks of immense subterranean abodes of large corridors with tiles and cylinders..."

Madame Blavatsky based her published reports on statements from people she had met during her travels. She admitted that the subterranean crypts and underground cities might well be "actual fact" or "idle rumor."

Beasts, Men and Gods (E. P. Dutton & Co., New York, 1922) is another remarkable book containing information on the hollow earth mystery. Author Ferdinand Ossendowski also tells of Asian legends of Agharta. An excerpt from that book is reproduced here:

"... On my journey into Central Asia I came to know for the first time about the 'Mystery of Mysteries,' which I can call by no other name. At the outset I did not pay very much attention to it and did not attach to it such importance as I afterwards realized belonged to it, when I had analyzed and connoted many sporadic, hazy, and often controversial bits of evidence.

"The old people on the shore of the river Amyl related to me an ancient legend to the effect that a certain Mongolian tribe in their escape from the demands of Genghis Khan hid themselves in the subterranean country. Afterward, a Soyot from near the Lake of Nogan Kul showed me the smoking gate that serves as the entrance to the 'Kingdom of Agharta.' Through this gate a hunter formerly entered into the Kingdom and, after his return, began to relate what he had seen there. The lamas cut out his tongue in order to prevent him from telling about the 'Mystery of Mysteries.' When he arrived at old age, he came back to the entrance to this cave and disappeared into the subterranean kingdom, the memory of which had ornamented and lightened his nomad heart.

"I received more realistic information about this from Hutuktu Jelyb Djamarap, in Narabanchi Kure. He told of the semi-realistic arrival of the powerful King of the World from the subterranean kingdom, of his appearance, his miracles and of his prophecies; and only then did I begin

MYSTERIOUS DISAPPEARANCES: THEY NEVER CAME BACK

to understand that in that legend, hypnosis or mass vision, is hidden not only the mystery but a realistic and powerful force capable of influencing the political life of Asia. From that moment I began making some investigations.

"The favorite Gelong Lama of Prince Chultan Beyli and the Prince himself gave me an account of the subterranean kingdom.

"Everything in the world," said Gelong, "is constantly in a state of change and transition—peoples, science, religions, laws, and customs. How many great empires and brilliant cultures have perished! And that alone which remains unchanged is Evil, the tool of the Bad Spirits. More than sixty thousand years ago a Holy man disappeared with a whole tribe of people under the ground and never appeared again on the surface of the earth . . . Many people have visited this kingdom. But no one knows where this place is. Some say Afghanistan, others India. All the people there are protected against Evil and crimes do not exist within its bournes. Science has developed calmly and nothing is threatened with destruction. The subterranean people have reached the highest knowledge. Now it is a large kingdom, millions of men with the King of the World as their ruler. He knows all of the forces of the world and reads all the souls of humankind and the great book of their destiny. Invisibly he rules eight hundred million men on the surface of the earth and they will accomplish his every order."

"Prince Chultan Beyli added: "This kingdom is Agharta. It extends throughout all the subterranean passages of the whole world. I heard a learned lama of China relating to Bogdo Khan that all the subterranean caves of America are inhabited by an ancient people who have disappeared underground. Traces of them are still found on the surface of the land. These subterranean peoples and spaces are governed by rulers owing allegiance to the King of the World.

"You know that in the two greatest oceans of the east and the west were formerly two continents. They disappeared under the water but their people went into the subterranean kingdom. In underground caves there exists a peculiar light which affords growth to the grains and vegetables and long life without disease to the people. There are many different peoples and many different tribes.

"An old Buddhist Brahman in Nepal was carrying out the will of the Gods in making a visit to the ancient kingdom of Jenghiz—Siam—where he met a fisherman who ordered him to take a place in his boat and sail with him upon the sea. On the third day they reached an island

MYSTERIOUS DISAPPEARANCES: THEY NEVER CAME BACK

where he met a people having two tongues which could speak separately in different languages. They showed to him peculiar, unfamiliar animals, tortoises with sixteen feet and one eye, huge snakes with a very tasty flesh and birds with teeth which caught fish for their masters in the sea. These people told him that they had come up out of the subterranean kingdom and described to him certain parts of the underground country."

The Lama Turgut traveling with me from Urga to Peking gave me further details.

"The capital of Agharta is surrounded with towns of high priests and scientists. It reminds one of Lhasa where the palace of the Dalai Lama, the Potala, is the top of a mountain covered with monasteries and temples. The throne of the King of the World is surrounded by millions of incarnated Gods. They are the Holy Panditas. The palace itself is encircled by the palaces of the Goro, who possess all the visible and invisible forces of the earth, of inferno and of the sky and who can do everything for the life and death of man.

"If our mad humankind should begin to war against them, they would be able to explode the whole surface of our planet and transform it into deserts. They can dry up the seas, transform lands into oceans and scatter the mountains into the sands of the deserts. By his order trees, grasses and bushes can be made to grow; old and feeble men can become young and stalwart; and the dead can be resurrected.

"In cars strange and unknown to us they rush through the narrow cleavages inside our planet. Some Indian Brahmans and Tibetan Dalai Lamas during their laborious struggles to the peaks of mountains which no other human feet had trod have found there inscriptions carved on the rocks, footprints in the snow and the tracks of wheels. The blissful Sakkia Mouni found on one mountain top tablets of stone carrying words which he only understood in his old age and afterward penetrated into the Kingdom of Agharta, from which he brought back crumbs of the sacred learning preserved in his memory.

"There in palaces of wonderful crystal live the invisible rulers of all pious people, the King of the World or Brahytma, who can speak with God as I speak with you, and his two assistants, Mahytma, knowing the purposes of future events, and Mahynga, ruling the causes of these events.

"The Holy Panditas study the world and all its forces. Sometimes

MYSTERIOUS DISAPPEARANCES: THEY NEVER CAME BACK

the most learned among them collect together and send envoys to that place where the human eyes have never penetrated. This is described by the Tashi Lama living eight hundred and fifty years ago. The highest Panditas place their hands on their eyes and at the base of the brain of younger ones and force them into a deep sleep, wash their bodies with an infusion of grass and make them immune to pain and harder than stones, wrap them in magic cloths, bind them and then pray to the Great God. The petrified youths lie with eyes and ears open and alert, seeing, hearing and remembering everything. Afterwards, a Goro approaches and fastens a long, steady gaze upon them. Very slowly, the bodies lift themselves from the earth and disappear. The Goro sits and stares with fixed eyes to the place whither he has sent them. Invisible threads join them to his will.

"Some of them course among the stars, observe their events, their known peoples, their life and their laws. They listen to their talk, read their books, understand their fortunes and woes, their holiness and sins, their piety and evil. Some are mingled with flame and see the creature of fire, quick and ferocious, eternally fighting, melting and hammering metals in the depths of planets, boiling the water for geysers and springs, melting the rocks and pushing out molten streams over the surface of the earth through the holes in the mountains. Others rush together with the ever elusive, infinitesimally small, transparent creatures of the air and penetrate into the mysteries of their existence and into the purposes of their life.

"Others slip into the depths of the sea, and observe the kingdom of the wise creatures of the water, who transport and spread genial warmth all over the earth, ruling the winds, waves and storms. In Erdeni Dzu formerly lived Pandita Hutuktu who had come from Agharta. As he was daring, he told about the time when he lived according to the will of the Goro on a red star in the east, floated in the ice-covered ocean and flew among the stormy fires in the depths at the earth."

"These are the tales which I heard in the Mongolian yurtas of Princes and in the Lamaite monasteries. These stories were all related in a solemn tone which forbade challenge and doubt.

"Mystery . . ."

MYSTERIOUS DISAPPEARANCES: THEY NEVER CAME BACK

CHAPTER SIXTEEN

MONSTERS, UFOS AND BIZARRE BEINGS

Since Christopher Columbus returned to the Spanish court with stories about fantastic monsters, there have been reports of bizarre beings in the Triangle of the Lost. Often these monsters are from UFOs; their appearance coincides with UFO flaps in Central and South America and the Caribbean Islands. During the past two years, as an example, reports have come from throughout the island of Puerto Rico of weird, dwarflike little men landing in flying saucers. The reports are frequently so wild and far-out as to be almost unbelievable.

Recently, a businesswoman from Huntsville, Alabama, had a frightening experience on an interstate highway in Georgia that defies rational explanation. The woman, who requested anonymity from the news media, said she encountered a robot "four feet tall, wearing a metallic pewter-like outfit. The creature was capped with a head dome or 'Bubble' made of the same material."

While the land area of Georgia is not included in the Triangle of the Lost, we might presume that this weird, unexplainable incident is linked to the mystery area.

"I could only see the object from about waist up," she continued. "I was looking out the window of my stalled car. The bubble or dome had two rectangular slits for eyes. There weren't any other openings in the domelike device, which was about the size of a regulation football helmet."

The woman was traveling south of Atlanta on Interstate 75, north of Tifton, Georgia. She was alone in the car, having left Huntsville earlier for Tifton. South of Atlanta, the woman stopped her vehicle and obtained

MYSTERIOUS DISAPPEARANCES: THEY NEVER CAME BACK

gasoline at a service station. She also requested that her car be given a routine check. The attendant checked the battery, water, and oil, filled the tank, and the woman continued her journey.

Driving at peak speed on the interstate, the woman was approximately 30 minutes north of her destination where she planned to visit a relative. Without warning, the engine of her car suddenly stopped.

"The engine quit, my power brakes went out, and the power steering stopped working," the woman informed newsmen. "Nothing worked on the car. I would estimate the time this happened at about 3:30 p.m."

The woman guided the vehicle off the side of the road. "The country is fairly level in this area," she said. "The only strange thing that happened until then was that the car had stopped working."

Identified as Mrs. Robinson in several news stories, the woman reported a strange feeling came over her when she pulled off the road. "I was sitting numbly behind the wheel," Mrs. Robinson recalled, "when I sensed something weird and unexplainable. I turned my head slowly and almost mechanically toward the left. This was toward the road."

The thing was there!

Standing close to her automobile!

She was too afraid to look the thing in the eyes, even though her window was rolled up.

"It was so close that I could have touched it if I'd rolled down my window," Mrs. Robinson related. "I didn't know what to do. I didn't really think it was real, but I could glimpse it out there beyond the window. It was dressed in some sort of metallic material. It sort of looked like pewter. The dome, or bubble, was made of the same material. There were two openings, two rectangular slits, for the eyes."

Mrs. Robinson was too frightened to look directly into the creature's eyes, presuming the slits were eyes. This entire incident took from five to seven minutes, according to Mrs. Robinson, and then the creature walked from the left of the car and around to the front. It stood there momentarily, then walked to the rear of the vehicle.

"The walk was pretty much like anyone else, although I couldn't see the legs," Mrs. Robinson related. "I couldn't see below the waist so I don't know if the creature had legs or what. I did notice that when it moved, the bubble dome also moved. This seemed to be more a me-

MYSTERIOUS DISAPPEARANCES: THEY NEVER CAME BACK

chanical motion, as opposed to a skeletal or fluid movement."

She reported the dome moved from right to left, then back again, and up and down, as if scanning the terrain. "It acted like a robot that had been programmed," she related. "I believe it could only see out of those rectangular slits and the head had to turn to see what was at the side."

After walking to the rear of her vehicle, Mrs. Robinson reported that the creature seemed to vanish. "I looked through my rear view mirror, but I was frightened of making any sudden movements or turning around," she stated. "After a long time passed, I got out of the car. I was seriously thinking that the car might explode or something. I really didn't know what to expect."

Standing outside her vehicle, Mrs. Robinson looked around for some sign of the creature. "I couldn't detect any unusual sounds or odors," she explained. "I didn't see any kind of a spacecraft or an aerial vehicle. Finally, I decided to open up the hood of the car in hopes of attracting assistance from a passing driver."

When the woman opened the hood of her car, large amounts of smoke poured out of the engine compartment.

"There wasn't a fire-just smoke," said the woman. "The smoke just billowed out of there."

Approximately an hour and fifteen minutes after the car quit running, and the creature appeared, a Georgia state patrolman stopped to assist Mrs. Robinson. "He called for a wrecker to take the car to a garage," she related. "When the car was pulled to the garage, the hood was almost at the melting stage. The hood was so hot that you couldn't touch it. I was so molten hot that it seemed as if you could poke your thumb through it."

While the metal was fiery hot, the paint was not affected!

It was another hour an a half before a mechanic could check the vehicle. "This was three hours after the car stopped before he could look at it. It was too hot to touch," she related. "I've never had an experience like that. I hadn't drank a drop. I wasn't taking drugs or tranquilizers. I just don't know what happened."

Mrs. Robinson told newsmen that the Georgia State Patrol man informed her that other motorists in that area had reported similar experiences that same day. "Whatever it was, I can't explain it," said the

MYSTERIOUS DISAPPEARANCES: THEY NEVER CAME BACK

woman.

After the story was published by ***Huntsville Times*** Science Writer Barry Carebolt, the businesswoman became extremely reluctant to discuss the incident. "She's just quit talking about it," said a UFO investigator. "However, there have been plenty of rumors concerning what happened to the car. Several scientists at the space center here went to Georgia to examine the car. This was on their own time; it wasn't an official investigation. Some of these men work with metals and they were interested in the phenomena of something that would heat metal to a high temperature and not affect paint. They reported the engine was melted. The entire engine had been melted down into a surrealistic looking mess."

What happened to the car?

There are unconfirmed reports in Huntsviile, and also in Georgia, that the vehicle was purchased by an agency of the U.S. Government. These rumors claim the car was placed under armed guard, then whisked off to a laboratory for secret analysis. "It has been impossible to learn which agency might have purchased the car," an investigator said. "Or if they did purchase it. No one seems to know where the car is at the present time. The lady involved in the incident refuses to discuss the case with anyone. She was rumored to be quite upset when the story appeared in the newspaper. Until more information is developed, we are left with an intriguing mystery."

Officially, a spokesman for the Georgia Highway Patrol discounted the incident. "We had a report on that," said the spokesman, "but we don't know anything about a melted engine."

Unofficially, a member of the Georgia State Patrol confirmed there were several cases similar to Mrs. Robinson's that same day. "Most of them were on or near the interstate highway running south of Atlanta," the patrolman said. "There was also a case that same night over by Stone Mountain. Another one popped up the next day on a county road in the northern part of the state."

The lawman said the State Patrol did not get involved except on a routine basis. "I understand the patrolman gave assistance, took down the reports, and called for a tow truck," he related. "What happened to the cars after they reached a garage was up to the individual owners. I did hear a rumor that these cars were brought to Atlanta and put in a warehouse under armed guard. However, I sure wouldn't swear to that

MYSTERIOUS DISAPPEARANCES: THEY NEVER CAME BACK

under oath. It is strictly hearsay, the kind of talk you hear on a coffee break. I also heard that the cars were collected in the warehouse and then flown off for analysis."

I was unable to obtain the names, or any other information, regarding these cases. The encounter by Mrs. Robinson was the only incident to be made public. While there were no signs of a UFO in the Robinson case, her vehicle reacted in a manner associated with the well-known UFO electro-magnetic effect. Many motorists reporting a UFO tell of their car engine and radio going dead, lights cutting out, and similar phenomena. Once the engine on the Robinson vehicle stopped running, the power brakes and steering would be affected.

There are also certain segments of the electro-magnetic spectrum that might melt metal. Depending on the materials, a high-powered micro-wave unit could melt certain metals without harming paint. However, a portable micro-wave unit able to melt an automobile engine in a few minutes would be beyond present earth technology.

This same flap also produced reports of little men in flying saucers. The first came from Mt. Airy, North Carolina, when a wave of UFO reports jammed the police telephone switchboards. A Mt. Airy couple, on the way to a football game, observed a blue, saucer-shaped object with rounded edges. The device was hovering about one hundred feet above their home when they stepped outside. At the same time, they noticed a creature about three feet tall standing in a nearby clearing. The UFOnaut was dressed in a gold metallic space suit. When the wife screamed, the couple hurried to their car and drove away. An investigation later revealed no trace of the UFO or its occupant.

That same week, Danville, Virginia was the scene of another encounter with a diminutive spaceman. Bill Hines informed the police that he and a friend were frightened, then chased down White Oak mountain by a creature about three feet tall. Hines said the aggressive little man had no eyes, a shimmering white body, and it "vanished" in a "green haze."

Raymond Ryan, 42, was fishing one night near the Gulf of Mexico when he spotted a strange underwater light following his boat. "I tried repeatedly to beat the thing away with an oar," Ryan said, "but the light only got dimmer. I finally went and got my twin brother, Rayme, and we went back to the river'."

The two brothers located the glowing light and poked at it again

MYSTERIOUS DISAPPEARANCES: THEY NEVER CAME BACK

with their oars. They then went to the U.S. Coast Guard station in Pascagoula, Mississippi, and reported the light. A 16-foot boat was dispatched to investigate the strange effect.

"The object was located in about five feet of water," the Coast Guard stated. "It was moving at a speed of about 5 or 6 knots. There was an amber beam, about six inches in diameter, attached to a shiny metallic object."

Coast Guardsmen attempted to capture what they termed "an unidentified submerged illuminating object." The device evaded capture by cutting off the light beam and moving away. As soon as the Guardsmen relaxed, the device reappeared. The report stated the USO travelled several different directions during the hour it was under observation. Finally the light went out and the object disappeared."

At the same time, people living in the boondocks of Puerto Rico were staying close to their homes at night. A rash of reports told of creatures with claw-like appendages, slit eyes, and a "gliding" way of walking, came from several regions of the island. A band of UFOlogists launched an expedition into the Sierra de Lugiuilo area after sightings reached epidemic proportions there. Their efforts to capture a UFOnaut or robot were unsuccessful.

Puerto Rico was also being buzzed at low levels by a saucer-shaped object, silverish in color, with rows of blinking lights in November. The device would suddenly pop into view at treetop level, alternately glowing bright, then dimming. A humanlike pilot could be observed through the row of windows around the craft. Reports of UFOs are fairly numerous in and around the Triangle of the Lost. As one investigator summed up: "It appears this area is under observation from some unknown group."

Strange creatures from UFOs are a part of this mystery in all areas of the world. In the Triangle of the Lost, however, are monstrous manifestations of "Things" that chill the blood of any ordinary mortal. Bristly-haired dwarfs, strange swamp monsters, and even beasts from prehistoric times have been encountered in the lands within or around the Triangle. As an example: There was a sudden movement in the bushes as Emelino Martinez walked back from his hunting trip in the hills of Venezuela on the night of April 10, 1954. Martinez stopped motionless, shotgun at the ready, when the threshing noise sounded again in the bush. He waited momentarily and then resumed his walk down the mountain path toward his parked automobile.

MYSTERIOUS DISAPPEARANCES: THEY NEVER CAME BACK

Sickening fear froze his blood when he heard a guttural noise, as if something was calling. Cold bumps of fright moved in a chilling blanket across his body. His pounding heart leaped against his throat. "I knew when I was the hunted and not the hunter,", Martinez reported later. He had parked his automobile in a small clearing along a dirt road on the mountain a few miles outside of Caracas, Venezuela. He dropped his day's catch of small game and ran for his car.

An unintelligible shout behind him indicated the thing was in close pursuit. Stumbling, falling, scrambling, Martinez fled down the trail. He stopped for an instant to glance back toward his pursuer.

"I almost dropped dead," he related. "Two things were running after me. The moon was out and I saw them very distinctly. They were short, about the size of a 2-year-old boy, and they looked like half-man, half monkey. They were covered with dark hair. One quick look and I picked up some extra speed in my flight."

Martinez reached his car, then fumbled in his pockets for the keys. The pounding footsteps of his pursuers racing down the trail caused the nervous hunter to drop the keys. "I picked them up and started to open the car door," he explained. "My mind was spinning with terror. I knew those things meant to harm me. Just as I opened the door, I was grabbed from behind. We fell together into a ditch beside the road."

Martinez dropped his shotgun as two powerful arms closed over his throat. "I broke the beast's grip and scrambled toward the car. It was on top of me, screaming, growling and biting like a mad animal," Martinez recalled, beads of perspiration appearing on his forehead.

"I tried to grab my shotgun and couldn't reach it," he said. His hands grasped a large rock and he repeatedly smashed his attacker on the head. Screams of pain slashed through the dark night. Martinez saw his attacker move backward, blood spurting from his head wounds. The frantic young hunter dashed to his car.

"I snapped the door lock as they banged against the car, pounding their hairy fists against the windows in frustrated rage," he explained. "I started the car and probably set a speed record coming down the mountain. I drove directly to the police station. They laughed and advised me to go home and stay out of taverns."

Emelino Martinez, 27 years old, was a construction worker. "I got some of my friends and we drove back up on the mountain the next morning," he said. "My new shotgun was still there where I dropped it. I tell

MYSTERIOUS DISAPPEARANCES: THEY NEVER CAME BACK

you, senor, we were really armed. The car was filled with weapons."

After they recovered the shotgun, Martinez and his friends collected several bloodstained leaves. They questioned the people who lived on the mountain. "They knew about the beasts," Martinez reported. "These farmers told about ships from the skies—flying saucers. Cattle, sheep, pigs, dogs and two young farm lads had disappeared on the mountain."

The farmers claimed the beasts were black, bristly-haired dwarfs who hid in caves and kidnapped both livestock and humans. "They advised us not to hunt for the beasts," Martinez said. "We agreed."

The bloodstained leaves were later analyzed at a laboratory, along with similar stains on the young man's shirt. "I have never been able to determine the specimens," Juan Valzez, a technician, said recently. "The blood is definitely not human. It doesn't match any known animals. We are still very puzzled."

The frightening experience is a vivid part of Emelino Martinez' memory. "I still have nightmares," he said. "I wake up screaming sometimes with a picture of those things in my mind. I hope to never see them again."

Encounters with a gigantic monster, which resembled a dinosaur occurred in 1948 by alarmed citizens in Florida. Fishermen, airplane pilots, tourists and startled beach picnickers said the beast was "... very big, short-necked, with a reptilian face and a blunt nose."

These descriptions, and tracks left by the marauding monster, matched those of a dinosaur supposedly extinct for more than sixty million years!

Tracks were found along beaches near Tampa and in the swampy marshlands along the Suwanee river. "The imprints were three-toed, with webbing between each toe," a newspaper man recalled. "There was about 25 inches between each foot print. I measured one of the toes. It was 13 inches in length!"

Working from these impressions, scientists estimated the hulking beast weighed approximately three tons and moved about on two legs.

The creature terrorized the Florida coast for nine months and then vanished as quickly as it appeared. Some investigators suggested the possibility that dinosaurs did not become extinct, as we believe, but moved into the sea where their secret existence has been shrouded for

MYSTERIOUS DISAPPEARANCES: THEY NEVER CAME BACK

limitless centuries.

Florida UFOlogist Joan Writenour told of a young woman, Miss M. B., who was driving on lonely route 481 near Brookevilie, Florida, at night.

Suddenly, a tire blew out and the young woman halted her automobile and started to change it. She had barely begun when a violent noise indicated something was stomping around in the nearby woods. Then Miss M. B. sniffed a nauseous odor.

At that moment, a large hairy creature walked from the woods and headed directly toward the stranded motorist. "It was big, heavy probably seven feet tall and weighed about four to seven hundred pounds," Miss M. B. estimated. The frightening visitor had sloping skull, an ape's face and "eyes as big as silver dollars." The body was covered with blackish hair.

Fortunately for the young woman, the monster did not appear hostile. It seemed curious about her presence and patiently settled down at the edge of the road. Miss M. B. was desperately trying to keep her nerves under control when the hum of an approaching car came down the highway. The beast grunted and disappeared into the wilderness. There were no signs of the hulking monster when the automobile stopped to help the young woman. "I shall never forget those large, glowing eyes," Miss M. B. reported.

Recently, residents of Holopaw, Florida bolted their doors, oiled their guns and stayed indoors after sundown when a southern version of the abominable snowman invaded the sunshine state. The creature was tagged "the abominable sandman" by Florida newsmen and "that awful creature" by eyewitnesses.

Something classified as "about five feet tall, covered with hair . . . twice as broad as a man and walking upright on two legs" raided garbage cans, invaded homes, frightened dogs and scared livestock. When the tiny crossroads community settled down from the bizarre invasion, no one was certain whether their uninvited visitor had been a bear, an escaped gorilla or, as many insisted, a real life midget monster.

Two young deer hunters first sighted the hairy monster. They took steady aim and fired their high-powered rifles at the beast. The creature roared with pain and scrambled away. The two young men followed a trail of blood into the dense Florida vegetation. Angry growls of pain sent the two men hurrying in the opposite direction.

MYSTERIOUS DISAPPEARANCES: THEY NEVER CAME BACK

Shortly afterward, the "sandman" invaded a garage, making a frightening noise as he prowled through the tools and jars stored there. The homeowner rushed to investigate and retreated rapidly when the growling beast tossed a tire tube at him.

From these initial sightings, stories about the grotesque monster mushroomed each year.

The sandman was here, raiding a garbage can and frightening children. He was there, breaking down a fence and frightening cattle. Like the wind, he was everywhere, growling at dogs, peering through windows, or chasing a housewife into her home. An atmosphere of terror was quickly generated in the community. However, Florida lawmen viewed the "sandman" sensation as highly exaggerated. "There's nothing to it," a policeman reported. "At the very most, the sandman is nothing more than an escaped gorilla."

Yet zoo keepers in Florida insisted there were no escaped gorillas on their wanted lists. Frightened people who encountered the beast were certainly not calmed by the gorilla tale.

Max Atwell, an Osceola county ranchhand, was parked in a pick-up truck in a pasture late one evening. He was waiting for a small herd of cattle to walk down to the fence gate. "Suddenly, this thing growled and came scrambling out of a patch of weeds near my truck," Atwell stated. "It ran directly toward the truck. I started trembling. I rolled up those truck windows and snapped the door locks."

The hairy beast approached the driver's side of the vehicle, peered into the window and growled again. "It was a low, guttural sound," Atwell wrote me. "My mind started working again and I remembered I was in the truck. I started the engine and the noise frightened the beast. It moved away. I floor-boarded that truck, buddy, and roared out of there. I must have been doing 90 mph all the way to my home."

Ashen-faced and shaken, Atwell returned to the scene, armed with a shotgun. "The creature had vanished," he wrote. "I've thought a lot about the incident since then. Our faces were only a few inches apart when the thing looked through the window. That was no gorilla. It was more of a combination of a human and a gorilla. An apeman."

Eventually, the sandman disappeared from Holopaw and, shortly afterward, other communities in Florida were alarmed by similar sightings. Even today, there are several sightings each month as the sandman ventures out of the swamps.

MYSTERIOUS DISAPPEARANCES: THEY NEVER CAME BACK

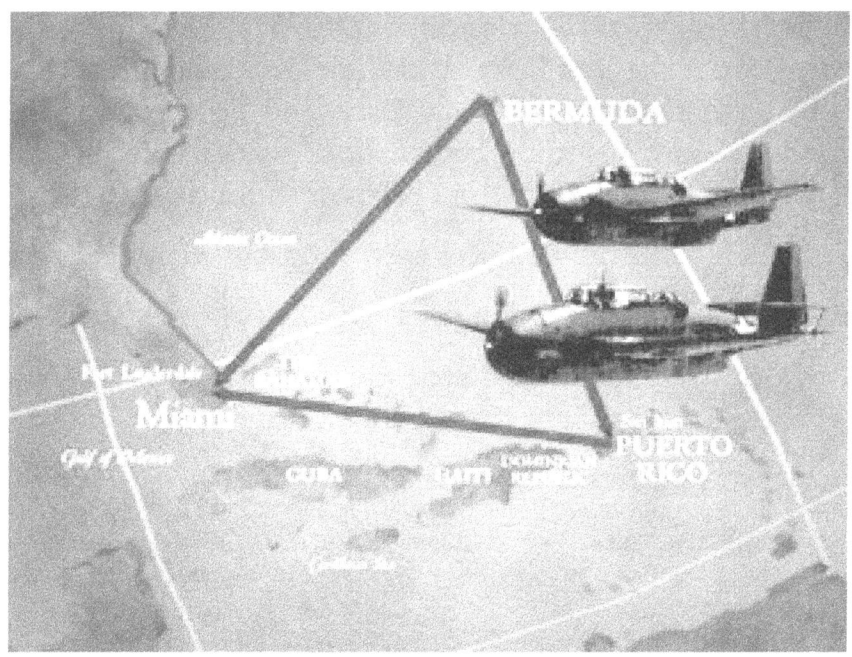

CHAPTER SEVENTEEN

FLIGHTS OF DOOM

The Triangle of the Lost leaped to world attention with the disappearance of five Navy Grumman TBM-3 Avengers torpedo bombers, a Martin Mariner rescue plane, and their crews. On the afternoon of December 5, 1945, the temperature at Ft. Lauderdale Naval Air Station, Florida, was a warm 64 degrees. Although there were scattered clouds in the sky, the sun was shining as the five planes prepared to take off at 2 p.m.

The airport, which has since been transformed into the Hollywood-Ft. Lauderdale International Airport, was a scene of intense activity that afternoon. Crews had checked the Avenger torpedo bombers in Flight 19 earlier that day. The 52-foot wings had been carefully inspected for signs of stress. The 1600-h.p. Wright Cyclone engines had been tuned. Both pilots and crewmen trusted the powerful airplanes, the Avengers, which could fly 300 mph carrying a 2,000 pound load of torpedoes or bombs.

A crew of three (pilot, radioman, gunner) planned to make the flight on the Overwater Navigational Training Patrol. They were to fly for 160 miles due east, turn north for 40 miles and return in a southwesterly direction to the base. Members of the crew had from 18 months to four years of flight experience.

MYSTERIOUS DISAPPEARANCES: THEY NEVER CAME BACK

In one barracks, three friends prepared to leave for the flight line. They were Corporal Allen Kosner of Kenosha, Wisconsin, PFC Robert Gruebel of Long Island City, New York and Sgt. Robert Gallivan of Northampton, Massachusetts. About an hour before takeoff, Gallivan and Gruebel got off their bunks, pulled on their flight gear.

Gallivan looked down at Kosner, who rested on his bunk.

"Aren't you going?" the sergeant asked.

"I've got my flight time in for the month," Kosner answered. "I don't feel like going and there's no reason I should."

"Lucky guy," Private Gruebel responded.

"I'll write my folks. We can catch the movie when you get back," said Kosner.

"What's playing?" asked Gruebel.

"What Next, Private Hargrove?" said Gallivan.

Gallivan and Gruebel closed the door as they left the barracks. Private Gruebel was known on base as an "eager beaver," an enthusiastic airman who enjoyed flying. After they arrived on the runway, pilots and crew members checked out their powerful planes.

The preflight check was a routine to make sure that each plane was fully equipped for the mission.

"Fuel?" asked the control tower.

"A-OK," replied each pilot. The planes carried 18,250 pounds of high-powered fuel, enough for more than 1,000 miles of flying.

"Radio?" queried the tower.

"Functioning fine."

"Life saving equipment?"

Each pilot responded positively that Mae West life jackets and a self-inflating life raft was aboard their planes. Precisely on schedule, the five torpedo bombers roared off into the skies at two o'clock. The pilots gathered into formation and flew into the Triangle of the Lost toward the Bahamas. After a series of scheduled torpedo runs over a target near Bimini, the planes regrouped and turned toward home.

Back at the naval air station around 4 p.m, a bored air controlman idly read a comic book. Suddenly, an astonishing message came crack-

MYSTERIOUS DISAPPEARANCES: THEY NEVER CAME BACK

ling over the radio.

"Calling the tower . . . this is an emergency . . . Calling the tower. . . this is an emergency!" The voice belonged to Lieutenant Charles Taylor, commander of Flight 19.

"What's your trouble?" asked the tower.

". . . We seem to be off course," Taylor blurted out. "We can't see land. Repeat. We cannot see land."

"What's your position?"

"I'm not sure," Taylor answered hesitantly. "We seem to be lost."

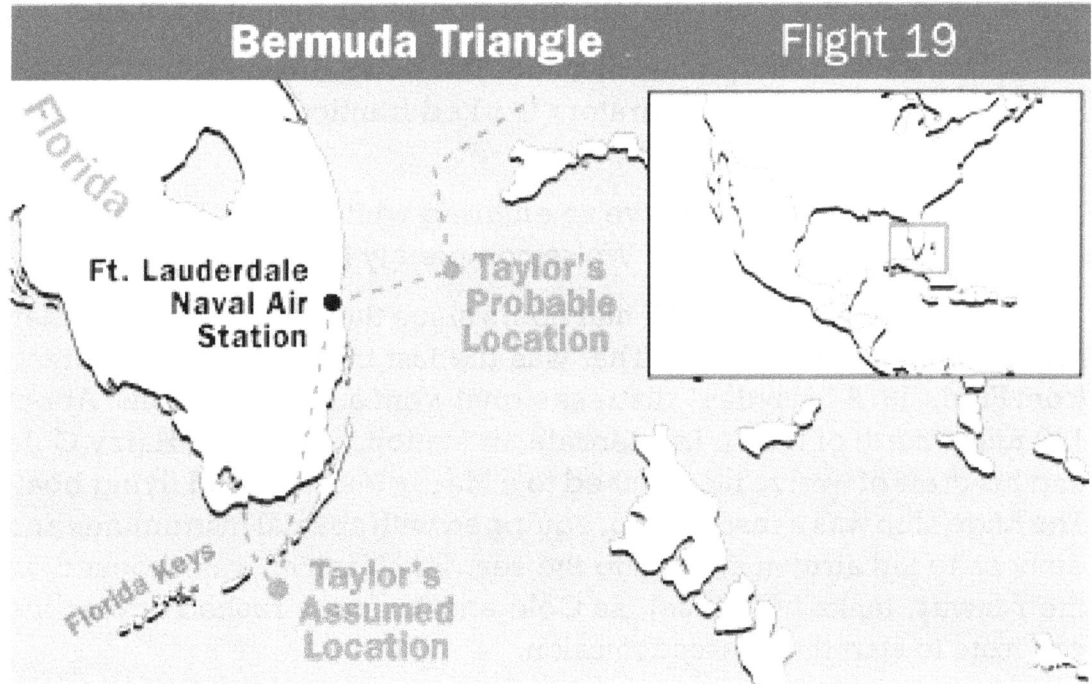

Radiomen were astonished. "That's impossible!" said a pilot who was lounging in the radio control room. "Nobody gets lost on a good flying day like this." The air controlman went into action. "Fly due west," he stated.

Lieutenant Taylor's reply came back instantly. "We can't be sure which way is west," he radioed. "Everything is wrong. Things are strange up here. Even the ocean doesn't look right."

"What's wrong with those guys," demanded the exasperated pilot in the tower. "All they've got to do is head into the sun and they're flying west!"

During the following hour, the air controlmen at the naval air sta-

MYSTERIOUS DISAPPEARANCES: THEY NEVER CAME BACK

tion monitored the radio transmissions from the five torpedo bombers. The planes were flying close together in regular formation. All five pilots were confused. Although the planes were within easy sight of each other, they were unable to determine their position. As their frustration grew, air controlmen detected a tremor of fear in the pilots' voices.

Lieutenant Taylor, the flight commander, asked the pilot of another plane to assume command of the group. "Maybe you can get us straightened out," Taylor stated.

Marine Captain George Stivers came on the air.

"It's 1635 hours," he began. "We must be around 250 miles northeast of the base. We aren't certain where we're located. It looks as if..."

There was a sharp blast of static. The noise drowned out Captain Stivers' voice. The tower operators worked frantically over the equipment to pick up the weak signal.

"My god! It looks like we're entering white water," Stivers said, his voice cracking with fear. "We're completely lost!"

It was almost two and a half hours since the Lost Patrol had taken off on their routine mission. That was the last message ever received from Flight 19. A "mayday" distress signal went out to all stations. About 150 miles north of the Ft. Lauderdale air station, Lieutenant Harry Cole and his crew of twelve men rushed to a Martin Mariner PBM flying boat. The huge ship was a rescue ship, equipped with special instruments and devices to aid airmen down into the sea. The Mariner was chocked on the runway, tanks full of fuel, as Cole and his crew rushed across the concrete to start their rescue mission.

Within minutes, Cole took off from the Banana River Naval Air Station (now Patrick Air Force Base, near Cape Kennedy). Their ship rose quickly into the evening skies, headed quickly out over the Triangle of the Lost. Within minutes, Lieutenant Cole radioed back to the base.

"We're about eleven minutes out, headed southeasterly," he reported. "No signs of anything yet!"

The Martin Mariner then went off the air.

Time passed. Minutes ticked away with leaden slowness. "What's wrong with that flying boat?" demanded a naval officer. "He should be checking in every few minutes." After an hour of trying to contact the huge bird, naval personnel knew they were now searching for six

MYSTERIOUS DISAPPEARANCES: THEY NEVER CAME BACK

downed planes. As it became apparent that all six planes and their crewmen had vanished, the U.S. Navy launched one of the most massive air-sea rescue operations in history. Nothing worked. Not a single trace of the missing planes or their crewmen was ever found.

"We're not able to even make a good guess of what might have happened," declared a spokesman for a review board that gathered later to investigate the tragedy. In ***Limbo of the Lost*** (Bantam Books; New York; 1969), author John Wallace Spencer discussed the unusual disappearance of the planes. He reported several theories were formulated to explain the disappearances. They include:

1. Engine Trouble: As Spencer pointed out, it would be beyond rational belief that six planes would simultaneously have engine trouble and crash without leaving a trace.

2. Air collision or a waterspout: Debris from a collision would have been found by the searchers. An encounter with a giant waterspout would leave evidence atop the ocean.

3. Magnetic fluctuations. There are erratic movements of compasses in the Triangle of the Lost. This is one of two places on earth where a compass will point to true, rather than magnetic north. Yet there was no reason for the planes to fly in circles. They could set a course toward the sun and pick up their bearings.

4. Unusual atmospheric aberrations: The U.S. Navy does not believe in a time-space "hole in the sky" that swallows up planes.

6. Bad weather: Strong winds, gusting up to 40 mph, were reported in the area just prior to the disappearance of Flight 19. These winds would not be strong enough to create problems for the powerful Navy planes.

A possible explanation exists for the strange disappearances of the five torpedo planes. In The Bermuda Triangle, author Charles Berlitz reported the following message was received shortly after Lieutenant Taylor turned over command of the flight to Marine Captain Stivers. "We are not sure where we are . . . we think we must be 225 miles north east of base," radioed Captain Stivers. ". . . We must have passed over Florida and we must be in the Gulf of Mexico . . ."

According to Berlitz, the captain then made a 180 degree turn and hoped to fly back to Florida. Shortly after that, radio signals from the planes grew weaker. This would indicate the Lost Patrol was flying eastward away from the base. The tragedy may have happened in this man-

MYSTERIOUS DISAPPEARANCES: THEY NEVER CAME BACK

ner:

1. The patrol made their bombing runs and started back toward base. On their return flight, they flew over an area that created a magnetic fluctuation in their compasses. This natural phenomena would cause compasses on all five planes to act in an certain manner. Intent on their compasses, the pilots would temporarily ignore the sun in the west.

2. After several minutes of confusion, panic would set in. The patrol might have passed over a small island or something that looked like land. When Captain Stivers took over, he ordered Flight 19 to turn east away from Florida. The planes were to land at 4:00 p.m. and, due to the confusion, had apparently not flown west long enough to reach the Florida coast.

3. Once they flew east away from the base, radio signals grew weaker. Reports indicate the last words received from Captain Stivers was something about "white waters.." This indicates the squadron may have flown as far as the Bahamas islands. Aerial views of this region reveal long watery trails of luminous white water contrasting vividly with the surrounding ocean. These long streams of bright water can be found in the Bahamas and in the mysterious Sargasso Sea, both part of the Triangle of the Lost. Astronauts on the Apollo 12 moon mission reported these "white waters" were the last light visible from earth as they sped off into outer space.

Once the patrol made a complete change in direction, their doom was sealed. Somewhere in the depths of the Triangle of the Lost lie the crashed remains of the Lost Patrol.

This scenario is admittedly a speculative answer to the disappearance of the five torpedo bombers. It does not allow for the missing Martin Mariner flying boat. Some UFO investigators have claimed the missing planes were attacked by UFOs. There is no evidence to indicate this is true. However, unsuspecting UFO buffs point to an unsubstantiated remark allegedly radioed back by the patrol. The comment is: "Don't come after us . . . they look like they're from outer space."

Several researchers have claimed to have seen a censored transcript of the messages between air control and the planes. Unfortunately, according to Navy authorities, such a transcript just doesn't exist. In an inquiry into the matter, a spokesman for the Navy reported that transcripts of air-to-ground conversations were not maintained until several years after the patrol vanished. "These were the days when we had very

MYSTERIOUS DISAPPEARANCES: THEY NEVER CAME BACK

crude, almost primitive, wire recording facilities," said the spokesman. "This was a routine patrol and there was absolutely no reason to make a recording. Ground-to-air facilities on a small base did not include any provisions for making a transcript."

The remark "... they look like they're from outer space" is also suspect. The patrol vanished in 1945, two years before the first post-war sighting of UFOs. "Outer space" was an unfamiliar phrase to the average person.

Due to a sensational radio broadcast by Orson Welles in 1938 concerning an invasion by Martians, most people related '"outer space" to "Mars." What a patrol leader might radio back would have been: "Don't come after us ... they look like they're from Mars!"

We have to conclude that the "outer space" theory of attack by flying saucers is suspect until it can be verified by documented evidence.

After World War II, there was a dramatic increase in the number of planes vanishing in the Triangle of the Lost. This may have been due, in part, to the increased use of airplanes over the area by both military and civilian pilots. Typical of these unexplained losses was a well-equipped, privately-owned DC-3 owned by the New Tribes Mission of Chico, California. An interdenominational organization, the New Tribes Mission recruited and trained missionaries for work in isolated areas around the world.

After a flight from their headquarters in California, the New Tribe's DC-3 took off from Miami for a destination at Maracaibo, Venezuela, with 15 crewmen and passengers aboard. The plane landed at Hamilton, Bermuda, after an uneventful flight from Florida, then soared into the sky for the final leg of their journey. Due to irregularities in international flight patterns, the plane was not reported lost for almost ten days. Date of the disappearance is listed as June 9, 1950, in perfect weather with calm, clear blue skies.

Forty-two people were on board a U.S. Navy four-engine Constellation airliner that vanished on October 30, 1954, in the Triangle of the Lost. The flight originated at Patuxent River Naval Air Station, Maryland, to fly service personnel and military wives to the Azores, then on to Africa.

The flight was piloted by Lt. Commander John S. Cole, an experienced airman and a cautious flight captain. After leaving the base early that morning, Captain Cole was more than two hours out over the Tri-

MYSTERIOUS DISAPPEARANCES: THEY NEVER CAME BACK

angle of the Lost when his craft developed engine trouble.

"We're having problems," the pilot radioed to the base. "I'm turning around. We've got trouble with one engine."

Ground crewmen waited anxiously for the big Connie to return. Finally, radar operators picked up blips from the approaching aircraft. Moments later, the airliner limped down on the runway for a perfect landing.

When the plane taxied to the hangar area, Captain Cole radioed to the tower. "Do you have another plane?"

MYSTERIOUS DISAPPEARANCES: THEY NEVER CAME BACK

"We've got a super-Constellation that's just been checked out and fueled," was the reply.

The crew and passengers had dinner at the base, then entered the Super-Constellation for their flight. The tri-tailed plane rolled down the runway at 9:30 p.m. and headed back into the Triangle of the Lost. Captain Cole planned a non-stop flight to the Azores islands that would require nine hours before touchdown.

Two hours after takeoff, the base received a position report from the four-engined airiiner. That was the last message from the plane. When the plane did not land on schedule, an air-sea search was quickly launched. Searchers returned with the same familiar complaint—no debris, no wreckage, no life rafts could be located from the missing airliner. The Triangle of the Lost had once again claimed a plane-load of victims.

The next disappearance also concerned a U.S. Navy plane. On the calm, tranquil evening of November 9, 1956, a powerful twin-engined Martin Marlin P5M patrol boat left the naval air station in Bermuda for a routine night patrol. At 8:30 p.m. that night, the control tower in Bermuda received a radio message from the flying boat.

"We're about 350 miles north of you," reported the pilot. "Engines are running good. Weather is fine. Nothing to report."

After an "over and out," the tower logged in the time for the plane's next position report. When the P5M failed to call in, another air-sea rescue operation was launched. Naval officers were not overly concerned about the plane's fate.

"That's a patrol bomber—a seaplane with strong pontoons," newsmen were informed. "If there's trouble with a plane like that, the pilot can simply land on the ocean and wait until he's rescued."

"What about fuel?" asked a reporter.

"They've got enough to last until morning," replied the officer. "There's no reason why they can't land on the surface and just wait for us."

The complacency of the search party was shaken when a radio message came in from the Liberian cargo ship, Captain Lyras. "'We've spotted a plane about four hundred miles southeast of New York City," radioed the captain of the freighter. "The plane is on fire. We're putting to and starting rescue operations for any survivors!"

MYSTERIOUS DISAPPEARANCES: THEY NEVER CAME BACK

Emergency rescue operations went into effect immediately. U.S. Navy, Coast Guard, Military Air Transport Command, and the Civil Aeronautics Administration's sophisticated planes were sent into the area where the Captain Lyras positioned the burning plane.

Before the planes could arrive, the Captain Lyras was back with another message. "We've got what appears to be a life raft about four miles away," radioed the ship. "We're headed in that direction. We can see a light out there in the darkness."

An aircraft carrier near the position launched planes that dropped flares. A fast aerial search crisscrossed the position, but nothing could be seen. The search continued for a week with the same sorrowful results. Seven enlisted men and three officers were never heard from again.

The Triangle grabbed another plane on the morning of January 8, 1962, when a large U.S. Air Force KB-50 flying tanker took off from Langley Air Force Base, Virginia. The flying service station planned to participate in air-to-air refueling operations. Major Robert J. Tawney and his crew of eight airmen planned to complete their aerial maneuvers and then go to the Azores. When the plane failed to radio a scheduled position, a search was started within minutes. Nothing was ever found of the missing four-engine plane or its crew.

It is remarkable when a plane vanishes without leaving a single clue. Air-sea rescue operations are conducted by trained personnel who follow a standard procedure to discover the whereabouts of a missing craft. When a plane goes down, air-sea rescue units are launched into the area of the last known position of the missing craft.

Fast airplanes take off with people trained to check the waters for signs of oil, debris, life rafts, and any floating matter. Even a school of sharks will alert air-sea searchers that survivors may not have gotten to a life raft. Some rescue operations will have a hundred or more airplanes patrolling the area.

When the planes are launched, ships closest to the last known position are diverted to the scene. Aircraft carriers, destroyers, and battleships steer a "full steam ahead" course in hopes of finding survivors. Civilian ships, foreign and U. S. freighters are often asked to look for survivors. Even high-flying U.S. "spy planes" have been known to help out in a search. Submarines are alerted and asked to cruise near the surface and look for signs of life.

Planes flying over international waters must carry sophisticated

MYSTERIOUS DISAPPEARANCES: THEY NEVER CAME BACK

radio equipment. When a pilot takes off from an airport, he must file his flight plan indicating time of departure and an estimated time of arrival. A search is launched when the pilot and plane fail to make their ETA. Commercial and military planes must carry life rafts, life preservers, flare pistols, and radios.

"This is what makes these disappearances so mysterious," remarked Gunther Rosenberg, founder and past president of the European Occult Research Society. "The planes are equipped with every possible type of lifesaving device. Most military and commercial pilots are trained in ditching procedures at sea. These aren't pilots out for a quick Sunday afternoon flight. These men are professionals. And a competent pilot knows the first thing he should do when trouble occurs is to send out an S.O.S. or Mayday signal with his position. Many of the planes that have vanished in the Triangle of the Lost carried radiomen aboard. While this is a vast region, with large areas of water, it seems inconceivable that so many planes could disappear without a single clue."

The next incident in the Triangle of the Lost fueled demands of an investigation into possible UFO interference. It was a calm, windless morning on August 28, 1963, when two Strategic Air Command Stratotankers lumbered down the runway and into the skies over Home-

MYSTERIOUS DISAPPEARANCES: THEY NEVER CAME BACK

stead Air Force Base, Florida. The big four-engine jet planes planned to conduct a normally routine air-to-air refueling operation between the Bahamas and Bermuda.

When the jumbo jets failed to make their scheduled position report at 1 p.m., the sea-air rescue teams went into action. The following day, an oil slick was reported on the ocean off Bermuda. A U.S. Air Force life jacket was also discovered in the same area. A U.S. freighter *Azalia City*, had been alerted to the disaster. All members of the ship watched the sea. They found a flight helmet with the name "Gardner" stenciled across the front, indicating it might have been owned by Captain Gerald Gardner, 28, of Lincoln. Nebraska.

Searchers found a virtual "sea of debris" around 350 miles southwest of Bermuda. A second "junkpile" was discovered about 400 miles off the coast of Florida, some 160 miles from the first sighting. The coast guard cutter *Chiola* rushed to the spot where the last wreckage was discovered.

While the *Chiola* was in that region, the captain was mystified by the sudden malfunctioning of his ship's sophisticated electronic communications equipment. There are areas in the Triangle of the Lost where even the most modern radio fails to behave in a normal manner. These "skip spots" and "ghost zones" frequently occur when atmospheric conditions create a magnetic "dead" zone. Experienced radiomen know these areas are seldom more than a few miles in size, that their equipment can be switched to a new wave-band for continued transmission.

Several UFO researchers claimed that the two Strategic Air Command planes were victims of flying saucers. "'There was a third craft in the skies that day," theorized Robert Shelton, editor of the now defunct UFO Newsletter, "That third aerial device was a flying saucer. The UFO, came into the area and sent out signals that caused a malfunction in the radios of both KC-135s. Then, this hostile alien ship blasted the first Stratotanker with a powerful ray. The second plane veered away and was 160 miles from the scene of the first crash when it was also blasted by the alien craft." Shelton pointed to a mysterious incident at the crash scene as evidence for his theory.

". . . The KC-135s carry two life rafts for their crews," reported Shelton. "No one can explain how three rafts came to be at the scene of the first crash. Where did this third raft come from? Is an outer space intelligence leaving clues to their hostile attacks on our most well-equipped aircraft?"

MYSTERIOUS DISAPPEARANCES: THEY NEVER CAME BACK

While no one could answer Shelton's question, there was little evidence to back up his theory of attack by flying saucers. Admittedly, it requires an unusual circumstance for two military planes to collide in the air. However, authorities believe that is exactly what happened in this instance. Eleven airmen lost their lives in this unfortunate mishap.

"Weather is excellent and everything is running smoothly" was the message from the pilot of a C-81 Cargomaster that vanished in the Triangle of the Lost on September 22, 1953. The pilot said his position was 80 miles from the New Jersey coast as the craft was flying through the Triangle toward the Azores. A week-long search failed to discover a trace of the missing aircraft.

More mystery was added when a C-119 Flying Boxcar disappeared on June 5, 1965. The huge cargo airplane was flying from Homestead Air Force Base, Florida, to a small island in the Bahamas. The final message gave the plane's position as 100 miles from Grand Turk Island with an Estimated Arrival Time of approximately 45 minutes. Another week-long search ended with no clue to the ship's ultimate fate.

As with some other planes, this disappearance was accompanied by faint, garbled radio messages. Some researchers have continued to suggest that "something" or "someone" was jamming or blocking the C-119's radio messages. Finally, the messages faded out completely and searchers wondered if the plane flew through a "rip" in the time-space continuum between the dimensions.

MYSTERIOUS DISAPPEARANCES: THEY NEVER CAME BACK

Another enigmatic occurrence happened on June 7, 1964, when pilot Carolyn Cascio and a passenger were flying in a small plane from Nassau to Grand Turk Island in the Bahamas. When she reached her ETA, Carolyn Cascio radioed that she was lost.

"I'm flying over two islands that don't look familiar," she reported.

Later, she added: ". . . There's nothing down there."

Still later, she radioed: "Isn't there any way out of this?"

Despite her problems, ground control on Grand Turk Island could see and hear a small plane flying around the island for about half an hour. Then, the plane turned and flew off in a northerly direction. Charles Berlitz in *The Bermuda Triangle* asks, "How was it that if observers could clearly see the plane, the pilot could not see the buildings on Grand Turk?"

Several pilots who make regular runs between Florida and the Caribbean Islands claim there is both magnetic and electronic disturbances within the Triangle. During one flight, a private pilot was over Andres near the deep water around the Moselle Reef when the compass began to spin erratically. The condition quickly ended after the plane flew away from that area. The reef, according to some pilots and fishermen, is a place where mysterious lights are frequently seen beneath the water at night. The area is the subject of much speculation by fishermen, who consider this region of the ocean around Bimini to be haunted.

The Triangle of the Lost is one of two places on earth where compasses point to true north. The Seventh Coast Guard District's report on the Triangle states: "The majority of disappearances can be attributed to the area's unique environmental features. First, the 'Devil's Triangle' is one of the two places on earth that a magnetic compass does point to true north. Normally it points to magnetic north. The difference between the two is known as compass variation. The amount of variation changes by as much as 20 degrees as one circumnavigates the earth. If this compass variation or error is not compensated for, a navigator could find himself far off course and in deep trouble.

"An area called 'The Devil's Sea" by Japanese and Filipino seamen, located off the east coast of Japan, also exhibits the same magnetic characteristics. As with the 'Bermuda Triangle', it is known for its mysterious disappearances."

MYSTERIOUS DISAPPEARANCES: THEY NEVER CAME BACK

CHAPTER EIGHTEEN

THE EVIDENCE FOR ALIEN INTELLIGENCE

Many investigators of humanity's origin have suggested that we may have been "seeded" here by beings from other worlds or dimensions. Their existence within the Triangle of the Lost is admittedly based on psychically inspired data. Yet, with reports of undersea cities, strange disappearances, and other enigmatic occurrences, we might investigate the possibility of alien intelligence on our planet.

If such an intelligence existed, we should be able to find clear evidence of visitations from these beings. We know that most records of past epochs have been destroyed. Therefore, we shall have to rely upon the myths and legends to see if there have been unusual creatures swooping down from the skies or rising up from the seas.

Currently, scientists are investigating ancient myths for a possible clue to the site of some cache of alien artifacts. In Russia, a panel of exobiologists have collected thousands of these myths from throughout the world. Their data is being fed into computers to see if a pattern exists, or if there is a central message from this multitude of legendary material.

"Alien objects on earth would be the greatest discovery in history," reported a Russian newspaper. "Such artifacts might be thousands-perhaps millions of years old. The cache might contain an automatic device that would signal intelligent life on other planets. Such a find could lead to contact with beings from other planets. Many scientists now know that legends have a habit of becoming reality. Our scientists hope to become another Schliemann."

The newspaper referred to Heinrich Schliemann, one of the most impressive amateurs to stamp his name in the annals of archeology. As a

MYSTERIOUS DISAPPEARANCES: THEY NEVER CAME BACK

child in North Germany, little Heinrich became fascinated with Homer's *Iliad* and the siege of Troy. Years later, Schliemann forgot the pressure of his prosperous business by reading a well-thumbed copy of the *Iliad*.

In the 1860s, Heinrich Schliemann was approaching an age when most men prepare to slow down. Despite the fears of his friends and relatives, he sold his business, moved to Greece, married a young Grecian beauty, and launched his search for Troy. "I don't understand why Troy can't be found," Schliemann explained. "Homer was the world's first war correspondent. He was reporting on a real war. There are precise directions in the *Iliad*."

Schliemann wandered through the cool valleys of Greece and over the tall mountains. He tried to find a terrain to fit the descriptions by Homer. An extraordinary man unconcerned with a few false trails, Schliemann was rewarded by finding the buried ruins of Troy. Later, he located other lost or buried cities.

"Read the old writers as if they were reporters," Schliemann informed a group of archeology students at a lecture. "The ancients had no reason to lie. Their stories are often true."

Brinsley le Poer Trench, author of **Men Among Mankind**, (Amherst Press, Amherst, Wisconsin) agrees with Heinrich Schliemann. "Mythology is shorthand," he declared. "It is condensed history."

This transformation of fanciful tales into historical facts intrigues many open-minded scientist. Are our legends simply a collection of embellished tales spun by imaginative liars of the past? Or is there a foundation of reality behind our myths? What guideline must be created to determine a genuine contactee myth? What is a lie? What is truth?

For centuries, scholars of Greek mythology dismissed the stories of a fierce tribe of bizarre warrior women, the Amazons. These aggressive women pillaged and rampaged through eastern Europe. The old storytellers claimed this ancient Women's Liberation Movement was headquartered in Russia's Caucasus mountains, near the homes of the Scythian tribesmen. In 1965, Ukrainian archeologists disinterred Scythian tombs and discovered the graves of Amazonian women.

"Legends say these women mingled with the Scythian men," reported Radio Moscow. "Female children were retained by the Amazons and raised as warriors. Boys were sacrificed, killed, mutilated, or given to their fathers. One of the oldest legends in history has been confirmed as fact. The Amazons were real. They lived in our country."

MYSTERIOUS DISAPPEARANCES: THEY NEVER CAME BACK

Legends of white gods have intrigued scholars who peer into the dark mists of African history. Dr. Henri Breuil, the world's foremost authority on cave paintings, lent credence to these white gods a few year sago. When he published his report on cave paintings in Damarland, near the Kalshair desert, Dr. Breuil declared the paintings were unmistakably the work of a mysterious race of white people.

Who were the ancient whites in Africa? Were they a band of ancient explorers? Or aliens from another world? A clue to their origin may be the Lady of Brandenberg, a cave painting in South Africa. This painting on a prehistoric cave wall continues to puzzle scholars. The "Lady" is dressed in tight slacks, gloves, garters, and shoes. She looks as if she just stepped out of the pages of a science-fiction magazine. Her male companion wears a helmet and visor, with an antenna. He looks like a primitive rendition of a modern astronaut. The evidence is admittedly slim. Could these paintings be clues to ancient visitors from space?

Man's history is shrouded with secrets, contradictions, and uncertainties. Who are we and where did we come from? Did we spring from the ape family, via Darwin's unproven theory of evolution? Or were we seeded by beings from the stars? Did astronauts from other worlds land on earth in prehistoric times and advise our primitive ancestors on how to establish a civilization?

Let's look at what history tells us of the origin of civilization. One day about seven or eight thousand years ago, according to the historians, our ancestors were living in caves and clubbing their way through a dangerous, brutal world. Without prior notice, a miracle occurred in the Mesopotamian Valley that was the origin of our civilization. Virtually overnight, a group of primitive tribesmen were transformed into skilled, educated citizens of Sumerian city-states. We are told that the Sumerian cities sprang up spontaneously.

Let's imagine that a primitive cave dweller has called a meeting of his neighbors. Nomads, shepherds, and a few hunters attend this unusual session.

Ogg, a visionary who lives in a cave, proposed to lead his neighbors on a new adventure.

"Fellows, my wife has been complaining about living in a cave," Ogg explained. "I'm sure your wives have grumbled quite a bit. Let's get down to the nitty-gritty and construct a few cities, build some houses. Pave a few streets. Put up a few towers and pyramids. We know hunting

MYSTERIOUS DISAPPEARANCES: THEY NEVER CAME BACK

is a risky business and a poor way of keeping meat on the fire. Let's start farming, raise our food. We'll sow grain, harvest our crops and store it in granaries."

A low-browed hunter in a bearskin stood up. He scratched his stomach and glared toward Ogg. "Farming sounds like something that needs a whole lot of water," he declared. "What happens if we have a drought?"

"We'll irrigate the fields."

The hunter growled and looked toward Ogg. "Suppose we build those things called houses. What do we put in them?"

"Tables, chairs, beds, furniture and all kinds of good things," Ogg replied. "We'll start making some nice pottery. Naturally, tables will require a few knives and forks. We'll have to start a metalworking industry. You fellows are smart enough to figure out alloys and things like that."

The reluctant hunter shook his spear at Ogg, the visionary. "Ogg, baby, this sure sounds like an awful lot of work."

Ogg answered quickly; he had no desire to argue with the tribe's best spearman. "There will be plenty of time for fun and games," he explained. "We will develop cuneiform writing. We can build a few observatories and start the study of astronomy. We can figure out how to build telescopes. Boys, we might even hire a couple of philosophers-in-residence. They can sit and think about ethics and good things like that."

History declares that these primitive humans walked out of their caves and established a flourishing civilization. Ogg and his neighbors shed their bearskins. They learned to weave, make furniture, build cities, and create hundreds of imaginative projects. There are immense complexities to a civilized, community. Could primitive humans achieve such remarkable results in a short span of time? Or were they assisted by exraterrestrial creatures?

We do not know where the Sumerians came from, although their astronomers were so accurate that their measurements on the rotation of the moon deviates only 0.4 from the modern figures. Even more impressive, at the height of the Greek Empire, man could not count higher than the figure 10,000. After that, the Greeks shrugged their shoulders and fell back on "infinity," but a tablet found on a slope near Kuyunjik a few years ago recorded a fifteen digit number: 195,955,200,000,000! Where did the Sumerians develop the knowledge to be masters of math-

MYSTERIOUS DISAPPEARANCES: THEY NEVER CAME BACK

ematics?

How were they capable of knowing that the planets revolved around the sun? This fact was not discovered until about five hundred years ago by Copernicus and Kepler. The old Sumer astronomers drew pictographs of the planets revolving around the sun eight thousand years ago! Their other drawings show the stars as accurately as a sketch drawn by a modern astronomer. There are also pictographs of human-like beings (aliens?) wearing a celestial crown of stars. Other human and animal figures are drawn flying through the skies on starred spheres.

History has dismissed the Sumerian account of how their civilization was established. Dr. Carl Sagen collaborated with the noted Russian scientist, Dr. Josef S. Shklovski, on *Intelligent Life in the Universe* (Holden-Day, 1966).

Discussing tablets known as *Ancient Fragments*, Dr. Sagen wrote: "... Ancient writers present an account of a remarkable series of events. Sumerian civilization is depicted by the descendants of the Sumerians themselves to be of nonhuman origin. A succession of strange creatures appears over a course of several generations. Their only apparent purpose is to instruct mankind. Oannes and other Apkulla (strange creatures) are described variously as 'animals endowed with reason', as 'beings,' as 'semidemons,' and as 'personages.' They are never described as gods."

UFOlogists have been mystified by reports of unidentified flying objects plunging into, or rising out of our oceans. Some investigators have hinted that the land beneath the seas would be a perfect site for a secret alien base on our planet. Occultists have discussed an undersea civilization for centuries. Some UFOlogists have attempted to link undersea saucers with the Sumerian legends of the "Oannes."

Berosus, a Babylonian priest and historian, wrote that the inhabitants of Sumer "lived like beasts in the field, with no order or rule." There appeared before them a bizarre creature, "an animal endowed with reason." This prehistoric "beast from the black lagoon" was an amphibian; it had the body of a fish, except there was a second head below the fish's head. If this wasn't enough to spark a nightmare, the benevolent being had humanlike feet on the end of its fish tail. It could walk about on land. The Oanne spoke with the primitive tribesmen in their own dialect. Each night the Oanne returned to his home in the ocean.

Berosus recorded: "... this being in the daytime used to converse

MYSTERIOUS DISAPPEARANCES: THEY NEVER CAME BACK

with men; but took no food at that season; and he gave them insight into letters, and sciences and every kind of art. He taught them to construct houses, to found temples, to compile laws, and explained to them the principles of geometrical knowledge. He made them distinguish the species of the earth, and showed them how to collect fruits. In short, he instructed them in everything which could tend to soften the manners and humanize mankind."

Oannes from the oceans . . . Ogg and his cavemen . . . a creature from the depths . . . primitive subhumans suddenly endowed with the knowledge to create a civilization. Either hypothesis for the origin of Sumer leaves us dangling on a slender thread of reality. Perhaps, we should poke about and read other reports on unusual beings in those lands.

The Epic of Gilgamesh, inscribed on twelve clay tablets, were discovered near the hills of Kulunjik in 1870. As they translated the tablets, historians were bewildered by references to "gods from heaven" and their visits to earth.

There is the familiar story of gods descending from the skies and breeding with earth women. Gilgamesh is the offspring of these unions, a man-god who dwells in a stately palace."

A tablet states that Gilgamesh heard a sudden roar one afternoon when the 'sun god' swooped down and carried off an innocent companion, Enkidu, into the skies," explained Gunther Rosenberg, a founder and former president of the European Occult Research Society. He discussed *Alien Beings in Myth and Legend* in a monograph published in 1968 by EROS Press.

"A tablet tells how Enkidu approached a door that talks. This could be frightening for a prehistoric human," wrote Rosenberg. "However, I have a two-way intercom system installed at the entrance of my home. Enkidu had many adventures in space and returned to earth. Shortly after his return, he becomes ill. He dies from a mysterious disease that Gilgamesh believes is caused by the poisonous 'breath of sun god's chariot.' I think immediately of radiation poisoning."

The tablets report that Gilgamesh becomes worried. He also has been close to the sun god's chariot and there is a possibility of his impending death. The saga recounts his journey to the land of the gods, where he meets the "father of man."

"The father of man tells Gilgamesh of a story that is very close to

MYSTERIOUS DISAPPEARANCES: THEY NEVER CAME BACK

the Biblical account of the Great Flood," Gunther Rosenberg related. "This ancient saga tells the story of Noah, thousands of years before the Bible was compiled.

The tablets tell how the 'father of man' frees the dove and raven to find land if the water has receded.

What is Rosenberg's view on the origin of civilization? "Aliens landed on earth and instructed the Sumerians," he concluded. "If these beings remained on earth for a prolonged interval, they may have selected the most beautiful, the most intelligent women as their companions. Man is a unique animal. He stands out like a sore thumb when comparisons are made with his cousins, the apes. The differences are more numerous than the similarities. Darwin's theory of evolution is simply unproven."

Rosenberg also has an admittedly far-out hypothesis that two distinct types of humans may live now in our society. "The first group could be the descendants of the primitive subhuman man that lived when the spacemen landed," he explained. "They would have been civilized and softened over the centuries. The second race might be the descendants of the sky people—offspring of the union between alien beings and earth women. Alien blood may course through the veins of many people. How else can we explain the unusual genius in our society? The Einsteins, da Vinci's, Kepler's, Teslas, and similar people endowed with tremendous knowledge. This may explain people endowed with psychic ability, ESP and things like that."

According to Rosenberg, the genetic strain from the sky people might remain strong and pure for hundreds of generations. "It could conceivably remain constant, or become stronger, as the earth blood lessens," he declared. "We know very little about genetics despite the recent breakthroughs by the biologists. This spaceman-woman strain could also be strengthened, or decreased, by periodic visits. The sky people, or their descendants on earth, may have manipulated our actions throughout history. We could use a little extraterrestrial maneuvering right now, considering the mess the world is in."

Manipulation of history and people? An impossibility?

The legends of the Eskimos tell of their ancestors being flown to the frigid northland for resettlement by gods with bronze wings. No one can provide a solid explanation for the origin of the Eskimos. Some claim a land bridge once existed in the Bering Straits. The Eskimos crossed

MYSTERIOUS DISAPPEARANCES: THEY NEVER CAME BACK

over into the northlands.

"This doesn't explain why the Eskimos remained in the polar region," declared Gunther Rosenberg. "Traditionally, people have migrated south to a warmer climate.

"Why did the Eskimos remain in the cold, terrible Arctic regions? Were they part of a vast resettlement project carried out by spacemen in ages past? Did some extraterrestrial, or ultra-dimensional, tribunal decide to test man's ability to survive in the frozen wasteland? Questions, questions, and very few answers."

There is a Mayan legend telling of a giant eagle plunging down from the skies with the "roar of a lion." The beak of the "eagle" opened and "four creatures, strange to our tribe, who did not breathe the air we breathe" stepped from the object. Peruvian myths claim the inhabitants of that country were originally born from gold, silver, and bronze metallic eggs which floated down from the skies. Are these the products of an overly-active imagination by ancient shamans, or an oral version of an actual event?

Another Mayan legend in the Popul Vuh, the Bible of the Quiches tribe of western Guatamala, tells of how these visitors knew the secrets of the universe, used a compass, and realized the earth was round. "These beings were upset because men were learning the secrets of the universe," reported Gunther Rosenberg. "So they fogged man's memory so he was not capable of knowing everything. Apparently, men's knowledge of certain universal secrets was reduced. On the other side of the ocean, universal language was lost after the Tower of Babel."

Throughout the world, we have myths of prehistoric visitations by white gods. Viracocha, a god believed to be so pure and powerful that only the most prestigious families were allowed to worship at his shrine, was an important figure in Peruvian history. Viracocha is said to have appeared mysteriously before the Incans. He educated them in the arts of civilization, taught them to be farmers and irrigators, and provided training in law, government, philosophy, religion and other endeavors.

Like the other mysterious figures in history, Viracocha promised to return to the Incans when they were in a crisis. "Cusi Yupanqui was one of the most important of the ancient Incan rulers," explained Gunther Rosenberg. "Cusi was apparently a benevolent fellow. He was unable to follow the rules of his cruel, greedy father, the king. The king was exasperated because his son expressed an interest in educating the Incan

MYSTERIOUS DISAPPEARANCES: THEY NEVER CAME BACK

nation. Cusi was banished from the royal court and sent back into the mountains to work as a swineherd."

Cusi was walking through a low valley one afternoon when a blinding flash of light caught his attention. The brilliant glare originated from the peak of a nearby mountain. The curious young man walked up to the slope and encountered a bearded stranger. The unusual visitor was clad in a flowing white robe and sandals.

"I am from the other world," announced the stranger. "We promised to return when your people were in danger. You must warn your people that a tribe to the west is marching to invade your city. Go! Warn your people at once!"

The ancient legend explained that Cusi dashed down the ridge, across the valley, and into the lowlands. Breathlessly, he rushed into the King's palace and blurted out his warning.

"The rebels are marching on us, father," he announced. "Alert the palace guard. Call out the soldiers."

The cruel king was unimpressed with the warning. "You have been living too long with the swine," the king laughed. "Your brain has been fried by the sun."

Less than an hour later, howling hordes of angry Chancas tribesmen roared down into the Quechua Valley. Within minutes, the Chancas rebels had overrun the capital city. Cusi's father was exiled from the kingdom.

"We must elect a new king," announced the leader of the Chancas tribe. "The wisemen must meet and select our new leader. Then we will withdraw back to our own lands."

A council of elders were summoned to the city square. They had overheard the whispers of Cusi Yupanqui warning of the impending invasion. They heard rumors of the warning delivered by a bearded stranger in a white robe.

"Those from the other world have chosen you," the tribunal informed Cusi. "Viracocha has picked you. You must accept the crown."

Cusi was known as "Pachacuti the First," or "He Who Conquers The World." During a long and benevolent reign as an Incan emperor, the legend claimed he journeyed frequently into the mountains to obtain counsel from the gods.

MYSTERIOUS DISAPPEARANCES: THEY NEVER CAME BACK

"These bearded strangers are found in the legends of every North American Indian tribe, in Mexico, and in South America," Gunther Rosenberg related. "They arrived unexpectedly to counsel the Aztecs, the Incans, Mayans, and Amerindians in the arts of civilization. They always claimed to be from another world. This could be a place of origin in the universe, inside the earth, or another dimension. We can only continue our investigation and hope for an eventual solution to the mystery."

In Russia, several scientists have hinted that the apocryphal book of the *Secrets of Enoch*, also known as the Slovonic Enoch, may be the story of an early-day UFO contactee. The manuscript was banned by early clergymen as heresy and was forbidden to Christians for centuries. Even today, there is an unsolved mystery surrounding the origin of the book.

Enoch was sleeping one night when two figures appeared in his dreams. "They were tall men. . . such as I have never known before on earth," he wrote. "Their faces shown like the sun. Their eyes glowed like lamps . . . They stood at the head of my bed and called my name."

Enoch awakened from his reveries, rubbed the sleep from his eyes, and discovered the two beings claimed to be messengers from God. "We have been sent down to you," they declared. "We are to bring you back to Heaven." Enoch related that the beings "took me on their wings and placed me on a cloud. And lo! the cloud moved. And going higher, I saw the air . . . Much higher, I saw the ether . . ."

Enoch said he was given a sort of grand tour of six "heavens," or planets. His observations of these worlds are quite detailed. In one "heaven," Enoch observed a world inhabited by bizarre flying creatures. He described these beings vividly as ". . . having the tails and feet of a lion and the head of a crocodile."

Ultimately, our ancient adventurer is taken to the Seventh Heaven and brought into the presence of God. Enoch is told the secrets of the universe and the mysteries of nature are explained. He is drilled in the complex nature of humanity and the history of mankind. Following this meeting with the Supreme Being, Enoch returned to earth and inscribed his wisdom in 366 chapters, or books, to bring his revelations to all of humanity.

Enoch tells of his reluctance to leave the Seventh Heaven. "We have only been here a few hours," Enoch complained. "I would like to see more."

MYSTERIOUS DISAPPEARANCES: THEY NEVER CAME BACK

"Our time is not as you know it," replied the messenger.

"A new generation has been born since you left home."

Enoch did not understand these words until he returned to earth. He had aged no more than a week on his journey; yet, his friends and companions of the same age had lost their robust zest for life. The glow of youth had vanished from their cheeks; it had been replaced by the pale, paraffin-like translucence of aging wrinkles. His friends were listless with age and they talked through a tired, filtered memory of the forty years that had passed since Enoch had disappeared.

"Modern science is attempting to probe the mystery of time and space," Gunther Rosenberg said. "Many believe that time slows down during a space voyage. A crew of astronauts might age less than twenty years in space. On their return, the earth would be a couple of million years older. The early church seized on this as an example of Enoch's heresy. Actually, in light of present knowledge, this lends credence to his story."

"Enoch was simply an early contactee," George Adamski remarked a few years ago. Several writers have told of an Egyptian papyrus from the reign of Pharaoh Thutmose III (1504-1450 B.C.) when "circles of fire" soared across the skies. The description on this disputed papyrus reads like a modern news report on a UFO sighting. Egyptian mythology is brimming with "sun gods" and "barges from the sun," which might be an ancient description of an Unidentified Flying Object. Horus, last of the "divine kings appointed by the Council of Gods" is said to have been the father of the first dynasties to rule Egypt.

Some occultists, like Gunther Rosenberg, believe the Grecian and Roman gods were actually spacemen; their supernatural powers were nothing more than an advanced technology in a primitive world. "There was frequent mention of union between earth women and the gods," explained Mr. Rosenberg. "We also read in mythology of many abnormal creatures and monstrosities. This half bull-half man known as the Minotaur is an example of this.

Perhaps these terrible creatures were the results of intergalactic bedroom Casanovas or experiments into genetic breeding which failed."

In his excellent book, *Flying Saucers Are Watching Us*, (Belmont Books, 1968), author Otto O. Binder theorized that a new team of spacemen may have landed. ". . . then, there landed a fresh team of gods (spacemen) led by dynamic young Zeus, or Jupiter, who could throw

MYSTERIOUS DISAPPEARANCES: THEY NEVER CAME BACK

lightning bolts (ray-guns?)," Binder wrote. "Jupiter brought with him such illustrious skymen and skywomen as Mercury, Saturn, Neptune, Apollo, Mars, Venus (Aphrodite), Athena, Hestia, and many others, and from their unions with earthly mates (prehuman anthropoids?) sprang the human race."

The monasteries of Tibet are said to be filled with many secrets. Ancient Tibetan legends claim that in ages past the sky people came down to earth on "steel birds and iron dragons." In China, there are sagas of the "sons of heaven" who soared through the universe on celestial clouds. The ageless myths in India brim with reports of sky chariots, celestial flying machines, and vivid accounts of gods who war against transgressors.

Legends of the American Indians also tell us that bizarre beings once landed from places beyond the stars. The familiar "sun disc" is important to many religious ceremonies. Legends tell of the "stick Indians," little men who kidnapped Indian children and whisked them to "other worlds."

If you are ever within driving distance of Sheridan, Wyoming, I suggest you stop at the local Chamber of Commerce and obtain directions to the enigmatic Medicine Wheel in the little Big Horn mountains. You will see thousand of limestone rocks laid out in a circular pattern, forming a circle approximately 245 feet in diameter. There are thirty spokes radiating from the wheel. At one time, hunters and cattlemen told of unbleached Buffalo skulls perched on the slabs, facing the east.

Ella E. Clark, Professor Emeritus at Washington State University, tells an interesting story about the Medicine Wheel in *"Indian Legends of the Northern Rockies,"* published by the University of Oklahoma Press. Red Plume, the famous Crow Indian chieftain, told of how he visited the Medicine Wheel and waited for four days and nights. On the final night, he was joined by three small men and women. These miniature beings led Red Plume to an underground cavern beneath the Medicine Wheel. For three more days and nights, Red Plume was tutored by the little people. He was taught the strategy of war; he was advised on the proper methods of leading his tribe to greatness.

When I visited the Medicine Wheel, I became intrigued with the mysterious monument and sought information from Indians in that state. While the older Indians were sometimes reluctant to discuss the structure with a "paleface," I obtained a considerable amount of facts, folklore, and information from younger Indians.

MYSTERIOUS DISAPPEARANCES: THEY NEVER CAME BACK

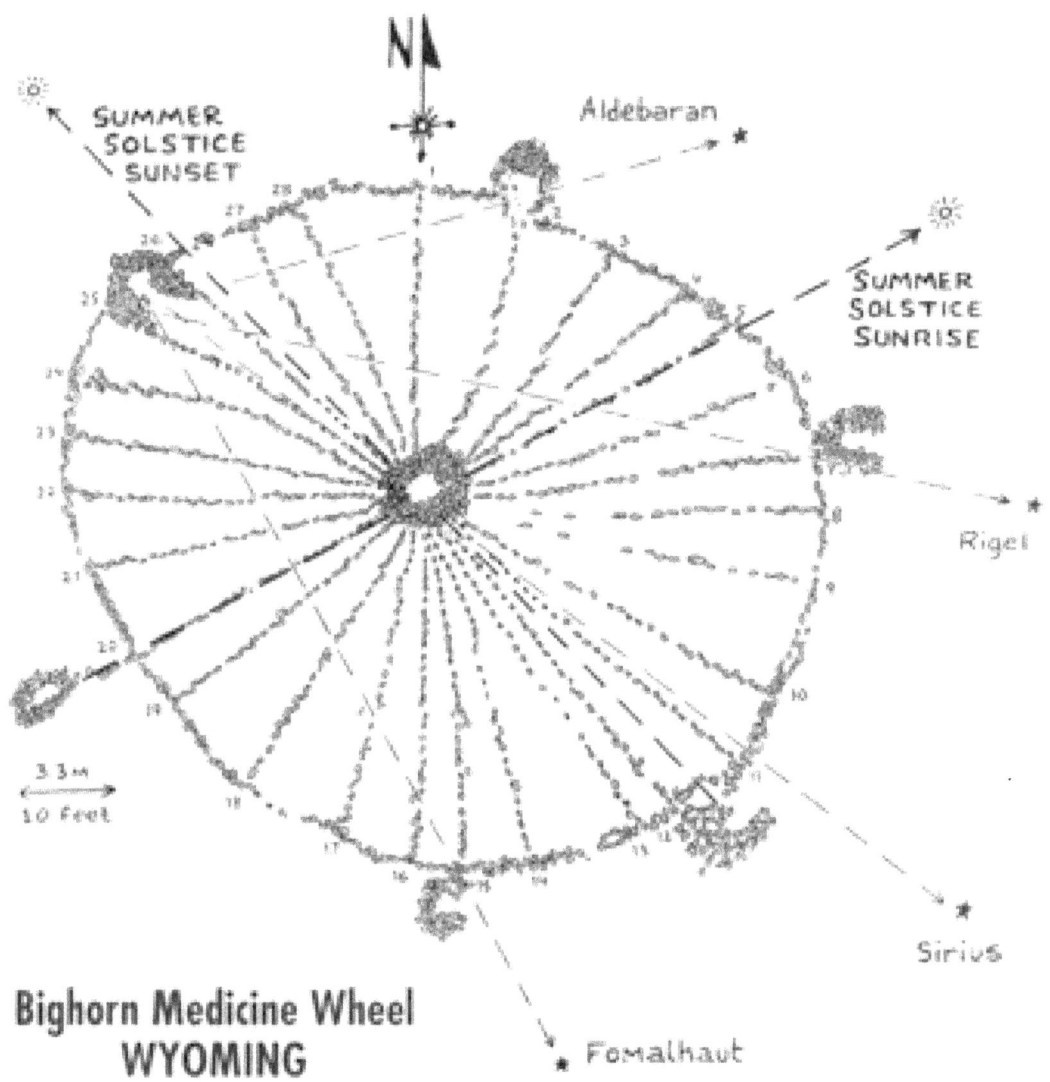

Bighorn Medicine Wheel
WYOMING

"It is difficult to believe but our forefathers claim the little people lived there," a college student declared. "I've talked with some of the older people in our tribe. It was a sacred place many years ago. The wee people supposedly created many paintings and rock carvings throughout the west. I believe they had a strong role in our tribal taboos and religion."

The "Star of Bethlehem" has been an impressive part of Christian theology for twenty centuries. Some UFOlogists believe the "star" contained considerable meaning for mankind. Others have dismissed it as a slice of Biblical fantasy. In an article entitled "*Visitors From Outer Space*," Russia's Vyacheslav Zaitsev wrote in Sputnik magazine:

"... Two centuries ago the mystery attracted the German astronomer, Johann Kepler, while more recently, scientists held an international

MYSTERIOUS DISAPPEARANCES: THEY NEVER CAME BACK

symposium to discuss the matter.

"But neither Kepler nor contemporary scientists found the key to the problem, which may turn out to have an altogether unexpected solution.

"In antiquity and the Middle Ages human imagination was stirred by an unusual star, now believed to be the Star of Bethlehem. The star was alleged to be able to move and stop.

"From that, let us turn to the Christian Apocrypha—books banned by church censorship from services and religious readings. The Apocrypha reflect man's efforts to explain the most dramatic mysteries of life. These books sometimes stand in direct contradiction of Church-approved texts.

"A familiar one about early Christianity is called *'The Tale of the Three Magi.'* The original version must have been written in Latin in the middle of the third century at the earliest, and later translated into many languages. A 15th century Byelorussian translation made five centuries before the space era contains a highly unusual interpretation of the tale. The star, it says, was watched by astronomers (that is the actual word used) in many Oriental countries. Once it appeared at night and lit up the whole of the sky as the sun does. Then the star hung over Mount Vans for a whole day, after which it alighted on the mountain like an eagle . ."

The Apocrypha also claims that Christ came down from the "Star of Bethlehem." This is such a fantastic story that we almost forgot that the books were written by early Christians. The "star," or space craft, is described as having wings. Long rays are said to whirl out behind the star-craft.

The sky people are often mentioned in myths and legends as emissaries of the "flying serpent." The dragon cult in China with its celestial serpents is not far removed from the snake-worshipping Aztecs in Mexico, who sacrificed young virgins to a pit of hungry vipers. When we inspect the legends of North and South America, we find these mysterious sky people popped up suddenly and advised our ancestors on the arts, science, agriculture, government, and religion.

Ptolemy, one of the greatest generals in the legions of Alexander the Great, wrote a history of his campaigns and described two dragons who appeared at the head of the army when it was lost in the Libyan desert. These celestial dragons spoke with Alexander and his generals. The Army followed the objects. Alexander was led to the temple of the

MYSTERIOUS DISAPPEARANCES: THEY NEVER CAME BACK

Oracle of Jupiter Ammon, where he obtained counsel for his future campaigns.

In *Men Among Mankind*, author Brinsley le Poer Trench writes:

"... The serpent has always been a symbol of wisdom, and from time immemorial has been regarded as a royal and celestial symbol. It has only been since the coming of Christianity that the serpent has been regarded as evil as a result of the misinterpretation of the Garden of Eden story ... The serpent is a representative of the two major arms of the spiral galaxy, in which we live and is, therefore, the symbol of the Galactic civilization as well as the sign of the Great Creator."

"The serpent then, is very much connected with the Sky and the Sky People. So, if we hear of 'serpents' or 'dragons' meeting and talking ... in a time of desperate difficulty ... it could conceivably have been Sky People who put in an appearance at that critical moment ..." he declared.

Quetzacoatl, a bearded white man in a long, white robe, was the messiah of the Aztec empire. He was considered an emissary from the serpent people. Legends tell of how he flew into ancient Mexico aboard a flying serpent.

"Quetzaccoatl was one of the greatest prophets in the Americas," declared Gunther Rosenberg. "His achievements have been handed down for generations. He was worshipped as a benevolent god in Mexico, Central America, and on south into South America. He is said to have appeared in Mexico many years before the Europeans landed in the New World. A tall, bearded white man with the powers of a magician and the wisdom of the sages, Quetzacoatl pacified the Indians, gave laws and ethics to their tribes, and taught them how to farm successfully."

The prophecies of Quetzacoatl directed the Aztec priests for hundreds of years. When he disappeared into the east, Quetzacoatl promised his followers he would return. This prediction led directly to the downfall of the Aztec civilization when Hernando Cortez and his band of white Spanish conquistadores marched inland from the sea. "There was jubilation and happiness in the Aztec capital," explained Gunther Rosenberg. "Reports of white men marching from the east could only mean that their savior, Quetzacoatl, was returning to fulfill his promise. While Montezuma kept his warriors in their barracks, the Spaniards captured the empire."

Are there any truths in these legends? Could these stories of be-

MYSTERIOUS DISAPPEARANCES: THEY NEVER CAME BACK

nevolent beings from the skies be the basis for stories about angels or demons? Is there an advanced super-civilization in space watching our progress? Will we someday blast off to the stars and discover that we are as gods? Or will man's aggressive instincts create an interplanetary war with our gods?

It is always possible that through these tales of sky people mysterious strangers, paradises and past visitations, a small thread of reality may actually exist. Yuan Ke, the Oriental scholar, wrote: "Many people hold that myths are products of human fantasy and have nothing in common with reality. This is a profound error."

"Generally speaking, there is nothing that man has thought up that does not have roots in the real world," said Maxim Gorky"

MYSTERIOUS DISAPPEARANCES: THEY NEVER CAME BACK

CHAPTER NINTEEN

WILL WE EVER UNRAVEL THE MYSTERIES OF THE SEA?

Who discovered America? Who were the first mariners to sail through the Triangle of the Lost? Did Columbus have charts indicating there was a New World existing beyond the Azore islands? These questions plague scholars who hope to solve these tantalizing mysteries. Whether ancient seamen crossed the Atlantic ocean before Columbus has excited the imaginations of scholars for centuries. Due to a lack of conclusive evidence, the debate continues to be a heated controversy.

Along with this mystery is the question of Atlantis. Of the many lost and fabled civilizations of man, Atlantis is undoubtedly the most popular. It is indisputably the most intriguing, the most debated. The enigma of this lost continent has been the subject of endless books, magazine articles, and theories. Both the writers of antiquity and modern authors have wondered where, when, and if fabled Atlantis actually existed.

As far as the surviving manuscripts allow us to judge, the first to write about Atlantis was the Greek poet, Hesiod. He lived about 700 B.C. and his account was accepted by the Roman poet, Horace. However, Aristotle looked upon Hesiod's tale of Atlantis as so much clap-trap. The undisputed champion of Atlantis was Plato. He made lengthy references to Atlantis in his two dialogues, *Timaeus* and *Critias*. Plato described how Atlantis reigned supreme in a golden age of humanity. The continent was said to have been destroyed by violent earthquakes "... and floods

MYSTERIOUS DISAPPEARANCES: THEY NEVER CAME BACK

... in a single day and night of rain... it sank beneath the sea".. and that is the reason why the sea in those parts is impassable and impenetrable.

Several researchers have suggested that Atlantis sunk beneath the Triangle of the Lost, that ruins discovered recently off Bimini are links to that ancient civilization. They also feel that these lands beneath the Triangle are rising, that in the future the coral-encrusted columns of ancient Atlantean temples will emerge to mystify modern science.

A careful reading of Plato's material indicates that Atlantis may have been a series of islands in the Atlantic. Or, as some medieval scholars suggested after Christopher Columbus' voyage to the New World, America may be the Atlantis of the ancients. Hundreds of books were written on this premise, developing the theory that ancient mariners sailed through the Triangle to discover the New World long before Columbus.

In the past century, controversial Ignatius Donnelly developed his hypothesis for Atlantis in *Atlantis: The Antediluvian World*. Donnelly believed Atlantis extended for 1,000 nautical miles through the Triangle, that the Azore Islands are the only surface remains of that legendary land.

Writing in the preface to his work, Donnelly listed the purposes of his scholarly research: "This book is an attempt to demonstrate several distinct and novel propositions. These are:

"1. That there once existed in the Atlantic ocean, opposite the mouth of the Mediterranean Sea, a large island, which was the remnant of an Atlantic continent, and known to the ancient world as Atlantis.

"2. That the description of this island given by Plato is not, as has long been supposed, a fable, but veritable history.

"3. That Atlantis was the region where man first rose from a state of barbarism to civilization.

"4. That it became, in the course of ages, a populous and mighty nation from whose overflowings the shores of the Gulf of Mexico, the Mississippi River, the Amazon, the Pacific coast of South America, the Mediterranean, the west coasts of Europe and Africa, the Baltic, the Black Sea, and the Caspian were populated by civilized nations.

"5. That it was the true Antediluvian world; the garden of Eden, the Garden of the Hesperides; the Elysian fields; the Gardens of Alcinous ... representing a universal memory of a great land, where early man-

MYSTERIOUS DISAPPEARANCES: THEY NEVER CAME BACK

kind dwelt for ages in peace and happiness.

"6. That the gods and goddesses of ancient Greeks, the Phoenicians, Hindus, and the Scandinavians were simply the kings, queens, and heroes of Atlantis; and the acts attributed to them in mythology are a confused recollection of real historical events.

"7. That the mythology of Egypt and Peru represented the original religion of Atlantis, which was sun worship.

"8. That the oldest colony formed by the Atlanteans was probably in Egypt.

"9. That the implements of the 'Bronze Age' of Europe were derived from Atlantis. The Atlanteans were the first manufacturers of iron.

"10. That the Phoenician alphabet, parent of all European alphabets, was derived from an Atlantis alphabet.

"11. That Atlantis was the original seat of the Aryan or Indo-European family of nations . . . as well as of the Semitic peoples, and possibly also of the Turanian races.

"12. That Atlantis perished in a terrible convulsion of nature, in which the whole island sunk into the ocean, with all of its inhabitants.

"13. That a few persons escaped in ships and on rafts, and carried to the nations east and west the tidings of the appalling catastrophe, which has survived to our time in the Flood and Deluge legends of the different nations of the old and new worlds."

Donnelly's impressive scholarship focused on the similarities between cultures in the old and New World. "Very few people will argue against those facts," said Dr. Gunther Rosenberg, founder of the European Occult Research Society. "There are indeed many remarkable similarities between the culture in pre-Columbia America and ancient Europe. Exactly how these similarities came about is the subject of much debate."

Scholars are divided into two opposing camps. "The Isolationists believe that similar cultures can develop simultaneously in widely separated areas," Dr. Rosenberg went on. "This means that people having no contact with each other may focus their energy and intelligence at the same time on architecture, religion, astronomy, and social order."

An archeologist expanded these beliefs. "I'm an Isolationist," he stated. "I think human minds will create often similar answers to problems, assuming there are equal challenges in the environment."

The opposing school are the Diffusionists. They list the many similarities in New and Old World cultures and claim there had to be early contact. Naturally, this early communication across the Atlantic would be due to voyages of ancient mariners. "The Diffusionists appear to have the best argument," reported Dr. Rosenberg. "They can point to the appearance of pyramid building in the two worlds, megalithic structures, mummification, sun worship, various games of entertainment, reed boats and the calendar systems as evidence of this early contact."

Dr. Rosenberg went on to explain that many Diffusionists dismiss accounts of Atlantis as a myth. "Ancient mariners may have returned to the Old World with stories of various societies in the New World," he explained. "These seamen may have felt the Americas were an island."

We might say that Atlantis does exist. It is now known as North and South America! If this is true we need evidence of exploration prior to the voyages of Christopher Columbus. We shall start our investigation by looking at Plato's description of Atlantis. He wrote:

". . . In those days (about 12,000 years ago) the Atlantic was navigable and there was an island situated in front of the straits of which you call the Columns of Hercules (Gibraltar); the island was larger than Libya and Asia put together, and was the way to other islands and from these islands you might pass through the whole of the opposite continent which surrounds the true ocean; for this sea, which is within the Straits of Hercules (the Mediterranean) is only a harbor, having a narrow entrance, but that other is the real sea and the surrounding land may be most truly called a continent."

There are several interesting points in Plato's description. First, he mentioned Libya (Africa) and Asia-but separated them from Atlantis. He pointed out that Atlantis was situated directly west of Gibraltar. By sailing due west from the mouth of the Mediterranean, we arrive in the New World.

Through the ages, scholars have placed Atlantis in such diverse places as the Sahara desert, Spain, Tunisia, Crete, the Azores, Canary and Madeira Islands, South America, Venezuela, Mexico, and Ceylon. Mystically oriented German tyrant Adolph Hitler hired a band of professors to prove his Third Reich was the true heir to Atlantis, which had been located in Germany! Name the ocean or the sea and, chances are, someone has claimed the submerged ruins of the legendary continent lies on their bottoms.

Modern authors have written many volumes on the inventions of the ancients. They point to these ancient arts and skills as evidence of an advanced culture, yet few researchers have delved into the art of prehistoric shipbuilding, navigation, and seamanship. As the sea was the most practical method of transport, we might discover the ancients were well-trained seamen.

The Bible lists the dimensions of the Ark of Noah as 300 cubits long, 50 wide, and 30 high. This translates out to a ship of 322 feet in length, 28 feet wide, and 14 feet in height. These dimensions compare favorably with sailing vessels of the last century. In *Canon of the Kings of Egypt*, historian Dioderus Siculus reported the Egyptian fleet that ruled the Red Sea was composed of 400 ships. He also related that the rulers of India had 4,000 ships to oppose any invasion by sea. These are mighty fleets by any standard.

Archimedes built a vessel for Hiero of Syracuse which contained the wood for fifty ordinary vessels. "This was a tremendous ship," said Dr. Gunther Rosenberg. "The vessel contained galleries, gardens, stables for horses, a fishpond, baths, and a mechanical device to throw stones up to 300 pounds in weight. There were archery batteries on board that shot 12-foot arrows. The floors were inlaid with precious stones that depicted scenes from Homer's '*Iliad*.' Also on board was a temple dedicated to the goddess of love, Venus."

Nevertheless, such giant ships would be useless for our purposes unless there was a method of navigation across the Atlantic ocean. Historians attribute the invention of the compass to a marine pilot from the Republic of Amalfi on the Mediterranean sea. He was known as Flavio Giola to ancient chroniclers. The date of his discovery is generally listed as 1302, although the inventor's history and other pertinent details are unknown.

There is a mass of documentation to show that the compass was used much earlier than the first notice of a compass appeared in the saga about the voyages of the Norsemen. "*The Landnamabok*" contains this passage in the second chapter of the first book: ". . . Floke Vilgedarson set out about the year 868 from Roraland in Norway to rediscover Iceland. He took with him three ravens to set as guides. It was the custom of our ancestors when looking out for land to let fly these birds. It they returned to the ship, it was presumed they were still far from land, but if they flew away they were watched. And the direction they had taken

MYSTERIOUS DISAPPEARANCES: THEY NEVER CAME BACK

was a sure guide to land. To consecrate the ravens to this use, Floke offered a great sacrifice to Smorsund, where his vessel was at anchor. For at that time the navigators of Scandinavia did not make use of the lodestone."

This passage was written in 1075. Showing that the magnet was well-known to the Norsemen, another early report of a compass is found in a satirical poem *La Bible* written by Guyot de Provins in France in 1190. The Pope, according to the poet, should be what the polar star was to ancient mariners, a conspicuous, fixed, and unchanging guide. He went on in the poem to speak of the magnet, the "levingstone," and describes the magnetic navigation. He wrote:

"The seaman knows an art that can't deceive/ The compass is his sacred oracle/ The potent charm of the magnet/ (A stone dark and ugly in look/ yet to iron it adheres,) gives its impulse to the needle/ Which then, cased, and freely suspended,/ Set in motion unhindered,/ True and certain points to that star."

Another mention of magnets is found in *History of the East and West* by Cardinal Jacques de Vitry, Bishop of Yuseulum and Ptolemais. He was a legate to the pope in the Fourth Crusade with Montfort's army. In those days the magnet was known as *Adamas*, a term used during the middle ages. He wrote: ". . . The adamas is found in India. The iron needle, after it has touched the magnet, always turns toward the north star, which does not move, as if it were the center of the firmament, the other stars revolving around it. Wherefore the magnet is very necessary to navigators at sea."

Another early authority on compasses in navigation was Brunette Latini, poet, philosopher, and astrologer from Florence. He was the instructor and patron of Dante and, after being exiled under threat of being burned alive, Latini settled in France where he wrote *Tresor de Sapience*, an encyclopedia in the Romance languages. He made several mentions of magnets and compasses in this work. Brunette also traveled to England where he conferred with Roger Bacon. At that meeting, Friar Bacon revealed his knowledge of compasses for navigation.

Going even further back into antiquity we discover that the Phoenicians and Egyptians had a knowledge of magnetic compasses for navigation. The Phoenician term for magnetized iron was the *Stone of Hercules*. The Egyptians called the compass the "*bone of Haroeri*," or "*the bone of Typhon*." They knew attraction and repulsion aspects of the magnet.

MYSTERIOUS DISAPPEARANCES: THEY NEVER CAME BACK

Let's assume that the compass has been around longer than our historians have admitted. A complete manuscript could be written on ancient knowledge of the compass as an aid to navigation. The compass would open the seas for ancient mariners to explore beyond the sight of land. Who then were some of the early explorers of North and South America? Who might have returned to Europe with stories of a legendary civilization beyond or within the Triangle of the Lost? A civilization that Plato might have chosen to call Atlantis? A brief glimpse of these early voyagers should include:

The Norsemen: The noted Norwegian archeologist, Dr. Helge Ingstad, made excavations at *l'Anse aux Meadows* in Newfoundland and uncovered indisputable evidence that the Norsemen established a colony there at least five hundred years before Columbus. Prior to this excavation, historians dismissed the Norse "Sagas" as fictitious accounts of Viking voyages.

The Norsemen may have ventured south into the Triangle of the Lost. Perhaps driven by storms or winds, or pulled by a strong sea, they may have found themselves far from home in an unfamiliar land. Columbus reported evidence of contact with Europeans during his second voyage. He recorded in his Journal of finding the wrecked hull of a large, European-style ship on the island of Guadeloupe. Several months later, while Columbus and his crew were sailing off the coast of Venezuela, they encountered a large canoe manned by eighty fair-skinned men. In his journal, Columbus described these canoeists as "of stout build, white skinned, with long blond hair and beards." The white natives failed to pull to when Columbus hailed them. They quickly fled from the Spanish ship, disappearing before their identity could be determined. Were these men the descendants of Norsemen who may have explored these shores hundreds of years before Columbus? Were they a band of Europeans from other countries who may have been shipwrecked in the Triangle of the Lost? We know they couldn't have been part of any existing Indian culture in North or South America. We might speculate they were linked in some unknown way to the "bearded white gods" who visited the Aztecs before the Spanish invasion of Mexico.

Prince Madoc and the Zeni Brothers: While they may sound like a name for a new rock band, these explorers may have sailed to the New World in the Twelfth and Fourteenth centuries. Cambrian chroniclers report that Prince Madoc made a voyage to a western continent in 1170 A.D., a land he said was fertile and populated with a race different in appearance from Europeans. '"We can also speculate about the similar-

MYSTERIOUS DISAPPEARANCES: THEY NEVER CAME BACK

ity of the name Madoc with that of the American tribe of Modoc Indians," reported Dr. Gunther Rosenberg. "Several investigators have noticed the similarity of customs among the Modoc tribe to certain aspects of Welsh culture."

Nicolo and Antonio Zeni were members of a family of warriors, navigators, and seamen who flourished in Venice during and around A.D. 1380. They added to their family's reputation as skilled seamen by sailing to the northern part of the New World. A contemporary historian of that time reported: ". . . Master Nicolo Zeni, being wealthy, and of a haughty spirit, desiring to see the fashions of the world, built and furnished a ship at his own charge, passing the Straits of Gibraltar, held on his course northward, with intent to see England and Flanders, but a violent tempest assailed him and he was carried he knew not whither."

According to the author, Purchas, in his *Pilgrimage*, Nicolo Zeni encountered a land inhabited by hostile natives. The Venetian saved himself and his crew from death from the warriors of a Chieftain named Zichmui. They set up a navy for the ruler. Several nearby islands were invaded and conquered. "After divers noble exploits," Purchas wrote, "Nicolo armed three vessels and visited *Engroland* (possibly Iceland). He founded a monastery there, built a church dedicated to St. Thomas, and then returned to Venice." He sailed back to the island ruled by the native chieftain in 1395. He died in his beloved, still unknown, land called "Freisland" on his second voyage. He said that to the west of Freisland was a place where "the people possess gold, grow corn, and make beer . . . further south they go naked . . . and in one region we visited a land where the ground was covered with eggs of wild fowl." Antonio Zeni buried his brother and returned to Venice in 1405.

Asian explorers: Oriental navigators may have explored the lands around the Triangle of the Lost many centuries before Columbus. Astonishing evidence has been uncovered by two archeologists from the Smithsonian Institution. Their find was unearthed in Ecuador, near the small town of Valdivia. This discovery consisted of pottery dating back to 3200 B.C. Even more incredible, the pottery has been positively identified as Jamonware from the island of Kyushu, Japan. "We've also found skulls near the pottery," said a spokesman at the site. "The skulls are definitely not those of the early inhabitants of this region. Instead, they have the physical characteristics of early Japanese."

There is additional documentation for early Asian voyages to the New World. "A cache of peanuts were unearthed some time ago in

MYSTERIOUS DISAPPEARANCES: THEY NEVER CAME BACK

Chekiang province in China," said Dr. Gunther Rosenberg. "This is the positive proof that ancient Chinese navigators must have reached the New World. Amazingly enough, the dating of the cache indicates it was placed there between 1200 and 1811 years before the birth of Christ."

Chinese brass coins dating back to 1200 B.C. have been uncovered at a remote spot in British Columbia, Canada. Archeologists also point to the remarkable decorative pottery of the Tajin culture around Vera Cruz, Mexico. "You would swear these early New World inhabitants were under the influence of Chinese teachers," said Dr. Rosenberg. Some years ago, Chinese authorities prepared a massive document to point out the similarities in language, social order, laws, and myths between the Mexican Aztec civilization and the Chinese culture around A.D. 450.

A stone bearing what was alleged to be Phoenician inscriptions was unearthed near Pariba, Brazil, in 1872. The stone was exhibited to archeologists and other interested scholars.

"It's a hoax," declared one eminent authority. "Everyone knows the Phoenicians couldn't have been here before Columbus."

The stone was forgotten until 1968 when Dr. Cyrus Gordon, chairman of the Department of Mediterranean Studies at Brandeis University, announced his conclusions following several years of investigation. He

MYSTERIOUS DISAPPEARANCES: THEY NEVER CAME BACK

reported the Brazilian stone is inscribed in excellent Phoenician script, which he has translated as follows:

". . . We are the sons of Canaan from Sidon, the City of the King. Commerce has cast us on this distant shore, a land of mountains. We set (sacrificed) a youth for the exalted gods and goddesses in the 19th year of Hitam, our mighty king. We embarked from Ezion-Gerber into the Red Sea and voyaged with ten ships. We were at sea together for two years around the land belonging to Ham (Africa) but were separated by storms and we were no longer with our companions. So we came here, 12 men and 3 women, on a new shore which I, the Admiral, control. But auspiciously may the gods and goddesses favor us."

We can only guess at what may have happened to this small band of Phoenician traders. Could they have been the ancestors of the white-haired men sighted by Columbus during his second voyage?

Around 200 A.D. Greek geographer Pausanias recorded that sail-

MYSTERIOUS DISAPPEARANCES: THEY NEVER CAME BACK

ing west into the Atlantic ocean would bring a mariner to islands where "the natives are red-skinned. . . whose hair was like a horse's mane." Another interesting sidelight in history points to knowledge of the New World at an early time. Martellus Coler was the Roman Consul in Gaul in 62 B.C. The ruler of a nearby province wanted to make a few points with Caesar's emissary.

"I have a group of strange and wondrous people," said the chieftain. "They come from an unknown land beyond the sea."

Martellus Coler grunted. "I have heard of people masquerading as strange beings to gain Caesar's favor."

The native chieftain protested loudly. "These people are truly a marvel."

"Bring them forth," was the counsel's reply.

At a signal from the chieftain, a band of warriors led several strange people into the counsel's chambers. They were described as people with black hair, red skins.

"How did you arrive here?" asked Martellus Coler.

"They don't speak our language," the chieftain said quickly.

Martellus shrugged. "Then we will talk through signs."

After several hours of deliberations, the Roman counsel learned the red-skinned people lived on a vast land beyond the Atlantic ocean. They had been fishing in a large reed canoe when an unexpected storm suddenly arose. The terrified Indians could only hold the sides of their canoe as it was swept out to sea. After a dangerous and terrible journey across the Atlantic, they were driven upon the beaches of France. Martellus Coler does not tell what the ultimate fate of these hapless Indians might have been. This incident indicates the Romans knew about the New World, that they may have sent explorers across the Atlantic in search of new territories and riches. There is considerable documentation, attested to by reputable archeologists, to believe that Roman war and trade ships reached the New World as early as 150 B.C.

We may never know which group of ancient Mariners first landed upon the shores of the New World. We can only speculate on their courage in braving the unknown boundaries of the Atlantic ocean. We can only speculate on the terrors they may have encountered within the Triangle of the Lost.

MYSTERIOUS DISAPPEARANCES: THEY NEVER CAME BACK

Those who returned to their homelands undoubtedly had stories of a wild, fantastic new land. Perhaps, these stories from the Ancient Mariners led to the Old World belief in Atlantis.

Perhaps, all we have to do to find Atlantis, is to look at North and South America.

MYSTERIOUS DISAPPEARANCES: THEY NEVER CAME BACK

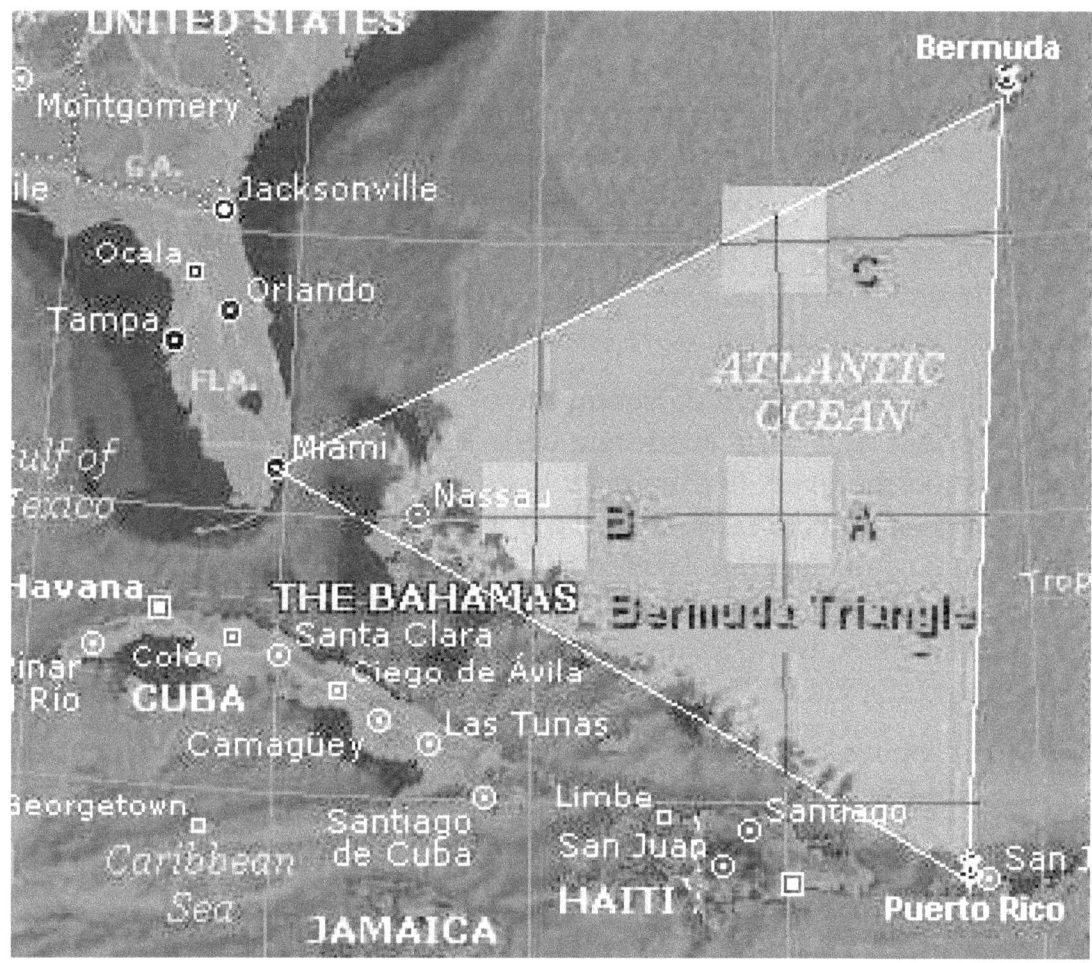

CHAPTER TWENTY

PSYCHICS PREDICT TRIANGLE MYSTERIES

Edgar Cayce, the remarkable sleeping prophet, was one of the world's most noted clairvoyants. Although he died in 1945, Cayce was the first psychic to give readings on the area we know as the Triangle of the Lost. During his lifetime, Cayce gave more than 8,000 readings to people concerned with health, marital, and other matters. Documents relating to his astonishing accuracy as a clairvoyant are in the archives of the Association for Research and Enlightenment, Virginia Beach, Virginia.

Researchers have always been intrigued by Cayce's references to the sunken continent of Atlantis. During a reading in June, 1940, the seer stated: "Poseidia will be among the first portions of Atlantis to rise again—expect this in 1968-69—not so far away." Poseidia, Cayce's term for Atlantis, is one of the most intriguing of all archeological mysteries.

Researchers quickly remembered Cayce's prediction when mas-

MYSTERIOUS DISAPPEARANCES: THEY NEVER CAME BACK

sive stone works were discovered on the sea bottom near the island of Bimini in 1958. Huge blocks of stone were discovered beneath the waters, laid in patterns suggestive of highways, temple platforms, and stone walls. Photographs of these underwater stones resemble other massive stoneworks in Peru, England and Italy. Unfortunately, it is impossible to determine the age of stones.

However, divers have returned to the surface with fossilized roots which indicate the stones were laid approximately 12,000 years ago.

These discoveries of Bimini have created a controversy among archeologists and their academic colleagues. Although few scientists have visited the area, the majority have dismissed any theory of man-made origin for the stones. One of the most interesting discoveries was the "Bimini Road" found in 1968 by divers Robert Angove, Jacques Mayol, Harold Climo, and Dr. J. Manson Valentine. Shortly after announcement of the discovery, Dr. Gunther Rosenberg, of the European Occult Research Society, visited in Bimini for an extensive investigation.

He reported seeing a road of oblong flat stones carefully shaped and aligned beneath the surface of the ocean. "These stones were evidently put there during prehistory," said Dr. Rosenberg. "The larger stones have their edges eroded by the ocean. They look as if they have been submerged for several thousand years. The unusual thing to remember about the Bimini wall, or road, is that accurate straight lines are seldom discovered in natural formations. These stoneworks look as if they were once a highway that was later submerged during some disaster."

Dr. Rosenberg hesitates to term the Bimini works a "road." Instead, he asks for additional study to determine exactly what lies beneath these blue-green waters. "This complex structure could possibly be linked to some ancient civilization," said Dr. Rosenberg. "Whether this would be Atlantis or some unknown culture must be determined. As many people know, there are similar formations of stones on the sea bottom off Cuba, Haiti, and Santa Domingo. During one voyage I saw what may be the truncated top of a pyramid submerged beneath the sea. We need to determine the origin of the structures."

Pilots who make regular flights through the Triangle of the Lost report seeing other stone works. A wall of stone has been photographed and investigated near Andros Island. Another undersea road appears to run atop a jagged submerged cliff off Cay Lobos. French Naval Captain Georges Horot and lieutenant Gerard Adefroville were diving in a bathy-

MYSTERIOUS DISAPPEARANCES: THEY NEVER CAME BACK

scaphe, the *Archimede*, off northern Puerto Rico when they found a series of steps cut into the Continental Shelf. We can only wonder at who carved this intriguing stairway in a rock cliff that is now at the bottom of the sea.

The world's deepest diving submarine, the *Aluminaut*, recently discovered an area 150 miles by 100 miles off the southern coast of the U. S. that is flattened like a terrace. This extends to the depths of 3000 feet and is paved with a layer of manganese oxide.

Arthur L. Markel, vice president and general manager of Reynolds Submarine Services Corp., operators of the submarine, informed newsmen that: "Gulfstream currents apparently keep the pavement swept clean of sediment so that it resembles a blacktop road. We attached wheels to the *Aluminaut* and actually rode along these deposits as though it was on a country road."

Scientist and UFO researcher M. K. Jessup, writing in *The Antiquity of Civilized Man* in *The Book of Saucer News* (Saucerian Publications, Clarksburg, West Virginia,) states that "It is becoming constantly less debatable that there was some 8,000 to 20,000 years ago a vast cataclysm on this planet which produced catastrophic changes on its surface. It has been called the flood; a collision of worlds; impact of a comet; shifting of the globe about its axis of rotation; movement of polarity, etc. . . . the exact nature is unimportant. Something did happen and annihilated worldwide civilization and almost exterminated our race."

Jessup states that debate upon the location of Atlantis is a waste of valuable time and energy. He feels that what should be considered is:

"(1) The worldwide similarity of stone works as to size, technique of workmanship, obviously installed before the catastrophe and before mountains were raised;

"(2) A block of intelligently worked meteoric steel buried in tertiary coal beds at least 300,000 years old:

"(3) A pitcher or vessel of strange alloy inlaid in silver of archaic design blasted out of solid stone in a quarry in Massachusetts;

"(4) A gold thread taken from solid stone fifteen feet below the surface in England;

"(5) A coin found 120 feet below the surface when drilling a well in Illinois;

MYSTERIOUS DISAPPEARANCES: THEY NEVER CAME BACK

"(6) A slate wall with inscription in a coal scene in Ohio; and perhaps

"(7) Records in Egypt, Nepal, and Tibet which actually describe some phases of cultural, literary and mechanical development of 70,000 to 270,000 years ago.

"Nothing but the common denominator of worldwide antiquity in man will solve the problems archeology has created for itself through a foreshortened time scale," he reported.

Another psychic who has made exclusive predictions on the Triangle for this book is Tenny Hale, a well-known Beaverton, Oregon seer. Miss Hale predicted the notorious Watergate scandal many years before this political fiasco appeared in print. She made her predictions concerning the apartment and office building complex in Washington, D. C. in a poetic prophecy published in 1971. This was a year before the actual burglary and break-in that destroyed the presidency of Richard M. Nixon.

"I didn't understand the prediction when it came to me as a child," said Tenny Hale. "However, I included it in the book as an important event for our nation around 1972."

The book, *The Seventh Panel*, was published by Tenny's own firm and is available directly by writing Tenny Hale, P. O. Box 125, Beaverton, Oregon 97005. Miss Hale's fascinating prediction about Watergate reads:

A capital land, the water, the gate

The east;

Where the leaned and famous gather

To feast;

This place no mortal designs

Many will lease.

The machine becomes

The beast.

"This cryptic message had no meaning in 1933, and it certainly didn't make much sense in 1971 when it was printed," wrote Tom Valentine in the *National Tattler*. "Now that the facts of the scandal are out in the open, the prediction is remarkably accurate." Valentine pointed out that the Watergate apartment and office building complex, located in

MYSTERIOUS DISAPPEARANCES: THEY NEVER CAME BACK

the nation's capital, was designed by a computer. "The reference that it is a place 'which no mortal designed' is truly remarkable," said Valentine.

Slender and chic and looking more like a fashion model than a psychic, Tenny Hale was raised in Iowa. She realized as a child that she had psychic ability. "It was something you did not advertise in those days," she explains. "Mostly I wrote my predictions down on scraps of paper and kept these in shoeboxes. Those scraps of paper were later the basis for my book, *The Seventh Panel*.

Miss Hale has been involved in psychic work for several years. She began to offer her services as astrologer and numerologist in 1967. "The general public does not fully understand the many difficulties of being a psychic," Tenny Hale said recently. "People often figure I can simply meditate and things come to me. Some mediums may actually work in that manner, but unfortunately it's very hard work for me. Sometimes things are very clear. Usually it's like being in a room with several telephones ringing at the same time. You can do it, but it takes considerable time, effort, and energy."

Asked for psychic impressions on the Triangle of the Lost, Miss Hale went into meditation and produced the following data:

"My psychic reading on the Triangle brought forth the fact that it is the place Edgar Cayce called Arcturus," said Miss Hale. "Edgar Cayce in his readings stated that Arcturus was the place where one had to go to leave this solar system. In one reading he said that he, Edgar, had gone through Arcturus to another solar system before coming down as Edgar Cayce to learn the new things he needed.

"Cayce also said that during what he called the time and a half, the Biblical Ones from Revelations, which he pegged as being during from 1958 to 1998, that the Atlanteans would gather to fight the old battle of good against evil," Miss Hale went on. "If good loses the battle again, said Cayce, they would find that the sons of Belial, or the evil guys, would fight them in space without a body but as souls. This, he said, would be difficult. He said that evil souls have already begun to hover over the earth and block the way to Arcturus so that souls dying are finding it hard to get through to other planes. They are being earthbound. My reading said that the Cayce definition of Arcturus was more or less correct. I also was told that the Triangle area we speak of is an opening to Arcturus. People and ships have been falling into it accidently, so to speak."

MYSTERIOUS DISAPPEARANCES: THEY NEVER CAME BACK

Another psychic who has provided data on the Triangle for this project is Larry E. Headrick, P. O. Box 683, Spearfish, South Dakota 57783. Mr. Headrick is a clairvoyant who has devoted considerable time to the study of occult subjects since his retirement from the U. S. Air Force three years ago. In addition to making personal and world predictions, Mr. Headrick also lectures extensively on subjects of healing, clairvoyance, prophecy. "I have had fair success in all of these areas," said the South Dakota seer. Among his most accurate predictions were forecasts of the fuel and energy crisis, continued strife in the Middle East, and the resignation of President Richard M. Nixon.

Results of Larry Headrick's psychic impressions are:

"The Triangle of the Lost has become a proverbial "thorn in the side" for modern-day science. As Allen Vaughn suggests, perhaps we should rephrase the question from "what happens," to "What influences are present when it happens." Answers then may be gained not only from the earth or ocean surface but also from the stars.

"As the smoke from a factory's chimney vanishes into the air, it becomes a reminder that particles of smoke merge with many particles of air, and merely seem to disappear. In turn, this also reminds us that water, left in a heated area, will evaporate with no visible trace once the transformation has taken place. These two phenomena can be understood with relative ease.

"Therefore, we might presume that the universe is also a part of this invisible nature. The sun's rays, the moon's reflections and the brightness of the stars are simply an extension of nature. While we have considerable knowledge about nature, we must take many steps to understand the intricate workings of the universe. If we conduct a search into the Triangle of the Lost, we will be taking a giant step forward the goal of understanding.

""Lunar and solar eclipses combine both light and energy in a different manner from singular projection of light-energy from either source. An eclipse will occur at specified times and can be observed under proper atmospheric conditions. It is logical to assume that other planets and/or solar systems have similar conjunctions at certain times. They may emit an energy equally dangerous to the eyes, and in the case of the Triangle of the Lost, these emissions may be powerful enough to absorb matter in much the same way in which smoke and water mingle and vanishes into the air.

MYSTERIOUS DISAPPEARANCES: THEY NEVER CAME BACK

"A conjunction, or eclipse of certain planets or solar systems, focuses a laser beam onto the earth at a specific time. This beam is either intensified or reduced by the atmospheric conditions around the earth at that moment.

"Through a study of times, dates, and events connected with the Triangle, we can formulate a chart. Additional studies of the times of these various disappearances can provide answers as to intensity of the energy being beamed to that location. We would also discover when to anticipate the next disappearance.

"The beam entering a triangle has an excellent chance of providing answers to the enigmatic question of why matter vanishes from a certain location without evidence of having been there. Scientists might point to the theory of an irresistible force meeting an immovable object.

"This would not be a force as we now know it, but an anti-force which would create a neutralizing effect. Mass is held together by force, or natural attraction, to a like kind. Consider what might happen if there was a sudden loss of gravity upon earth. Now, explore the possibility of a body of mass lifting without attraction to its own kind. The beam projected into the Triangle by a combined effort of two or more sources creates, not a force, but an anti-force which releases the electrons from around the atomic structure. This allows the atoms to be transformed into an invisible substance. Since matter vibrates onto its own kind with

MYSTERIOUS DISAPPEARANCES: THEY NEVER CAME BACK

various strengths, it provides part of the answer as to why some objects within the Triangle disappear completely and others remain seemingly untouched.

"Therefore, man has but to understand anti-force. Then he will understand fully that nothing exists that cannot be broken down to the infinite when a correct anti-force has been effective. Admittedly this is a tall order."

R. C. "Doc" Anderson has often been called one of the world's most gifted psychics. From his ESP studio at 302 Gordon Avenue, Rossville, Georgia, this robust giant is known throughout the world as a prophet, healer, hypnotist, and master of the paranormal.

A flamboyant man, Doc Anderson stands 6 feet, 2 inches in height. Dark twinkling eyes peer out at the world over a stylish mustache and beard. Anderson moves with the easy motion of a man considerably younger than his 66 years. During his forty years as a psychic, Doc Anderson has regressed many of his clients back in time to develop data on their past lives. Tapes on file in his studio indicate that a large number of people believe they were once living in Atlantis. Admittedly, both reincarnation and hypnotic regression are controversial subjects. However, due to his interests in these subjects and the Triangle of the Lost, we asked Doc Anderson to provide his psychic impressions of what may be happening within these bizarre boundaries.

"Buddy, a lot of the disappearances in the Triangle are due to natural causes," drawled Doc Anderson in his thick southern accent. "Such things as tidal waves, waterspouts, unusual weather conditions, and the natural forces of the sea, have led to many tragedies down there. Until you've been out on the sea for a considerable length of time, you may fail to realize the power of the mighty oceans. I went around the world as a young man, working my way as a seaman on various sizes of ships. Anyone who sails for any length of time as a merchant seaman realizes the sea is a powerful mistress."

The southern seer predicts there are occult forces behind some disasters in the Triangle of the Lost. "Within the next twenty years we're going to find remnants of a forgotten civilization in that region," Doc Anderson explained. "The discoveries off the island of Bimini are only a clue as to what lies under the sea down there. We're going to discover submerged temples, pyramids, and a vast hall of records in that area. In addition, we will also find that the mysterious lights frequently seen shining up from the sea are from machines that sank into the ocean more

MYSTERIOUS DISAPPEARANCES: THEY NEVER CAME BACK

than 10,000 years ago. These devices are activated periodically. They transmit a powerful beam of deadly intensity toward the surface. There is a link between the phenomena of long streaks of 'white water' and these subterranean devices. The 'white water' is created when enormous masses of gas are released from this equipment."

Anderson points to the occult belief in a network of subterranean tunnels as a clue to solving the enigma of the Triangle of the Lost. "Many people believe these tunnels are simply a figment of an overly active imagination," reported Doc Anderson. "I fervently believe in the existence of the tunnels. I've seen maps in the old Tibetan temples that reveal the continents are linked by these subterranean passages. A mighty race that existed many thousands of years ago were the builders. They wanted a fast, efficient method of traveling throughout the world. The tunnels were built to allow them free access to travel without harm from their enemies on the surface. I've traveled all over the world and there are folk tales in every land about the existence of these tunnels. In addition to the tunnels, there are vast underground rivers, broad lakes, and cities hidden deep in the interior of the earth. My psychic impressions indicate there is an interchange, or link-up point, of these tunnels beneath the Triangle of the Lost."

In an interview with Doc Anderson, he agreed to enter his psychic trance state to obtain more information on the mystery surrounding the Triangle of the Lost. I tape recorded his remarks. A portion of the transcript is as follows:

Who built the tunnels?

Anderson: They were built by the Old Ones, the race that built an advanced civilization on this planet many thousands of years ago. While those who live now may feel humanity has reached the pinnacle of technology, we are but children compared to those who have gone before. Look to the old scripts for evidence of their existence. They are what is now referred to as "the Masters." Their influence is still apparent upon our present society.

Do these tunnels intersect beneath the Triangle?

Anderson: There, and in many other places as well. The tunnels served as a transportation system when a conjunction of planetary forces made it impractical to live on the surface. The catastrophe that struck this ancient civilization destroyed most of the evidence of their existence. A few items still remain. Check the statues on Easter Island and

MYSTERIOUS DISAPPEARANCES: THEY NEVER CAME BACK

look for a cave in South America with an underwater entrance. Within that cave rest metal plates that contain a history of this forgotten civilization.

What happened on the surface that made the tunnels necessary?

Anderson: The sun moved closer to the earth. Enormous amounts of radiation poured down upon this planet. Those who survived had to move underground. There is a vast hall of records beneath the great Pyramid at Giza in Egypt. Many of our finest religious, political, and social leaders have studied there before ministering to the needs of our people. A priesthood of masters continues to maintain the archives. As the radiation intensified, it was necessary for all who would survive to leave the surface. Those who remained became warped in both body

MYSTERIOUS DISAPPEARANCES: THEY NEVER CAME BACK

and mind. Animal life was virtually destroyed or else evolved through a process of natural selection toward a new form. The dinosaur at that time was one of the problems upon the earth. It was radiation from the nearness of the sun, not natural selection, that destroyed the dinosaurs.

How do these things affect people who may travel through the Triangle?

Anderson: Check your statistics. Most disappearances are from natural causes, not from any hidden forces. A few have encountered the phenomena called time-space warp. This is where one may enter the other worlds due to a magnetic disturbance that does occur within the Triangle on infrequent occasions. But as the Masters will tell you, these magnetic errors occur infrequently. Those who have entered the time-space warp are in other worlds, other dimensions.

How can we learn more about this time-space phenomena?

Anderson: Look to your physics and particularly to Einstein's unified field theory. You will find that the unified field, which relates to minute atomic particles, sets up a condition that leads to invisibility. They, the scientists of our world, have just recently discovered a new form known as the psi particle. Their research into this will lead to more understanding of anti world. There are various other dimensions coexisting with us in this space. We also need a more complete understanding of time.

Submerged tunnels. . . strange beings from outer space . . . ancient civilizations . . . and the Old Ones are some of the interpretations given by our panel of psychics. Like everything else in life, we can choose to either believe or dismiss the impressions of our seers. Our psychics emphasized that thousands of people transverse this area each day. To cancel a vacation trip to one of the Caribbean Islands because of fear would be irrational. The essence of their message is that an "occult something" does exist in the Triangle.

MYSTERIOUS DISAPPEARANCES: THEY NEVER CAME BACK

CHAPTER TWENTY-ONE

MYSTERIES OF THE DEVIL'S ISLAND

This island of Bermuda is named after Captain Juan de Bermudez, a Spaniard who anchored his ship, *La Garza* (The Heron) offshore in 1515. A dense bank of fog prevented Bermudez from sending a landing party ashore. It was 1527 before a plan was formulated by the Spanish crown for the settlement of the island. Hernando Camelo, a Portuguese, received a commission from King Philip of Spain to establish a colony on the island. There is no evidence to indicate that Camelo followed the King's instructions.

Camelo was possibly scared off by tales of evil on the island. These frightening stories were passed from ship to ship, depicting Bermuda as a place inhabited by the spirits of darkness. "It is a place where the evil ones dwell," insisted Spanish sailors. "Their presence attracts the demons of the storms. The thunder roars there like the devil's horns scraping on a church door. There are hidden rocks where you least expect them. To go near Bermuda is to court Satan's bad luck."

These unseen wraiths created a new name for Bermuda— *"The Isle of the Devils."* The superstitions about the area grew until the Spaniards gave up all hope of settling the island. No one cared to venture on land and settle down.

It was 1593 when Henry May, an Englishman, sailed on a French ship from Hispaniola on a calm morning of November 30. Seventeen days later, the ship's captain and pilots congratulated themselves on passing the dangerous island.

"We need the wine of height," demanded a pilot. He referred to a drink given on ships when safe latitudes had been reached.

MYSTERIOUS DISAPPEARANCES: THEY NEVER CAME BACK

"Roll out a barrel of the finest wine!" shouted the captain, M. de la Barbotiere.

The crew drank long and deep. Discipline was relaxed and the ship sailed through the water with a bleary-eyed crewman at the helm. Most of the sailors were sprawled on the deck in a drunken stupor. Others were sleeping deeply in their berths. At midnight, the craft sailed head-on into a sharp reef. There was a sickening crunch as the coral-encrusted rock ripped through the ship's bottom. Seamen cried out in horror as waves rolled over the decks, sweeping sleeping sailors out into the waters of the ocean. There was a sickening lurch as a strong wave pushed the ship even higher onto the reef. More men lost their precarious grasp on the ship's railing. They vanished into the darkened waters. It was morning before the survivors were able to regroup on land. Twenty-six men had reached shore, including the captain and Henry May. An equal number had drowned when the ship struck the reef.

"There's no need to cry about our misfortune," announced M. de la Barbotiere. "We'll be stranded here forever unless we build ourselves another ship."

Carpenter's tools, block and tackle, and other equipment was salvaged from the wrecked ship. During the next few weeks, cedar trees were downed and their massive trunks sawn into planks. A seaworthy ship of eighteen tons began to take shape on the isolated beach.

"The activities of our party reveal the ingenuity of sailors," Henry May reported after his arrival in London in the summer of 1594. "The seams of our vessel were caulked with a mixture of lime and turtle's oil. This hardened into a mixture that resembled the strongest bonding agent. We sustained ourselves on a diet of fish, turtles, and rain water. There was an abundance of wild hogs on the island but we did not disturb them."

On May 11, 1594, the shipwrecked sailors pulled anchor on their ship and sailed toward Cape Breton. Once again, Bermuda was left as a land inhabited by the devils. Mariners avoided the island. It took another shipwreck before another human would step onto the shore.

It was a cheerful morning in Plymouth, England on June 2, 1609, when seven ships and two pinnacles, or small sailing boats, raised their canvas and moved slowly out of Plymouth Sound toward the open sea. On board were a group of English adventurers setting course for Vir-

MYSTERIOUS DISAPPEARANCES: THEY NEVER CAME BACK

ginia, the "infant plantation" in the New World. One ship; *Sea Venture*, sailed under the flag of Sir George Somers. In his narrative of their adventure in Bermuda, William Strachy described Somers as "a gentleman of approved assuredness and ready knowledge in seafaring activity."

The fleet kept close together as they crossed the Atlantic. Then, on July 23, an unexpected gale struck with tremendous fury. The first victim was the pinnace being towed by the *Sea Venture*. The storm roiled the ocean surface into a fierce maelstrom. Winds howled. Lightning flashed. Thunder roared overhead. The pinnace was cast loose to avoid a mid-sea collision with the *Sea Venture*.

When morning arrived, the *Sea Venture* was alone on a turbulent sea, fighting its way through a dreaded West Indies hurricane. "Winds and the sea were as mad as fury and rage could make them," wrote William Strachy in his *True Reportory*, (Published with Jourdain's "*Discovery of Bermuda*" by The University Press of Virginia, Charlottesville; 1964 under the title of *A Voyage To Virginia in 1609*). "Our clamours were drowned out in the winds and the winds in thunder. The sea swelled above the clouds and gave battle unto heaven. It could not be said to rain; the waters like whole rivers did flood the air."

The pounding fury of the ocean caused the *Sea Venture's* caulking to give way below the water line. Nine feet of water flooded the ship's hold. Sir Thomas Gates, another member of the party, reported this unsettling news to Sir George Somers. By then, Somers was on the poop deck advising the steersman on how to maintain a true course through the storm.

"Do what you can," advised Somers" Gates nodded. "I'll get the passengers and crew down below. We can try and hold the water at its present level."

Gates and his band of frightened passengers found gaping holes in the ship's timbers. They shoved dried beef into these open seams in an attempt to stop the onrushing water. Another group manned the ship's pumps.

"Set up a bailing line," commanded Gates. "Use buckets, scoops, whatever you can find. We're doomed unless we keep the water in check!"

The exhausted crew and passengers bailed furiously, knowing their lives depended on their efforts. Gates walked through the ship,

MYSTERIOUS DISAPPEARANCES: THEY NEVER CAME BACK

ordering cargo jettisoned over the side. Furniture, barrels of water, food, tools and equipment were thrown overboard.

Gates came up on deck, saw a cannon lashed to the bow of the ship. "Get that thing overboard!" he yelled. "Otherwise we'll never make it to Jamestown!"

Although tons of equipment had been tossed into the ocean, the *Sea Venture* still rode dangerously low in the waters.

"Passengers' luggage," Gates shouted above the howling wind. "Throw everything into the sea!"

For three days and nights, without sleep or rest, the men aboard the *Sea Venture* fought the storm. The ship plunged forward into the Triangle of the Lost, under bare spars and settling deeper into the water. A mountainous wave appeared suddenly on the starboard on the afternoon of the third day. Somers saw the monstrous wall of water rushing toward his ship. He shouted a warning and everyone grabbed a secure handhold. The giant wave swept the ship's deck. There was a sickening moment when the *Sea Venture* seemed suspended in time and space, as if debating whether to falter and sink. Then, the vessel recovered and continued battering a path through the storm, her timbers strained be-

MYSTERIOUS DISAPPEARANCES: THEY NEVER CAME BACK

yond all measure.

The ship's last night of suffering was on July 28. A seaman glanced up into the stormy sky, noticed a tiny pinpoint of glowing light. He called Sir George Somers and, together, they stood on deck and watched as the bizarre glowing light manifested above the ship. ". . . like a faint star trembling and streaming along with a sparkling blaze, half the height upon the mainmast, and shooting sometimes from shroud to shroud," reported William Strachy. "At which, Sir George Somers called everyone about him and showed them the same, who observed it with much wonder and carefulness; but upon a sudden toward morning, they lost sight of it and knew not which way it went."

It was only a matter of hours until land was sighted a few miles beyond the ship. By sunset, the *Sea Venture* had been worked into shallow water, lodged between two shoals, on what is now known as St. George's Island. The ship went to her final rest at a place marked on the charts as *Sea Venture Flats*.

The strange dancing light that accompanied the *Sea Venture* to her resting place was not the only mystery to befall the 150 men and women who clambered ashore. A longboat was taken from the *Sea Venture* and prepared for the voyage to Virginia. A month after the shipwreck, first mate Henry Ravens and a volunteer crew of seven sailors pushed their tiny craft away from the beach.

"We'll be back to get you!" called Ravens to the crowd on the shore.

That was the last anyone ever saw of the tiny boat or the eight men aboard. The turquoise sea swallowed them up without a single clue to their fate. It was one of the first recorded disappearances within the Triangle of the Lost. Another two months of intensive labor was needed to build two more boats for the long, dangerous trip to the Virginia colony. The shipwrecked group labored hard, creating a stout ship with heavy timbers. The two ships took two weeks to cover the 580 miles to Jamestown—ending their dangerous adventure in the Triangle of the Lost. During their time on Bermuda, Sir George Somers never told his fellow voyagers the name of the island. Bermuda's reputation as the "isle of the devils" was so feared that he felt secrecy was the best course during their ordeal.

Following the publication of their adventures in England, playwright William Shakespeare became intrigued by the wreck of the *Sea*

MYSTERIOUS DISAPPEARANCES: THEY NEVER CAME BACK

Venture. His play, The Tempest, is based on Sir William Somer's adventures. Shakespeare was intrigued by the strange appearance of St. Elmo's light while the ship battled against the storm. His imagination transformed the eerie light into the spirit, *Ariel*, in the play.

When Sir William and the other castaways reached Jamestown, they learned the other voyagers had reached the "infant plantation." They were appalled to find many settlers had died from an epidemic of disease, that others were suffering from near-starvation. Under siege by hostile Indians, the colonists could not hunt or fish. A man risked death to go outside the stockade and gather firewood.

Eventually, the colony was reinforced and Sir William Somers sailed to Bermuda for additional supplies. He died there in 1610, a year after his shipwreck.

During the next two hundred years, the Triangle of the Lost devoured ships, people, and travelers at an alarming rate. Colonizing the New World was a dangerous task. Small ships in the Triangle were victims of sudden squalls, dangerous storms, and the strange appearance of St. Elmo's light. Spanish galleons sank without a trace of their crews. Ships carrying immense treasures within their holds vanished inexplicably. English merchant ships disappeared mysteriously. Shiploads of

MYSTERIOUS DISAPPEARANCES: THEY NEVER CAME BACK

immigrants to the New World sailed into the Triangle and were never heard from again. Stories of "ghost ships" running under full sail popped up in the Triangle. These doomed ships were said to be steered by phantom helmsmen, their crews and passengers having vanished into some unknown Valhalla.

Another baffling disappearance in the Triangle occurred in 1812 when the daughter of controversial vice president of the United States, Aaron Burr, sailed into the Triangle. Theodosia Burr Alston was the lovely wife of Governor Joseph Alston of South Carolina. Although her father had tried to provide a tranquil environment for his daughter, Theodosia's life was marred by tragedy. Her mother died when she was a child. She married at age 17 and moved away from her home.

Always close to her father, Theodosia became depressed after Aaron Burr's duel with Alexander Hamilton. His office as vice president did not prevent duelist Burr from being charged with Hamilton's murder. A warrant was issued and Burr became a fugitive. After months of hiding, Burr gave himself up to the authorities; a stormy trial acquitted him of all charges. Nevertheless, the public opinion turned against the tempestuous politician and his mercurial temper. Burr was forced into exile for four years. He returned from England in 1812.

Hearing of her father's plan to sail to New York, Theodosia Alston's moodiness turned to a bright gaiety. Tragedy marred this brief moment of happiness when her 10-year-old son fell ill with dreaded malaria fever. Doctors were called to the Alston's summer home on Pawley's Island, but they were unable to cure the fever. The boy died on June 30, 1812.

By then, Aaron Burr had returned to New York and established a practice as attorney. Theodosia wrote to her father: "I have just lost my boy. My child is gone forever . . May heaven, by other blessings, make you amends for the noble grandson you have lost."

MYSTERIOUS DISAPPEARANCES: THEY NEVER CAME BACK

The death plunged Theodosia into a deep depression. She lost her will to live, complained of the hot, humid climate of South Carolina. She remained in her bedroom in the governor's mansion, living with the memories of her dead son.

Governor Alston called the state's most respected physician to examine his wife. The doctor found Theodosia sitting up in bed, tearfully holding a portrait of her son. After the examination, the physician conferred privately with the governor.

"She needs a change of scenery," advised the physician. "If your wife remains here, she's going to get sicker in both mind and body."

Governor Alston said: "I can't leave now."

"Let her visit her father," explained the physician. "That might snap her out of it."

Governor Alston called an aide, who started to arrange for a charter ship to take Theodosia to New York. While these arrangements were being made, Timothy Green arrived in South Carolina. A friend and political ally of Aaron Burr, Green offered to escort the ailing governor's wife to New York.

"We'll sail on *The Patriot*," Green announced. "She's a good ship. Used to carry the mail and cargo between here and the northern ports. Since the war with England broke out, she's been a privateer."

Governor Alston looked worried. "I don't want my wife sailing on a warship."

"Don't worry," said Timothy Green, a note of assurance in his voice. "We've removed the guns from *The Patriot*. They've already been stored below decks. I've also secured permission from the British to gain entrance into New York harbor. There are a dozen ships blockading the port, but they've agreed to let *The Patriot* enter under a truce." To further emphasize the peaceful mission of *The Patriot*, Timothy Green loaded the ship with several tons of Alston rice. This grain was raised on the Alston plantation, *"The Oaks,"* and was known for being a superior food. Although these preparations were impressive, Governor Alston was still concerned for his wife's safety. He made arrangements with his uncle, William Algernon Alston, to sail on *The Patriot* as Theodosia's bodyguard. On December 13, 1812, Governor Alston stood on the dock and watched *The Patriot* head out to sea. He waved to his wife, who stood on the deck, a fragile woman bundled against the cold breeze, her blonde hair con-

MYSTERIOUS DISAPPEARANCES: THEY NEVER CAME BACK

trasting vividly beneath the black mourning bonnet.

On the day *The Patriot* was to arrive in New York, Aaron Burr anxiously scanned the sea for some sign of the vessel. Day after day, Burr returned to the Battery and paced the docks. "You've got to accept reality," counseled a friend. "Something's happened to the ship."

Burr cast a dark glance in the man's direction. "But my daughter can't disappear," he said in a choked voice. "My grandson has died from fever. I can't go on if Theodosia doesn't show up."

Burr's prayers, and those of the Alston family in South Carolina, went unanswered. *The Patriot* vanished in the Triangle of the Lost. Some claimed the ship had been deliberately shot up and sunk by British warships. Others claimed the vessel had blown up during a storm, yet, as Aaron Burr pointed out, the weather was calm and serene during the week. Governor Alston felt someone had slipped aboard *The Patriot* and sabotaged the vessel.

After weeks of mourning for his wife, Governor Alston wrote to Aaron Burr:

"Your letter of the 10th, my friend, is received. This assurance of my fate is not wanting ... My boy ... my wife ... gone! Both! This then is the end of all hope we had formed. You may well observe that you feel severed from the human race. She was the last tie that bound us to that species. What have we left? ... You are the only person in the world that I can commune on that subject; for you are the only person whose feelings can have any community with mine. You know those we loved. Here, none know them; none valued them as they deserved. The talents of my boy, his rare elevation of character, his already extensive reputation for so early an age, made his death regretted by my family ... but though certain of the loss of my no less admirable wife, they seem to consider it like the loss of an ordinary woman. Alas, they knew nothing of my heart. They have never known anything of it. After all, he is a poor actor who cannot sustain his little hour upon the stage, be his part what it may. But the man who was deemed worthy of the heart of Theodosia Burr, and who had felt what it was to be blessed with such a woman, will never forget his elevation."

Saddened by his grief, Governor Alston was dead within three years after writing to Aaron Burr. Theodosia's father lived another twenty-six years, spending considerable time and energy in trying to discover what happened to his daughter. He listened to hundreds of stories, paid

MYSTERIOUS DISAPPEARANCES: THEY NEVER CAME BACK

thousands of dollars to seamen rumored to know something about *The Patriot's* disappearance. Nothing was solid enough to conclusively show what happened to the ship.

As the years passed, reports came in of men dying in taverns and making a deathbed confession about Theodosia's death. The dying men swore they had been aboard a pirate ship that captured *The Patriot*, scuttled the ship and killed the crew and passengers. Aaron Burr followed up many of these leads, but an aura of mystery always remained.

An article written by Foster Haley in the February 15, 1959, magazine section of the Charleston, South Carolina, *News and Courier* may have solved the perplexing mystery. The author claimed to have discovered documents in the "*Archives of the State of Alabama in Montgomery*" a century and a half after they were filed there. The documents reported the deathbed confession of John Howard Payne, an ex-pirate who was dying in Tunis, Africa. Tunis was then a headquarters for Pirates, plunderers, and scoundrels from throughout the world.

"... I was sailing on a pirate ship when we took *The Patriot*," gasped Payne. "We murdered everyone on board, including the captain and a lady of high birth. She was forced to walk the plank like the rest of them. I've never been able to forget her death. I was the man who put the blindfold over her eyes."

John Howard Payne was a man without a country, a homeless wanderer. Strangely enough, the man who never had a home, was the au-

MYSTERIOUS DISAPPEARANCES: THEY NEVER CAME BACK

thor of the song, "*Home Sweet, Home*"!

Another, equally romantic version of Theodosia's fate appeared in the Charleston *News and Courier* on August 4, 1963. According to the author, R. J. Cannady, Theodosia kept a diary that told what happened to *The Patriot*. Before she died, the diary was placed in a bottle with her wedding ring and thrown into the sea.

Cannady told of how the ship was attacked by pirates led by Thaddeus Boncourt, then the wildest and most bloodthirsty buccaneer sailing in the Caribbean. Theodosia's diary was washed ashore, then purchased by a Colonel Justin Dane.

The one fact we know about Theodosia's disappearance is that she sailed on *The Patriot* into the Triangle of the Lost. Like many others before and since that time, her disappearance may never be explained. The bizarre boundaries of this dead stretch of water holds many secrets.

MYSTERIOUS DISAPPEARANCES: THEY NEVER CAME BACK

CHAPTER TWENTY-TWO

GHOST SHIPS IN SATAN'S SEA

The roll call of vanishing ships within the Triangle of the Lost is a baffling record of unusual marine disappearances. The fate of these unfortunate vessels, their crews and passengers, is shrouded by an impenetrable mystery. Altogether, more than six hundred large ships, submarines, and small boats have vanished without a trace within the bizarre boundaries of this deadly zone. No one knows what happened to them; we can only speculate on the reasons behind their disappearance.

One of the most mysterious areas within the Triangle is the legendary Sargasso Sea, a strange stretch of calm waters about the size of France. This portion of the North Atlantic contains an unusual floating seaweed, Sargassum, which drifts alone or in huge dark masses. When Columbus sailed into the Sargasso Sea during his first voyage, he mistakenly decided he was approaching land. Besides the huge amounts of floating seaweed, the Sargasso Sea is characterized by an almost supernatural calmness. Wind is virtually nonexistent in these latitudes.

Since the early mariners first sailed out of Gibraltar into the Atlantic, seamen have talked about the dangers of the Sargasso Sea. If you drop into a waterfront bar anywhere in the world, chances are you'll find a seaman willing to talk about this bizarre sea. Sailors call this region a *"Graveyard of Lost Ships,"* a *"Sea of Danger,"* and *"Sea of Lost Ships."*

Perhaps the first mariners to sail into the Sargasso Sea were ancient Phoenician traders. There is considerable evidence to show these hearty sailors reached the New World several hundreds of years before Columbus. The Phoenicians were followed into the Triangle of the Lost by Carthaginian seamen. Admiral Himileo, of Carthage, made the fol-

MYSTERIOUS DISAPPEARANCES: THEY NEVER CAME BACK

lowing report on the Sargasso Sea about 500 B.C. He wrote: "... No breeze drives the ship, so dead is the sluggish wind of this idle sea ... There is much seaweed among the waves, it holds back the ship like bushes... the sea has no great depth, the surface of the earth is barely covered with a little water ... the monsters of the sea move continuously to and fro, the fierce monsters swim along the sides of the sluggish and slow moving vessels ..."

My first knowledge of the Sargasso Sea came from a young schooner captain a few years ago in Key West, Florida. A happy-go-lucky adventurer, George Rollins graduated from college with a degree in law and an opening in his family's prestigious law firm in New England. He worked as an attorney for several months. "I was sitting in my office one morning going over legal papers for a lawsuit," he related. "The offense was slight, except my client was paranoid. A wealthy paranoid, I might add. I happened to look out the window and a couple of birds were perched on the limb of a tree. Suddenly, they flew off into the sunshine. Something snapped inside me. I laid down the papers said 'so long' to law partners and went out and bought a schooner. My family thinks I'm crazy. But I enjoy knocking around the world, taking a little time to live and enjoy life."

In those days, George Rollins financed his sailing excursions by sailing down into the Bahamas, bringing back a load of liquor. "Taxes aren't so high down there," he explained. "So I make a run occasionally. No big wholesale deal or anything like that. I come back and sell a case here or there to keep myself in spending money." During one voyage, George Rollins swore he was swept up by a sudden storm and driven into the Sargasso Sea.

"It was touch-and-go out there," he related. "I didn't know where the storm was taking me. The ship was knocked about for several days after the auxiliary engine quit. Finally, the storm subsided and I found myself in what is known as the Horse Latitudes. I'd heard about the Sargasso Sea and the stories didn't exaggerate.',

Legends claim that ships from every era of sailing have been trapped in the Sargasso Sea. Immobilized by the seaweed, unable to sail away because of the lack of wind, these vessels are said to drift sluggishly through the deadly fields of seaweed. The decayed vessels are reported to be manned by skeleton crews, sailors who died on these doomed vessels.

"I've heard seamen tell of seeing everything from Viking warships

MYSTERIOUS DISAPPEARANCES: THEY NEVER CAME BACK

to Yankee whalers in the Sargasso," George Rollins explained. "They swear these ships are floating around out there—doomed to rot away in that calm sea."

Rollins claimed to have been becalmed in the Sargasso for several days. "The engines wouldn't work, there wasn't wind for sails," he went on. "I hadn't planned on being out for more than a few days. My supply of water was limited. However, food was no problem because I always carried several cases of freeze dried meals aboard."

The incredible Sargasso was as calm as a dead sea. "I remembered then how these parts became known as the Horse Latitudes," said George Rollins. "When the Spanish galleons were carrying gold back to Spain, many of their ships became enmeshed in the seaweed. As they drifted through the calm sea, praying for wind, their water supply often ran low. They had to drive their horses overboard to conserve water. Hence the name of Horse Latitudes."

Rollins was sleeping one afternoon below deck when a bumping noise sounded against the side of his schooner. "It was like someone hitting the sides with a baseball bat," he reported." I rushed up on deck and almost died of shock!"

Rollins gasped when he saw a large, rotting ship pressed against the side of his schooner. "There were wormholes in the wood and the sides were covered with a green, slimy growth," he said. "It looked like a ship from the bottom of the sea. She was a sailing ship, fairly large, probably a brigantine. The tattered folds of a rotting flag were hanging limply from the mast. I couldn't make out what country the flag belonged to because of the rotten fabric."

Rollins wanted to board the ship, then decided against this action.

"It would take some effort to scale the slimy sides," he admitted. "I didn't have any way of hooking my schooner to the ghost ship. The other ship had drifted into me. I could imagine myself getting on board that doomed vessel and, without warning, drifting away from my own ship. Later, I realized that there might have been a plague or some other deadly disease germs on board that ghost ship."

Rollins attempted to push his schooner away from the doomed ship. "Something told me to get away from there," he related. "I didn't want to end up like the crew aboard the other vessel. I was depressed and more than a little frightened by the ship's presence."

MYSTERIOUS DISAPPEARANCES: THEY NEVER CAME BACK

He was unable to push away from the unwelcome ship. "The next two or three days were like a nightmare," Rollins recalled. "The brig loomed up over my schooner. Whenever there was a little wave action, the two vessels bumped against one another. I became quite alarmed and wondered if the ghost ship might pound a hole in the side."

After more than a week trapped in the Sargasso Sea, Rollins awoke one morning to find a slight wind blowing from the east. "I raised the sails and prayed," he explained. "Within a matter of minutes I was headed west away from the ghost ship. She remained there, moving sluggishly about, her sails hanging down in tatters from the masts. I wished I'd had the courage to go on board. I couldn't see a name on the ship's side. I've always wondered what she was and how she came to be there."

While some mariners may have embellished reports about the Sargasso Sea, there is no reason not to believe the story told by George Rollins. Other seamen have been becalmed in this ocean of seaweed and returned with similar tales. Alan Villers, an Australian, has been a seafaring man for most of his life. Villers also sighted a ghost ship in the Sargasso Sea while crossing the dangerous waters in a sailing ship. Villers felt that a ship trapped in masses of seaweed might use up her supplies and eventually grow grass and barnacles until she would become virtually unable to sail."

Villers went on to state that borer worms would begin to eat into the wood. The sides of the ship would become riddled with wormholes until ". . . a rotted and putrid mess, manned by skeletons . . . slipped below the heated surfaces of the calm sea."

During the golden age of sailing ships, many disappearances within the Triangle of the Lost were undoubtedly due to piracy, bad weather, or being trapped in the Sargasso Sea. Today, such incidents are even more ominous because most vessels are equipped with auxiliary engines. Even the masses of Sargassum are no match for a powerful, well-tuned marine engine.

Some of the ships that have mysteriously vanished in the Triangle include:

U.S.S. Insurgent disappeared in August, 1800, with 340 men on board.

The *U.S.S. Wasp*, commanded by Captain Johnston Blakeley, sailed into the Triangle with a crew of 140 men. No word was ever heard from the *Wasp* again.

MYSTERIOUS DISAPPEARANCES: THEY NEVER CAME BACK

U.S.S. Wildcat sailed from Cuba with a crew of fourteen. The ship never reached its destination on Thompson's Island.

H.N.S. Atalanta left Bermuda for England with a crew of 290. The ship was staffed with England's top naval cadets. The vessel vanished in January, 1880.

Rosalie, a commercial ship under French registry, sailed for Havana in 1840 with a full crew and numerous passengers aboard. The ship was found with cargo intact. The only life aboard was a lone canary in the captain's cabin. There was no clue to explain the disappearance of the people on board.

James B. Chester, was found drifting in the Sargasso Sea in 1885 with both crew and passengers missing.

Freya, a German ship, was found abandoned after leaving Cuba for a port in Chile in 1902.

That "something" may be kidnapping people from ships has been theorized by many investigators. In 1881, the American ship *Ellen Austin* was enroute west of the Azores when a drifting schooner was sighted. A boarding party found the ship to be abandoned and, under maritime law, a fair prize for anyone who brought her to port. A group of enthusiastic sailors volunteered to sail the derelict ship and follow the *Ellen Austin* to port. They had just boarded the ghost schooner when a storm arose. The two ships drifted away from each other.

Two days later, the captain of the *Ellen Austin* sighted the schooner. A crew rowed over to the drifting ship. An ashen-faced mate reported back to the captain. "'They're gone!" the sailor blurted out. "Every man on board has disappeared."

The captain was puzzled. "What happened?"

"There's no sign of a struggle," answered the mate. "It's as if they vanished into thin air."

The captain of the *Ellen Austin* decided to put a new crew on board the abandoned ship. His seamen mumbled ominously about jinxed ships, whispering among themselves about death ships. Finally, a crew of four men succumbed to the visions of a large bonus for bringing the derelict into port. Within minutes after they boarded the schooner, another squall roared out of the west. The two ships became separated and the *Ellen Austin* once again lost sight of the prize ship. The derelict was never sighted again and neither were the men in the second crew.

MYSTERIOUS DISAPPEARANCES: THEY NEVER CAME BACK

Mention ghost ships of the North Atlantic and almost any sailor will tell you about the puzzling disappearance of the crew and passengers aboard the *Mary Celeste* in November, 1872. After sailing from New York with a cargo of alcohol, the *Mary Celeste* was found abandoned north of the Azores by a British brig, *Dei Gratia*. Crewmen from the *Dei Gratia* found the ship's sails were up. Food and water supplies were intact. All personal belongings of the crew and passengers were undisturbed. The only unusual thing on the *Mary Celeste* was that the captain's cabin had been boarded up, as if someone might have wished to fight off some unknown peril. Despite a century of theorizing, no one knows what happened to the ten people who vanished from the *Mary Celeste*. Whatever the reason, people have a way of vanishing from ships in the Triangle of the Lost. Another classic incident occurred in February, 1921, when the *Carol Dearing* ran ashore in North Carolina. There was no one aboard, although a partially eaten meal was found on board the ship. The *John and Mary* was found drifting 50 miles off the Bermuda shore in 1932. The crew and passengers had vanished. A 112-foot schooner, the *Gloria Colite*, was found abandoned near the same area eight years later. In 1944, the *Rubicon*, a Cuban ship, drifted aimlessly off Key West, Florida, until a boarding party took charge of the ship. The only living thing on board was a half-starved dog.

Large freighters have also disappeared without a clue left for searchers. *The Cotopaxi* left Charleston harbor in 1925 en route for Havana, Cuba. The ship vanished without a trace. Forty-three people were on board the *Stavenger* when the ship sailed into the Triangle of the Lost in 1931. No one has ever heard from the ship again. "All is well," was the signal radioed to a harbor master on the Azores when the freighter *Anglo-American* steamed westward in 1938 toward the Triangle. The ship was never seen again.

One of the most enigmatic disappearances took place in 1924 when the Japanese freighter *Raiuke Maru* was sailing from Bermuda toward Cuba. A frightened radioman got off a message before the vessel vanished. That unusual call for help has intrigued investigators since then. "Danger like a dagger now . . . come quickly . . . we cannot escape," was transmitted from the stricken ship. The operator failed to give a location for the ship, something any seaman would do under even such desperate circumstances.

Another baffling mystery occurred in March, 1918, when the *U.S.S. Cyclops* left Barbados for a trip to Norfolk, Virginia. There were 309 navy seamen aboard the ship, a coal-carrying vessel that was a sister ship to

MYSTERIOUS DISAPPEARANCES: THEY NEVER CAME BACK

the *U.S.S. Langley*. After the ship failed to arrive in Norfolk, a U. S. Navy investigator revealed the *Cyclops* left the harbor at Barbados and turned south instead of north to Virginia. Further digging revealed the captain of the *Cyclops* was a German-born despot who drove his crew unmercifully. The captain, realizing the anti-German sentiment during World War II, had changed his name from Wichmann to Worley. A Naval inquiry concluded the Cyclops had probably been torpedoed by German U-boat submarines working out of a South American harbor. After the armistice, an examination of German records showed U boats were not in that region when the *Cyclops* sailed.

German espionage agents in South America claimed to have put several time bombs in the hold of the *Cyclops* prior to her departure from Barbados. The *Cyclops* was carrying a load of manganese ore, a cargo that could easily hide a time bomb. However, U. S. Naval authorities reported that the *Cyclops* vanished without leaving debris, an oil slick, or similar evidence of a mid-ocean explosion.

Captain Wichmann (or Worley) may have been responsible for the vanishing ship. A strange man, the German-born captain of the *Cyclops* was probably insane "His treatment of the crew was cruel, almost inhuman. One of his favorite habits was to stroll along the bridge of the *Cyclops* dressed only in his long woolen underwear and a derby hat.

MYSTERIOUS DISAPPEARANCES: THEY NEVER CAME BACK

The possibility of mutiny was also developed. The *Cyclops* passenger list included three U. S. sailors who were being indicted for murder. Along with two AWOL marines, the sailors were being taken to fleet headquarters at Norfolk for a trial. A Navy board of inquiry stated:

". . . Since her departure from Barbados on March 4, 1918, there has been no trace of the vessel. The disappearance of the ship has been one of the most baffling mysteries in the annals of the Navy. All attempts to locate the *Cyclops* have failed. All efforts to learn what may have happened to the ship have been unsuccessful. Many theories have been advanced but none that satisfactorily accounts for her disappearance."

U. S. Vice Admiral M. S. Tisdale advanced his theory for the reason behind the disappearance of the *Cyclops* in an article called *Did The Cyclops Turn Turtle?* Admiral Tisdale felt the cargo of manganese ore may have caused the ship to flop over in the sea. Once manganese ore starts shifting, the load will continue to move until the source of the movement stops. "I have seen the *Neptune* flop ten degrees for no apparent reason," he wrote. "If, in so flopping, something occurred to accentuate the list, is it not perfectly plausible to assume that this accentuation might have increased to such a degree as to cause the ship to turn turtle?"

A seiche wave is a mammoth ocean phenomenon caused by atmospheric or seismic disturbances. In the movie, *The Poseidon Adventure*, a large ocean liner is suddenly turned upside down by a mountainous wave. Author Paul Gallico was sailing across the Atlantic many years ago when a large wave smashed into his ship. There was a frightening moment, then the liner rolled back to its original position. From that incident, Gallico created his suspenseful *Poseidon Adventure*.

Admiral Tisdale and several other investigators felt the *Cyclops* could have been hit by an enormous seiche wave, been turned over on its back by the force. The manganese ore cargo would have shifted, plunging the vessel to the bottom of the sea.

A mad captain . . . German U-boats . . . bomb-planting spies . . . and a disgruntled crew are part of the ingredients of the *Cyclops* mystery. One or more of these combinations could have caused disaster on the ship. The only absolute certainty is that the *Cyclops* sailed into the Triangle of the Lost. . . and vanished forever.

The first man to sail alone around the world was Joshua Slocum, a Boston seaman who left Boston Harbor on his 51st birthday in April, 1895. On a three-year voyage around the globe Slocum sailed more than 46,000

MYSTERIOUS DISAPPEARANCES: THEY NEVER CAME BACK

miles in a 36-foot *Spray*. The *Spray* had once been a beached hulk. Slocum was given the ship as a practical joke. He took several months and $500 and, with the assistance of several retired sea captains, transformed the rotting hulk into an outstanding craft with excellent speed and sailing ability. Slocum sailed around the world alone, then returned to Boston harbor on June 27, 1898.

A sailor who was unable to swim, Slocum wrote *Sailing Alone Around the World*. The book was an instantaneous best seller. In his book, the hearty old sailor describes sailing in the Triangle of the Lost near the Azores when he became sick. He was suffering from fever and painful stomach cramps in the cabin when a fierce storm struck. Slocum was too feeble to lower his sails. He tried to raise himself off the cabin floor, then fell back into unconsciousness.

Gradually, the old sailor drifted up out of the darkness. The storm was howling, but the *Spray* held a straight course through the turbulent ocean. Slocum glanced up on deck and saw a specter at the helm of the *Spray*. The incredible visitor was dressed in ancient garments. Slocum walked unsteadily out on the deck. "Who are you?" he asked. The specter introduced himself. "I sailed with Christopher Columbus," the ghost announced. "I was the pilot aboard the Pinta" I have come to you because you're in trouble tonight. Go below and rest. I'll keep the ship on course until morning." Shaking his head in wonderment, Slocum retired below to his cabin. When he awakened the following morning, he discovered the spectral sailor had vanished. The storm had ended. The *Spray*'s sails were spread out, set for maximum wind. The *Spray* had crossed more than 90 miles of ocean during the night, a journey that only a good helmsman could have accomplished. After writing his book, Slocum crossed the country on a lecture tour. But fame and adoration failed to dim his love of the sea. In October, 1909, the old man was 65 years old. He decided to sail the *Spray* into the West Indies for a winter's vacation. He pulled out of Miami on November 14 and headed into the Triangle of the Lost. That was the last anyone saw of the man called "the greatest sailor of all time." He vanished somewhere in the Triangle of the Lost with his beloved *Spray*.

Recent developments within the danger zone include the disappearance of the 20,000-ton German freighter *Anita* in March, 1973. The ship carried a thirty-two-man crew. The *Anita* was sailing from Virginia to Germany.

On Christmas Eve, 1967, the owner of the *Witchcraft* cabin cruiser

MYSTERIOUS DISAPPEARANCES: THEY NEVER CAME BACK

and a lone passenger disappeared less than a mile offshore from Miami. That same month the *Revonac*, a 48-foot racing yacht, also disappeared off Miami a week before Christmas.

With few exceptions, modern craft disappearing in this dangerous zone are equipped with radio sending and receiving equipment. A spokesman for the U. S. Navy admitted they are puzzled as to why emergency messages are not sent out from boats in distress.

"Naturally, many of these disappearances are due to natural causes," he related. "A sudden squall can swamp a small boat. The owner may not have time to send a message because he's fighting to keep his boat afloat. By the time the owner realizes he should send a message, the boat may be sinking."

The Navy spokesman admitted to being baffled on the disappearance of larger ships. "There's no reason why a large ship with a well-trained crew should disappear," he announced. "These ships have the best radio equipment. At least two men on board can send and receive radio messages. We've speculated about the problem. We've even theorized that an electronic 'net' or jamming system may be in use out there. This gets you into undersea cities, UFOs and other far-out phenomena, which the top brass doesn't appreciate."

Mariners have been superstitious about the Triangle of the Lost for centuries. Perhaps, when the mystery of this danger zone is solved, we may discover there was a good reason for their fears.

MYSTERIOUS DISAPPEARANCES: THEY NEVER CAME BACK

CHAPTER TWENTY-THREE

WHAT'S HAPPENING OUT THERE?

In 1969, a 32-year old Englishman embarked on an unusual ocean adventure. John Fairfax became the first man to successfully row his way across the Atlantic Ocean alone. The courageous sailor took six months to row his 21-foot *Britannia* from the Canary Islands to Ft. Lauderdale, Florida. After he arrived in Florida, Fairfax held a press conference to describe the most exciting moments of his adventure. Newsmen scribbled furiously when Fairfax said an encounter with two flying saucers was the high point of his voyage. "I was looking up one night and saw two bright lights about 20 degrees above the horizon," Fairfax said. "I saw two bright lights that were at least ten times more brilliant than Venus. These objects absolutely were not stars. They climbed into the sky hanging close together and then they separated."

Fairfax reported one object was flying low, the other high. "The high one moved toward the constellation of Ursa Major," he went on. "Then the two objects vanished. While these two objects were in view, I had a strange feeling come over me. This would be like a hypnotic trance. It was strange because I had the feeling of being told to go away. I kept replying "no" to this feeling." When the objects disappeared, the strange feeling also left Fairfax. He came out of the trancelike state and found he was sweating profusely. He also saw that the cigarette he had been smoking was nothing but a long ash.

Dr. Gil E. Gilly, an industrial psychologist from Phoenix, Arizona, is also known as "Mr. ESP", due to his psychic ability. He believes extraterrestrial beings have kidnapped people in the Triangle for experiments on flying saucers. "I attribute a lot of these disappearances in the Triangle to just this sort of thing," said Dr. Gilly. "Just as we dissect animals to learn what's inside, these beings from other worlds are looking into us. They dispose of the bodies here on earth. I look for some of these

MYSTERIOUS DISAPPEARANCES: THEY NEVER CAME BACK

bodies to start turning up within a few months due to the result of tornadoes."

Page Bryant is a Jacksonville, Florida psychic who recently flew over the Triangle while in a trance. She also says the area is a UFO base, that disappearances are caused by an "unknown energy force."

". . . Her record for accurate psychic predictions is clearly established," reported the *National Tattler* recently. During an appearance on Allen Moore's radio talk show on Jacksonville radio station WAPE, Page Bryant interrupted her host to say she was receiving strong impressions of an airplane crash in the north. Moments later, a news service teletype machine typed out a bulletin that a Northwest Orient plane had crashed.

Page Bryant made a prediction "that another ship would vanish in the Triangle within a few months." Shortly after the prediction was proclaimed, a Greek ship *The Persistence*, a 375-foot vessel, vanished without explanation.

The desire to fly over the Triangle occurred to Mrs. Bryant recently. "I don't know why that idea came to me," she said. "One night I just blurted it out to a group of guests in my home. They sat there staring at me, wondering what had happened."

Mrs. Bryant later decided that her psychic senses could get in touch with "vibrations of that area and gain some definite insight as to what in the world, or out of this world, is going on down there."

She explained, "All of the people missing down there may not really be gone from us forever. It's possible that whatever is behind these mysteries can be understood. If we don't reach out to contact, to see, to feel their presence, then they may just stay lost forever."

Mrs. Bryant, witness Cynthia Stanley, and pilot Bob Burr took off in a Cessna 172 from St. Petersburg for a flight over the Atlantic to the Bahama islands, down to Walker Cay, then across the Bahamas again before returning to Florida. The flight went well in calm, cloudless weather. After crossing over the Bahamas, Mrs. Bryant went into a psychic trance.

". . . In my psychic self, I left the Cessna and was suddenly physically flying in a smaller, private plane," Mrs. Bryant stated. "I was flying toward a mass of storm clouds. The thunder roared terribly, drowning out the plane's engine noise. I was unable to maintain my sense of direction. The compass stopped functioning. I couldn't tell what direction I

MYSTERIOUS DISAPPEARANCES: THEY NEVER CAME BACK

was headed. I couldn't tell the sky from the water. I was lost with blackness all about.

"Suddenly, I saw several bright flashes of yellow-gold lightning. These were extremely powerful flashes. The plane was now bouncing about and I frantically tried to send out an emergency Mayday! on the radio. There was no reply.

"I struggled to gain control of the plane and fly it through an opening visible through the dark clouds. The opening looked like a slit, like light shining under a door. Then the plane was tossed sideways. It seemed to be sucked through this opening. At that precise moment, I felt an immense pressure pushing on my chest, almost crushing me. I felt as if I was being forced out of my bursting skin, being blown apart and flattened. This feeling came as the plane entered the white slit in the sky."

Mrs. Bryant suddenly snapped out of her psychic trance. "I was crying," she related to newsmen, "and I felt nauseous. All around me the sky was serene and blue. Yet, I've never been so scared as I was coming out of the trance that afternoon."

Mrs. Bryant had considerable emotional upheaval involved with her trance experience. She decided hypnotic regression would be the most practical method of reliving the psychic experience to find out more about the Triangle. Al Miner, an Arizona hypnotist who had recently moved to Florida, agreed to induce hypnosis. Two sessions brought out startling revelations about the Triangle. "These were so unusual that I flew over the Triangle again with pilot Bob Burr," said Mrs. Bryant. "I went into a light trance and confirmed the psychic impressions we uncovered during hypnosis."

The Florida psychic feels the Triangle of the Lost is a vortex from an unknown energy field. This energy source draws power from the earth's magnetic field and also from other planets. While our most sophisticated instruments cannot detect this energy field, she predicts its force will be measured by 1983. She has also concluded that this unknown energy source allows Unidentified Flying Objects to enter and leave the earth's atmosphere. "Before I made those flights over the Triangle I didn't put much credence into the stories about UFOs," Mrs. Bryant informed newsmen. "Now I'm convinced that the Triangle is an entry and exit point for them. The entire area is the vortex of a magnetic disturbance that enables a UFO to enter or leave our atmosphere."

MYSTERIOUS DISAPPEARANCES: THEY NEVER CAME BACK

Mrs. Bryant, like other psychics and UFO contactees, believes there is an underwater UFO base under the Triangle. "On the initial flight I saw below us—in my mind, while I was in a trance state—an undersea base or cave. I had a very strong psychic impression that this underwater facility was being used as a UFO base. However, I don't want to give anyone the wrong impression. I'm not saying there is a strong and direct connection between the UFO base and the disappearance of all these people."

Mrs. Bryant doesn't feel there is a Triangle involved in the mystery.

"It's actually a tunnel of energy that extends through the earth," she related. "It shoots out through the Atlantic Ocean in the region known as the Triangle. There is a corresponding sector in the Pacific Ocean, south of Japan. This is known as the Devil's Sea and there have also been many disappearances there under unusual circumstances."

In fact, the baffling losses of planes and ships in the Japanese version of the Triangle led to a government financed investigation of that region. Scientists loaded down the *Kaiyo Maru No. 5* with the most advanced electronic detection equipment. They planned to cruise the Devil's Sea, take soundings, record temperatures, magnetic fluctuations, and make a record of any unusual weather disturbances.

Their investigation ended on a frightening note. The survey ship, along with the crew and all scientists aboard, sailed into the Devil's Sea in 1955. Despite the presence of several radio transmitters aboard the ship, the vessel and everyone aboard vanished!

Mrs. Bryant went on to explain that a few smaller boats and planes have been taken by UFO occupants for purposes of scientific research. "But the vast majority of the ships and planes have disappeared because they sailed into the heart of this energy beam," she related. "The surface point of this energy field varies from one spot to another within the Triangle. This is why ships and planes have disappeared at different locations. The nature of the energy field is such that anyone entering the force is disoriented. There is tremendous confusion to whatever and whoever enters the heart of the beam. That explains why many missing ships and planes have reported their last positions at such varying points."

Mrs. Bryant believes the missing ships or planes actually dematerialize and go into another dimension. "They're dead to us on this plane

MYSTERIOUS DISAPPEARANCES: THEY NEVER CAME BACK

of existence," she went on. "But their energies and their spirits go on. I know because on the initial flight over the Triangle, I made transmedium contact with a gunner who vanished on December 5, 1945."

"The Twelve Devil's Graveyards Around the World" by Ivan T. Sanderson was published in the October, 1972, issue of *Saga Magazine*. Saga's editor, Martin Singer, has consistently published regular reports on UFOs, keeping his readers well informed on all aspects of the mystery. Using Lloyd's of London files for his research, Sanderson plotted the disappearance of planes and ships around the globe. He discovered that most of the missing craft vanished in six lozenge-shaped areas. These danger spots were located between 30 and 40 degrees latitude north and south of the Equator. Both the Bermuda Triangle and the Japanese Devil Sea were included in the list.

Working with his theory for several months, Sanderson came up with twelve "*Devil's Graveyards*" or "anomalies." They were focused around 36 degrees north and south latitudes. Five each were located in the north and south hemisphere. The north and south polar regions made up the final two danger zones. "All of these lozenge shaped areas have a high incidence of missing ships," Sanderson said. "The Bermuda Triangle is the best known because it has more traffic. The others are located in areas with a lesser amount of surface or air traffic. Yet they also appear to have considerable evidence of being the center of some type of space-time anomaly."

Summing up his research, Sanderson said: "The result of all this is that we now have concrete evidence that there are 'time anomalies' (of airplanes flying in and out of these danger zones) . . . If these blobs are situated where they are alleged to be, they form a precise (Trigonometrical) grid covering our earth like a vast fish net of triangles with equilateral sides, thus there ought to be—or must be—some logical explanation. Since no other physical cause fits the case, we can but fall back on the only one that has proved out so far. That is, something goes wrong with time in these areas."

During a debate on the Dick Cavett television show, Sanderson discovered the entertainer Arthur Godfrey had difficulty flying into the area of the "Devil's Sea." Godfrey explained he was flying around the world in a two engine jet. When he was over the "Devil's Sea," his instruments, compasses, and radios went dead for more than an hour. Godfrey said: "When you've only got about four hours of fuel, that's not a nice thing to have happen to you."

MYSTERIOUS DISAPPEARANCES: THEY NEVER CAME BACK

Godfrey was also supposed to fly back to the mainland on a large experimental plane called the Mars. His flight to the air field was late on arrival and the Mars took off without him. "I was watching the plane on radar when... suddenly-" Godfrey snapped his fingers- "She just wasn't there any more!" He added that investigators never found a trace of the giant ship.

"They never found anything," Godfrey emphasized. "Not even a tiny bit of debris or a little oil slick. There just wasn't anything left of the plane."

On another occasion, Sanderson reported on a number of sightings of giant underwater domes. These transparent devices allegedly were seen by commercial divers near the coast of Spain. Sanderson reported that lobster fishermen have seen similar domes beneath the waters of the U.S. Continental Shelf. He theorized these might be part of a worldwide grid being built by undersea terrestrials for combatting the pollution of the oceans by homo sapiens.

The idea of an underwater civilization, giant domed cities beneath the sea, and UFO bases under the Triangle is enough to boggle anyone's mind. It doesn't matter where the occupants of such a facility originate; they can be terrestrial or extraterrestrial. The very thought of their existence would drive most people to the nearest cocktail lounge.

We can enjoy the forecasts and impressions from psychics, speculate on the various theories, and wonder about other dimensions, other worlds. Until more facts have been generated about the Triangle of the Lost, we must withhold judgment. A logical explanation of the Triangle phenomena has been released by the commander of the U. S. Coast Guard, Seventh District. It reads:

"... Mysterious, mystic, supernatural... unlikely! This area, commonly bounded by Bermuda, Florida and Puerto Rico might have on the surface what would be considered a high disappearance rate, but you have also to consider the amount of air and sea traffic in this area. Thousands of ships, small boats, and commercial and private aircraft transit the waters off Florida's east coast. The majority of disappearances in this area can be attributed to its unique environmental features: first, the Gulf Stream with its turbulence and swiftness, can quickly erase any sign of disaster; and second, the weather in the Caribbean-Atlantic area, with its ability to change rapidly, can produce thunder storms and waterspouts without warning, making pilots and navigators face sudden catastrophe. "The topography of the ocean floor in the area between San Juan and

MYSTERIOUS DISAPPEARANCES: THEY NEVER CAME BACK

Bermuda varies from extensive shoal areas in the islands to some of the deepest trenches in the world. With the interaction of strong currents over many reefs, the topography is constantly changing and hazards to the mariner can be swift.

"There are some possible justifications for frequent accidents and so-called mysterious disappearances within the area, but the Coast Guard is not impressed with explanations from the supernatural. The combined unpredictable forces of man and nature are sufficient to supply unexplainable occurrences.

"A problem we face here in south Florida is the large number of boaters transiting the waters between Florida's gold coast and the Bahama Islands. Too many times, people will try to make the crossing with a boat too small, a lack of knowledge of the area, and a lack of good seamanship, but they insist on trying. That's what keeps the Coast Guard Air Station at Miami the busiest search and rescue facility in the world. When people exercise less than mature judgment, show no respect for the sea, and venture into it, the odds are against them.

"The Coast Guard feels there is nothing mysterious about disappearances in the particular section of this ocean. Weather conditions, equipment failure, and human error, rather than something from the supernatural, are what have caused these tragedies."

In compiling data for this project, I telephoned U.S. Navy officials in Washington for their reaction on the Triangle of the Lost. I was finally connected to an Admiral in the Pentagon. "We don't believe in supernatural reasons for these disappearances," he announced. "We've found that the people who believe in the Triangle also believe in UFOs, sea serpents, alien entities, and a lot of other claptrap. I've even read about a 'hole in the sky' where planes are supposed to fly into another dimension. Until someone comes up with a fact—just one single fact—we'll attribute these happenings to natural causes."

Dr. M. K. Jessup would have disagreed with the admiral's statements. An astronomer and an expert on the moon, Dr. Jessup's book *The Case for UFOs* (Citadel Press; New York, 1955) advanced the opinion that ". . . our aerial age on earth has become of great interest to our space neighbors." Jessup discussed disappearing ships, crews, and the mysteries within the Triangle. He wrote: ". . . I believe that the space between the earth and moon is occupied, however thinly, by large navigable constructions of a rigid nature, whose size may range from one to many miles in diameter, and which have a planetary appearance when

MYSTERIOUS DISAPPEARANCES: THEY NEVER CAME BACK

seen in telescopes. There are other bodies of a cloud-like nature which cast shadows on both the earth and moon, and which may range the entire solar system accompanying comets. These also, or their smaller components, sometimes approach earth. All of these objects evince evidences of control by intelligence, as do the more recently sighted UFOs."

Jessup believed that UFO occupants were inhabitants of, or associated with, these giant spheres in the sky. "They are of many types," he explained, "and in fact it does seem that many of them have the ability to change shape. They seem to be of two sorts: the solid or material, and the massless or ethereal. All exhibit elements of control, but the weightless ones seem more to have the appearance of remote control. Solid types seem to be discoid or to be spherical or spindle shaped, and these shapes, in themselves, are indicative of intelligent construction."

Jessup felt it was not necessary to identify UFO occupants as space visitors from Mars, Alpha Centauri, or some other planet. "They are a part of our immediate family," he insisted, "a part of the earth-moon binary-planet. They didn't have to come here from millions of miles out there. They've been around on our planet for thousands of years. Whether we belong to them is debatable—we might be owned like cattle. Perhaps, we belong to each other by common origin and association in a complex problem. If we keep our head, this problem may soon be settled."

Before his death in 1959, Jessup stated UFOs were a connecting link with the first wave of civilization on earth. "They've been used against us in a few minor and relatively insignificant cases," he said. "But they have primarily been friendly or indifferent to the fate of homo sapiens."

Vanishing ships and crews . . . airplanes that fly into some unknown zone . . . UFOs and the hint of undersea cities . . . strange spectres, ghost ships and the Sargasso Sea . . . These are just a few of the ingredients in the mystery of the Triangle of the Lost. We've looked at a massive amount of evidence going back to the earliest exploration of the New World. We've discovered that "something" is happening to people who enter the Triangle. Whether this is from natural or other causes is debatable. We can only investigate and speculate on the mystery until new evidence is brought forth that may solve the mystery of what happened to everyone.

You are the jury on the case of the Triangle of the Lost.

What is your decision?

MYSTERIOUS DISAPPEARANCES: THEY NEVER CAME BACK

CHAPTER TWENTY-FOUR

IS IT POSSIBLE WE WILL NEVER SOLVE THE MANY PUZZLES OF THE SEAS?

Strange disappearances in the Triangle of the Lost have perplexed even the most skeptical investigator. Altogether, according to Dr. Ivan T. Sanderson, there are twelve equally baffling triangles located around the globe. One of the most mysterious is the frightening Devil's Sea—a vast stretch of dangerous water in the Pacific Ocean. This deadly zone stretches from the corner of Japan to the Philippine Islands, over to Guam and back to Japan. Thousands of giant steamships, airplanes, fishing vessels, and helicopters have vanished in the Devil's Sea. There is a frequent absence of wreckage to provide a clue to what may have happened to the victims of these disasters.

Typical of the strange events that plague navigators in the Devil's Sea was the case of the *Tiki Maru*, a Japanese fishing vessel. The *Tiki Maru* was in the Devil's Sea on April 6, 1965, and the six-man crew was casting their nets into the Pacific Ocean for another day's fishing.

Suddenly, the serenity of the morning was shattered by a deafening explosion. The violent noise caused several of the crewmen to be deaf for several hours. The ocean waters suddenly began to churn and the 65-foot fishing boat rocked precariously in an onslaught of high waves.

"It was beyond anything I've ever seen," recalled the captain of the *Tiki Maru*. "When we heard the explosion, the sky was clear. There wasn't a cloud anywhere. The horizon was devoid of any sign of life. There wasn't another ship in the area."

The captain and the crew had served in the Imperial Japanese Navy during World War II. Curious about the origin of the explosion, they con-

MYSTERIOUS DISAPPEARANCES: THEY NEVER CAME BACK

sidered the possibility of a secret nuclear bomb test by the United States. "I discounted an atomic bomb test at once," the captain reported when his vessel arrived in the Japanese port. "If they were testing some awesome new weapon, there would have had to be a blinding flash in the sky."

The radioman on the *Tiki Maru* broadcast queries in international morse code. His message received a radioed reply from a U. S. Navy destroyer. There were no other ships in the area, no weapons tests were being made, and unusual aerial or sea phenomena were not reported. "To this day we don't know what happened to create an explosion of such magnitude," reported the skipper of the *Tiki Maru*.

Strange ocean noises within the Devil's Sea have been reported since sailors first sailed into the region. The Japanese called the sounds by the unusual name of "*uminari*." The *uminari* are most often heard close to shore. Several investigators have advanced the theory that the loud explosions are created by undersea earthquakes. Others state the thunderclap-like sounds may be due to some phenomenal wave action. These explosions might also be caused by the pressure of subterranean gases being released under great pressure from the bottom of the sea.

The strange sounds are sometimes accompanied by an unusual fog that rolls in shortly after the explosive noises. A yacht captained by R. C. Burton sailed from Manila toward Japan in 1952. The 90-foot yacht was headed for a Japanese shipyard for repairs and the installation of new electronic equipment. Midway in the Devil's Sea, Burton and his crew were terrorized by the sound of "strange popping noises" around the vessel.

"At first we thought we were being bombarded by another ship," Burton reported after the incident. "We were cranking up the radio to send a mayday signal for help when the fog moved in."

Captain Burton and his crewmen were scrambling over the deck when they began to glow like bright phantoms. The sailors' hair stood on end as they dashed around the deck in near panic. The fog was accompanied by unusual disturbances in the yacht's navigating equipment. Burton reported that the compass spun wildly. Later, he reported the craft was possibly magnetized. "Metal objects were locked together," he said. "There was a metal door attached to the iron frame. We attempted to open the door, but it was sealed tight. However, the door opened easily when the fog vanished."

MYSTERIOUS DISAPPEARANCES: THEY NEVER CAME BACK

Captain Burton explained that the fog enveloped the vessel for approximately ten minutes. Engines stopped working. Compasses gyrated wildly. The craft was totally disabled by the unusual vapor. "There was another factor to the phenomena," Burton said. "The ship and everything on it glowed brilliantly. There appeared to be a fluorescent brightness to any living organism."

When the ship sailed out of the fog the magnetic phenomena vanished. The glowing disappeared. The engines resumed working. The navigational equipment functioned normally. "I discussed the incident with the authorities when we arrived in Japan. They were unable to provide any reasonable explanation."

Captain Burton got in touch with me several years after the incident. "I'd like to know if you've heard of similar phenomena," he related.

He was referred to the case involving the British steamship *Mohican* on a voyage to Philadelphia on July 31, 1904. Captain G. F. Urquhart and his crew were victims of a similar fog that contained magnetic properties. Several of the *Mohican's* crewmen were allegedly paralyzed while they were surrounded by a strange vapor. Records do not indicate whether this paralysis was due to the fog or fear.

"My men were in absolute terror," Captain Urquhart informed newsmen. "I attempted to keep them calm, but they ran around the ship like ghosts. Several men were paralyzed by the fog. The *Mohican* glowed as if it was on fire!"

Captain Urquhart said the ship's voyage had been uneventful until fog appeared on the horizon. "We didn't expect trouble," he went on. "It looked like any other bank of fog you might run into. We remained in the fog for approximately one-half hour. Then the vapor lifted away from the ship, moving eastward out to sea."

The *Mohican* underwent wild magnetic effects on the ship's compass. There were also some problems with the ship's engine, although records do not indicate the nature of the disturbances. To date, these are the only incidents brought to my attention about these mysterious fogs.

Charles Devlin and I became acquainted several months ago while attending a seminar on paranormal subjects. Devlin is a former World War II fighter pilot who established a trading company in Asia after the war. He prospered as Japanese products were exported to other nations.

MYSTERIOUS DISAPPEARANCES: THEY NEVER CAME BACK

During a visit to the United States, Devlin and I discussed the Devil's Sea.

"I wouldn't have given a thought to flying saucers a few years ago," Devlin stated. "The thought that the Bermuda Triangle or the Devil's Sea was dangerous areas seemed like fantasy. That was before my flight from the Philippines in 1967."

Devlin explained that he was in his private jet aircraft on a return flight to Japan. "The night was clear, the weather was excellent. It was a perfect night for flying," he reported. "My pilot was relaxing while I flew the plane. It started when I saw a light flicker in the corner of my eye. I turned and looked out the window and saw a strange glowing object pacing the plane. Seconds later, my pilot nudged me and pointed to a similar object on the right side of the plane."

The businessman described the objects as translucent, round in shape, and glowing with a brilliant intensity. "Imagine a soap bubble that's six foot in diameter and able to fly along at several hundred miles an hour," he went on.

"That's what the thing looked like. The objects were too bright to see what might have been inside."

Devlin and his pilot were both terrified by the objects. "They were pacing us at close range," he reported. "They were totally unlike anything I'd ever seen. I banked the plane in an attempt to get away from the objects. They must have been locked in on the plane in some fashion. I banked sharply and they changed course with me. I cut back on my air speed; they did the same. In fact, they seemed to almost anticipate what I was going to do. They just rode along beside the plane, not moving closer or going away."

Throughout the incident, Devlin experienced no problems with his navigational instruments. "Everything worked," he related. "The globs flew along with us for about twenty minutes. Then, they vanished. One moment they were there beside us, glowing as bright as a streetlight. The next instant they were gone."

Devlin and his pilot started to relax. They were discussing the unusual objects when another device popped up in the night sky ahead of the plane. "This was also spherical in shape," Devlin stated. "At first, it looked like a tiny white spot in the sky. A distant star or something like that. Then, the object increased in size. It moved swiftly across the sky in front of us. The speed was faster than that of any known aircraft."

MYSTERIOUS DISAPPEARANCES: THEY NEVER CAME BACK

After a series of aerial maneuvers, the UFO dimmed. The device hovered and started changing colors. "Blue seemed to be the predominant color," said Devlin. "But it seemed to be undergoing a constant change of color. When the device turned orange, it tossed off a fiery tail of sparks. That's when the light turned into a metallic disc-shaped object."

Devlin described the disc as round, definitely metallic, and approximately thirty feet in diameter. "There was a cockpit rising above the body of the object," he related. "As we came closer we could see someone-or something-moving around inside the cockpit. It seemed to be lighted from the inside. We couldn't distinguish a form too well because of the distance."

As Devlin and his pilot watched, the disc cast off another fiery tail of sparks, then streaked off in a westerly direction. Both men were shaken by the sightings. "I decided to make a report when I got back to Japan," Devlin went on. "However, I discovered there isn't an agency to handle an investigation of a sighting in international territory. I dropped the idea. Since then, however, I've become interested in UFOs. I think they're responsible for the disappearances in the Bermuda Triangle and the Devil's Sea. These areas may contain underwater bases for aliens from outer space."

Devlin's sighting is not the first time that UFOs have popped up out of the Devil's Sea. On July 25, 1957, Russian antiaircraft batteries on the Kuril Islands engaged in open warfare with hundreds of UFOs. According to eye witnesses, the night skies were filled with saucer-shaped objects.

Reuters News Service reported: "Last night the batteries of Kuril Island opened fire on UFOs. Japanese authorities reported that the whole Soviet artillery was in action and that powerful searchlights lit up the sky."

The antiaircraft guns boomed throughout the night; they failed to shoot down a single UFO. The United States Air Force hastened to inform the suspicious Russians that there was no American aircraft flying near the Kuril Islands. Radio Moscow broadcast the American communique to subdue growing rumors about an impending invasion of the Kurils by the United States.

Kuril Islanders witnessed the invasion of these strange sky visitors. Some reported the UFOs were so numerous as to almost blot out the dark sky.

MYSTERIOUS DISAPPEARANCES: THEY NEVER CAME BACK

...Strange fogs!

...Unusual explosions!

...Visitors from the land of UFOs!

These are just a few of the mysterious phenomena in the Devil's Sea. Thousands of ships have vanished in this deadly triangle. It would require another book to list the roll call of unusual happenings in the Devil's Sea and other triangles throughout the world.

Yonaguni off the coast of Japan

MYSTERIOUS DISAPPEARANCES: THEY NEVER CAME BACK

MYSTERIOUS DISAPPEARANCES: THEY NEVER CAME BACK

ADVERTISEMENT

Angels Of The Lord

MORE PAGES! LARGE FORMAT! BONUS DVD! ADDED INFORMATION FROM THE PEN OF WILLIAM ORIBELLO!

LEARN THE METHODS NECESSARY TO CALL UPON YOUR GUARDIAN ANGEL FOR GUIDANCE AND PROTECTION

PSALMS 90:11-13 DICTATES: "The Lord hath given his Angels charge over thee, to keep thee in all thy ways."

NOW FOR THE FIRST TIME YOU CAN LEARN ALL THERE IS TO KNOW ABOUT GOD'S SPECIAL MESSENGERS AND COMMAND THEM TO DO YOUR BIDDING

ADD THIS POWERFUL AMULET TO YOUR ORDER

Join Spiritist William Alexander Oribello, Plus Tim Beckley, Rev. Frank Stranges, Arthur Crockett and Sean Casteel As They Reveal The Truth About The Angelic Kingdom. Learn:

- Why Angels Were Created.
- How Smart Angels Can Be.
- The Role Of The Angel Of Death (NOT Evil).
- What Their Purpose In The Lord's Scheme Of Things Really Is.
- The Actual Language Of The Angels And How To Speak It.
- How You Can Call Upon Them Directly For Guidance And Protection In Order To Make Your Own Life More Blissful.
- How It is Possible To Keep The Devil At Arm's Distance.
- How Angels Are Ranked.
- How To Get Them To Utilize Their Fiery Swords.
- Learn The Differentiation Between The Various Angels And Their Individual Functions There Are: Archangels. Seraphim. Cherubian. The Thrones. The Dominations, The Virtues. And The Powers.
- What Unspoken Blessings You Can Expect To Receive.
- Get Them To Fight Your Battles And Bring About Victory In Your Life.
- How Angels Are Ranked.
- How To Use Them As Your Personal Messenger To Turn In Your Favor The Thoughts And Minds Of Others.
- The "Ruling Class" Of The Archangels.
- Getting The Attention Of Master Teacher Angels.
- The Days And Hours Angels Are Closest To You.
- Angels Of The Spirit World.

Order Now: enables you to "call out" to your Guardian Angel in ordinary as well as times of great need. Here is everything you are required to know to bring about a stronger than ever bond with your angel guides and have them answer your cry for help and assistance in matters big and small. Send **$22.00 + $5.00 S/H** now and receive a BONUS DVD with more valuable information.

Timothy Beckley · Box 753 · New Brunswick, NJ 08903

ARCH ANGEL MEDALLION FOR YOUR GUIDANCE, PROTECTION AND PERSONAL GAIN

Love! Finances! Dependence! Reliance!—$38.00

This powerful Arch Angel Amulet, consists of a wide circle exterior, with an Arch Angel spell engraved along the outer edge in a magical script reading "Before me, Behind me, to my right and to my left, I am surrounded by protection." It comes with a small sheet explaining the names of four major Arch Angels as well as the wording with which it is inscribed. Though it does not come with a chain, this amulet is approximately 1 3/8" in diameter and made of the finest lead-free pewter. Design may vary from that in ad.

SAVE WITH THIS SPECIAL OFFER Angel Of The Lord Expanded Edition and your own Arch Angel Amulet for just $55.00 + $5.00 S/H

ADVERTISEMENT

NEWLY EXPANDED, LARGE FORMAT EDITION WILLIAM ALEXANDER ORIBELLO'S
CANDLE BURNING MAGIC WITH THE PSALMS
THE SCRIPTURES TEACH US THAT... "IT IS FAR BETTER TO LIGHT A CANDLE THAN TO CURSE THE DARKNESS."

IF YOU ARE LOOKING FOR SPIRITUAL GUIDANCE IN YOUR LIFE THIS MAY BE THE MOST IMPORTANT BOOK YOU WILL EVER OWN!

All you need to fulfill your inner most desires, dreams and wishes is a match, ordinary candles, oils and the ability to recite a specific Psalm from Scripture. Candle Burning Magic with The Psalms is the only book to combine both of these important elements.

In an easy to read style, William Oribello – one of the most dynamic spiritists of the past century — unlocks for the serious learner the secret code encrypted in the Psalms which will bring about positive results in the area of personal spiritual growth, as well as with everyday matters. Here are Psalms you can read aloud or to yourself along with the specific colored candles you need to burn.

OVER 150 PROVEN RITUALS USING GOD'S INSPIRED WORDS
OVERCOME DEPRESSION · EXPERIENCE GREAT JOY · OVERCOME ATTACKERS AND ROBBERS · BE PROTECTED FROM SUFFERING · KEEP BAD LUCK AWAY · RECEIVE INSTRUCTIONS IN DREAMS · RECEIVE GREAT STRENGTH · REGAIN PEACE WITH A PERSON YOU HAVE HAD A FALLING OUT WITH · RECEIVE DIVINE GRACE, LOVE AND MERCY · HELP IN COURT CASES · OBTAIN GREAT FINANCIAL REWARDS · HAVE A STRONG WILL · ATTRACT LOVE AND FRIENDSHIP · BANISH MARRIAGE PROBLEMS · · BRING ABOUT GOOD FORTUNE · DRAW PROSPERITY AND MONEY INTO YOUR LIFE

☐ Order the new large format, 200 page, edition of
CANDLE BURNING MAGIC WITH THE PSALMS for just $20.00 + $5.00 S/H

WANT TO LEARN MORE? FOR THE SERIOUS STUDENT ONLY!
NOW HEAR FOR THE FIRST TIME REV. ORIBELLO DELIVER A DRAMATIC LECTURE/SERMON ON THE MAGIC OF THE INNER LIGHT

☐ This special **MAGIC OF INNER LIGHT** package includes (1) Rare **Audio CD-MAGIC OF THE INNER LIGHT**, available no where else, on which Rev Oribello delivers a firey sermon/lecture. Two personal monographs available here only. (2) **COSMIC MYSTERIES UNVEILED** which provides a concise means of getting on "The Path," utilizing a simplified system of inner development, mental imagery and symbolic illustrations.

And ☐ **PERSONALITY UNMASKED**, revealing how you can find out what other people are really like. This entire *"For Serious Students Only"* package is just $29.95 + $5.00 S/H

( ) **SPECIAL COMBO** - All items this page - Candle Psalms Book, and Inner Light package — just $45.00 + $5.00 S/H

Timothy Beckley · Box 753 · New Brunswick, NJ 08903

ADVERTISEMENT

NEWLY OFFERED: THE SECRET HISTORY OF EXTRATERRESTRIALS EXPLORES THE INFLUENCE AND ROLE OF ETS IN THE MILITARY, GOVERNMENT, TECHNOLOGY, HISTORY, AND THE COMING NEW AGE.

Includes the Iraqi Stargate, the Hybrid Project of alien interbreeding. Surveys contact with ETs, abductions, alien technology and exopolitics, genetic tampering by ETs, and the history behind the Nazis and UFO and their link to underground bases in the Antarctica. This book sketches out a breathtaking vision of the planetary revolution just around the corner. — 328 pages. 8 color pages.
Order Secret History Of ETs by Ken Kasten,
$18.95 + $5.00 S/H

Timothy Beckley • Box 753 • New Brunswick, NJ 08903

WHO WAS THE "MYSTERIOUS ALIEN" WITH AMAZING POWERS?

FIND OUT THE SECRETS OF THE "STRANGER AT THE PENTAGON"

**70 MINUTE DVD
And Rare Report:
MY FRIEND BEYOND EARTH**

The late Dr. Frank E. Stranges says Val Thor was a guest of the U.S. military for several years.

Left to right: Jill, Donn & Valiant Thor. All three were reportedly from Venus. Photographed in 1959 at Highbridge, New Jersey.

LEARN: WHY HE HAD NO FINGERPRINTS
THE REASON HE CAME TO EARTH
WHY HE COULD NOT BE HARMED
WHAT HIS RELIGIOUS BELIEFS WERE
WHERE HE IS TODAY

For your copy of STRANGER AT THE PENTAGON THE VIDEO VERSION, send $17.50 + $5.00 S/H and we will include a bonus of the very rare booklet *My Friend Beyond Earth.*

Timothy Green Beckley • Box 753
New Brunswick, New Jersey 08903

PSYCHIC GEM FROM SPACE
Researchers claim Moldavite opens Interdimensional Doorways

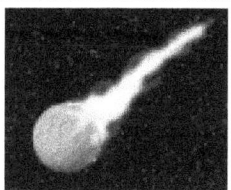

The rare stone Moldavite can only be found along the remote Moldau River in Czechoslovakia. Scientists have determined that it fell to Earth 15 million years ago.

The stone is believed to give its wearer enhanced "powers of perception" bordering on the supernatural. It vibrates 80 times faster than quartz and enables the participant to tie a direct line into the higher dimensional communique systems.

It is also a way of immediately clearning and aligning the entire chakara system and, according to the level of awareness reached, it will make the connection to the so-called 8th chakra or "telepathic receiver band."

❏ **MOLDIVATE GEMSTONE KIT** - Includes a small pendant and a copy of the 178 page *MOLDAVITE STARBORN STONE* by Robert Simmons as well as the remarkable *"Divine Fire"* audio CD narrated by Brad Steiger. — $42.00 + $5.00 S/H
❏ **LARGER STONE AND KIT** — $62.00 + $5.00 S/H

Timothy Beckley • Box 753
New Brunswick, NJ 08903

Credit Card Hotline:
732-602-3407.
PayPal orders may be addressed to
MRUFO8@hotmail.com

ADVERTISEMENT

AVAILABLE AGAIN IN THREE POPULAR SIZES!
Nikola Tesla's "Miracle" PURPLE ENERGY PLATES

The Plates Function As Transceivers, Creating A Field Of Energy Around Themselves That Will Penetrate Any Material Substance. This Energy Is Very Beneficial To All Life...Plant, Animal Or Human!

In the 1940s, electrical engineer Ralph Bergstresser met the wizard Nikola Tesla in an effort to explore the energetic options to help end WWII. Bergstresser was impressed with the knowledge and deep humanitarian ideals of Tesla. Tesla gave Ralph inspiration regarding his knowledge and access of "free energy" when he offered a curious clue. "If you want to understand the secrets of nature look to vibration and frequency."

Tesla died shortly after the meeting but Bergstresser spent the next 20 years breaking through the veil of matter to access Tesla's ideas. In 1965 he introduced the Tesla Purple Energy Plates to the world. He chose an inexpensive medium that, when altered, would act as a transceiver to draw in and radiate Universal Life Force or "Free Energy."

The Tesla Purple Energy Plates are a beautiful violet color and are a window into the 4th and 5th dimensional fields. They radiate their energy for a distance of 10 to 18 inches.

Experimentation has shown there are many uses for the plates. Here are only a few of them:

- Place a small size plate into a pocket or purse for more energy. Actual physical contact is not required.
- Place a large plate in refrigerator (center shelf is best). Food, except meat and fish, will stay fresh longer.
- Place a plate beneath a sick houseplant, or water sick plants with water that has been place on a plate overnight.
- Place a small plate in dog or cat bed, or under food dish.
- To energize crystals, place on a Purple Plate for 12 hours.
- Use a plate on injured area of any living thing.
- Under computers to block harmful radiation.

IMPORTANT NOTICE: The FDA and AMA prohibit making claims related to the mental or physical illness of individuals using unapproved methods of treatment. Purported "benefits" have been reported by private users employing no medical training. Users of Tesla Purple Plates should, under no circumstances, terminate any professional care they may be currently undergoing.

- Travelers can carry a small plate to energize their drinking water and eliminate illness or upset stomach.
- Small plates placed on forehead to alleviate headache, on joints to alleviate gout and arthritis, on stomach to stop nausea.
- Place on forehead to help remember dreams and promote deeper meditation.

ORDER YOUR PLATES TODAY IN ANY ONE OF THREE SIZES

❏ **PURPLE DISC—1½ INCHES IN DIAMETER**—Attach to pet collar or under water dish. Create a necklace for yourself or put one in each shoe. Carry in purse, wallet or pocket.
—$17.00 OR 3 FOR $40.00 + $5.00 S/H.

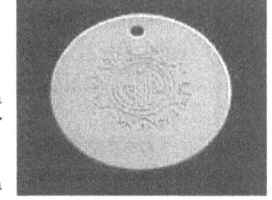

❏ **SMALL PLATE—4½ INCHES X 2¾ INCHES**—Best for using on a painful area. Put under glass or bottled water, or under your sheet, on pillow, or in your favorite chair
—$25.00 OR 3 FOR $68.00 + $5.00 S/H.

❏ **LARGE PLATE—12" X 12"** (approx)—Because of its size, this plate carries more energy. Excellent for refrigerator shelf. Under a bag of groceries. Under a gallon of water to drink or to feed plants. Multiple uses—**$75.00 OR 3 FOR $200.00 + $8.00 S/H.**

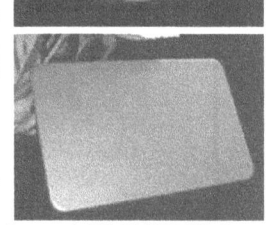

NOTE: Each plate comes with report on how best to utilize the awesome power of the plates.

WANT TO LEARN MORE ABOUT TESLA?

❏ **THE LOST JOURNALS OF NIKOLA TESLA—Time Travel, Alternative Energy, And The Secret Of NAZI Flying Saucers.** New edition. 4 chapters added. Author Tim Swartz investigates the stolen files of Tesla, removed ny the FBI following Tesla's death. **—$24.00 + $5.00 S/H**

❏ **THE SECRETS OF NIKOLA TESLA DVD COMBO**—Two full length features on one DVD tells the complete story! Here is the truth personified about an amazing man that big business tried to silence.—**$18.00 + $5.00 S/H**

Timothy Beckley • Box 753 • New Brunswick, NJ 08903

Credit card payment through PayPal • All cards accepted • No registration email: MRUFO8@hotmail.com and we send PayPal invoice. Fastest method, safe, secure, easy • USA bank checks, Int'l or postal money orders or Western Union

ADVERTISEMENT

OVER 900 PAGES OF SUPPRESSED BIBLICAL HISTORY FROM THE ORIGINS OF HUMANKIND TO THE LAST JUDGEMENT!

THE FORGOTTEN BOOKS OF EDEN
THE LOST BOOKS OF THE BIBLE—Large Print Edition
Suppressed By The Church ... But Now Fully Revealed
The Uncensored Truth About The Origins of Humankind And The Ageless Conflict Between Good And Evil

Here is the story of Adam and Eve which is the most ancient in the world; a story that has survived because it embodies the fight between man and the Devil. Adapted from the work of unknown Egyptians parts of this version are found in the Talmud, the Koran, and elsewhere, showing the vital role it played in the original literature of human wisdom. This adaptation has been passed down and was first written in Arabic and then translated into Ethiopic. It is a detailed history of Adam and Eve and their descendents found nowhere else and how the "Family Tree" ties all of the Old Testament together.

This large print edition also includes 26 Apocryphal books from the first 400 years of Christianity that were not included in the Testaments. The question remains: Why were these divinely inspired works kept out of the Bible by the church? You will find the answers within these pages.

We have combined *THE LOST BOOKS OF THE BIBLE* with another forbidden work known as *THE FORGOTTEN BOOKS OF EDEN* which includes the true story of Adam and Eve's conflict with Satan, as well as the Psalms of Solomon, the Testaments of the Twelve Patriarchs and the Secrets of Eden.

Order your copy of *FORGOTTEN BOOKS OF EDEN/LOST BOOKS OF THE BIBLE* now for just **$39.95 + $5.00 S/H.**

THE FORBIDDEN BOOKS OF THE NEW TESTAMENT

THE MATERIAL IN THE FORBIDDEN BOOKS OF THE NEW TESTAMENT HAS BEEN TRANSLATED FROM ITS ORIGINAL TONGUES BY THE WORLD'S GREATEST SCHOLARS, THE TASK TAKING WELL OVER 100 YEARS

There have been many facts about the life and times of Jesus which have not been included in the New Testament. The documents contained in this large size—8.5x11—450 page edition, were written soon after Christ's crucifixion during the early spread of Christianity, but before the church was able to censor some of the documents for a variety of reasons. Now after over 1500 years of suppression, the shroud of secrecy has been lifted and sincere students of the Bible will be able to read these original chapters and verses, and decide for themselves their authority.

The Birth of Christ — The Early Life of Mary — The Birth of John—The Virgin Birth — The Baptism of Jesus in the Jordan— Christ Praying In The Garden—Peter Cutting Off the Ear of Mulches—The Kiss of Judas — Christ on the Cross—The Resurrection of our Lord — Jesus Ascending to Heaven—The Red Sea Swallowing Up the Army of Pharaoh—Christ's Descent Into Hell — The Last Judgment.

450+ pages 8.5x11 Format Large print Edition — $39.95 + $5.00 S/H
978-1-60611-028-7 • 1-60611-027-6

Timothy Beckley • Box 753 • New Brunswick, NJ 0890
Credit Card Customers Call 732 602-3407
PayPal **MRUFO8@hotmail.com**
Please refer to the order form inside the back cover of this isue for detailed ordering and shipping information. NJ residents add sales tax.

TWO HUGE BOOKS. BUY THEM AS A SET FOR $62.00 + $8.00 S/H OR PURCHASE THEM INDIVIDUALLY

ADVERTISEMENT

A FILM BY TIMOTHY GREEN BECKLEY
SECRETS OF THE VATICAN

FILMED WITHIN THE WALLS OF THE HOLY CITY WITH SECRET CAMERAS

THE VATICAN has been shrouded in mystery and intrigue for centuries. Except for the highest Cardinals and Bishops, the public and even members of the priesthood are not privy to the inner workings of the church. It is rumored that there are, in secret archives, centuries-old artifacts that, if revealed, could embarrass the standard-bearers of the faith.

SEARCHING for the truth has always been Conspiracy Journal's main goal. With this in mind, we recently "invaded" the walls of the Vatican with our hidden cameras on a fact-finding mission. On our return, we followed up our investigation by interviewing such astute researchers as Jordan Maxwell, Brad Steiger and Patricia Ress. The result is an astounding professionally produced video which is available for immediate shipment.

SOME OF THE EXCITING CONTENTS INCLUDE:

· Does the Vatican conceal knowledge that the crucifixion was a fraud? · Is there a secret cabal of Satanists within the Vatican to further the evil conspiracy of the New World Order? · Learn about strange events today! · Can exorcism be a futile effort that often results in the death of the possessed? · What secrets is the Vatican keeping about the perilous future of our world? · Is the Vatican link to the Hubble Telescope evidence that they are aware of a world-destroying comet headed our way?

EXAMINE with these researchers the reports of Vatican conspiracies, anti-semitism, the sinking of the Titantic, the assassination of Lincoln, the true author of Mein Kampf, Satanic Rituals, Celibacy and Madness, Demon Possession, Mystery Cults of Babylon and MORE!

SECRETS OF THE VATICAN—$20.00 + $5.00 S/H

WANT TO LEARN MORE?—THE SECRETS OF THE POPES—This illustrated book by Arthur Crockett includes: St. Malachi's stunning prophecies about the Last Pope · The Pope who tried to turn worthless metal into gold · The Pope who claimed he had a conversation with Jesus · The Pope who professed to read minds · The Pope who forsaw the end of the world · And the startling story of "Pope Joan", who is believed to have been a woman!

ORDER "SECRETS OF THE POPES" FOR JUST $17.50 + $5.00 S/H

SUPER SPECIAL OFFER! SECRETS OF THE VATICAN DVD WITH 2 AUDIO CDS AND THE BOOK, SECRETS OF THE POPES FOR ONLY $32.00 + $5.00 S/H

Payment via PayPal (easiest way) Order by email to MRUFO8@hotmail.com. We will send a PayPal invoice. Or send USA bank check, International or Postal Money Order or Western Union. NO CASH!

ORDER FROM:
Timothy Beckley · Box 753
New Brunswick, NJ 08903

ADVERTISEMENT

CIA AND NAZI COLLABORATION EXPOSED! GERMAN SCIENTISTS UTILIZE TESLA TECHNOLOGY TO CONSTRUCT FLYING SAUCERS

Soon after cessation of hostilities closed World War II, hundreds of former Nazi and SS members were secretly smugged into America to work on military and space programs. They were employed by nearly every one of the military-industrial complex companies, developing bombs, missiles, rockets, aircraft and advanced ground vehicles.

Many former Nazis went to work for the CIA, and, indeed, actually formed the foundation of that agency because they kept accurate records of their enemies (Russia), and the CIA purchased this knowledge and contact information from them.

Both the U.S. and USSR made adequate use of Tesla technologies to create weapons and communications devices previously undreamed of, including — if the records are true — aerial disc platforms, or "Flying Saucers." Intelligence records show that German scientists had built and test-flown several different types of flying discs. The complete plans for one type were captured at the BMW auto factory in Prague at the close of the war.

FIRE FROM THE SKY exposes how it all happened and the consequences with which we all must live today. It also explains the circumstances under which UFO researchers and the public have been manipulated into certain belief patterns, including aspects of the abduction phenomenon which utilizes a high degree of mind control.

OUR SPECIAL PRICE:
$25.00 + $5.00 S/H

EXCLUSIVE BOOK & AUDIO CD SET

( ) WANT TO KNOW MORE?? EVIL AGENDA OF THE SECRET GOVERNMENT — EXPOSING PROJECT PAPER CLIP AND THE UNDERGROUND UFO BASES OF HITLER'S ELITE. Tim Swartz reveals how the Controllers have imitated REAL alien abductions and are breeding a Hybrid Zombie Race.
Add $15.00 to your order!

Timothy Beckley
Box 753 · New Brunswick, NJ
08903

PARTIAL LIST OF CONTENTS: In The Begining; USS Thresher and the U-2; Total Russian Defense; Project Paperclip; Operation Sunrise; Project Overcast; German Scientists and Aliens; NICAP; Then Came 1947; Antarctica; Admiral Byrd and Operation Highjump; Hitler Escaped!; Polar Defenses; UFOs: Nazi or Alien?; Russian Space Program; Scalar Weapons Activated; Rudolph Hess and Secret Space Base; Werner Heisenberg; Who Created The Atomic Bomb?; German Submarines in the South Atlantic; German Flying Saucers; Falklands Islands War; The Kennedy/Nazi Connection; Cover and Concealment; Nikola Tesla: The Forgotten Genius; Nikola Tesla— The Greatest Hacker Of All Time & MORE!

ADVERTISEMENT

NEW AMAZING BOOK!
VISIT THE MOST MYSTERIOUS PLACE ON EARTH!

Sacred Site? Entrance To The Inner Earth? Doorway To Another Dimension? Hidden UFO Base? Time Warp? "Black Hole?"

MYSTERIES OF MOUNT SHASTA
Home Of The Ancient Gods And Underground Dwellers!
ADVENTURE IN WONDER AND TERROR

Come along with paranormal journalist Tim Beckley as he explores what has a reputation for being the most Supernatural locale in North America, if not the world.

You can visit Mt Shasta, climb high up if you are able to take the thin atmosphere and don't mind carrying well needed supplies. What you may find could be nothing unusual (believers say a hypnotic cloak clouds the minds of "non deserving" souls.) Or you could come away with an entirely new attitude on life, just like author Dana Howard who stated, "Mount Shasta is one of several conditioning stations for visitors from outer space." Those who live near the base of the mountain report blue-white lights glowing through the tall pines, and huge mother ships have been seen hovering over its highest peak, flashing in and out of this dimensional reality.

· Here are stories of Lemurians and survivors of other "lost civilizations" who roam the woods freely and occasionally wander into n town to trade gold for supplies.

· Little men who seldom come out except at night to collect edibles and then return to their cavern homes.

· Native Americans residing in the backwoods say they have not only heard the screams of Bigfoot, but have seen these hairy creatures closeup!

· The location of the capitol of the subterranean world known as Telos, occupied by the Ascended Masters of Wisdom. This city is connected to the Hollow Earth through a worldwide network of secret tunnels.

· Accounts of miraculous healings, including those whose eye sight have been regenerated after being struck by mysterious blue beams of light coming from inside the mountain.

The number of unexplained events associated with Mt Shasta are now literally in the hundreds. This large size book of nearly 200, 8x11 pages, makes for exciting reading as well as information you won't find being printed even in the nearby daily and weekly newspapers. Order **MYSTERIES OF MT SHASTA** for just **$29.95 + $5.00 S/H** and join us on an exciting journey into the nether world.

**Mount Shasta Book
Just $29.95 + $5.00 S/H**

Global Communications
Box 753 · New Brunswick, NJ 08903

ADVERTISEMENT

EXPLORE A STRANGE AND HIDDEN REALM KEPT SECRET FROM THE PRYING EYES OF THE PUBLIC. HERE IS PROOF THAT A VAST, UNCHARTED, CIVILIZATION EXISTS INSIDE THE PLANET

PLUS REVELATIONS ABOUT THE SECRET DIARY OF ONE OF THE GREATEST ADVENTURERS WHO EVER LIVED

☐ **Etidorhpa: Strange History Of A Mysterious Being And An Incredible Journey INSIDE THE EARTH**

by John Uri Lloyd with introduction by Timothy Green Beckley— THIS IS THE ONLY FULLY AUTHORIZED — COMPLETE — EDITION OF THIS RARE MANUSCRIPT THAT HAS BEEN UPDATED AND CONTAINS ALL MISSING TEXT AND ILLUSTRATIONS! For decades over 60 pages of this fascinating manuscript had gone missing — or were they mysteriously "removed" because of the nature of their content? "This book," maintains Beckley, "is a masterpiece. It is a mystery within a mystery so intriguing that it has endured for well over a century as a mater piece in occult literature." There are various explanations as to the nature of this tale. . .Is it an absolutely true story of a trip to the earth's interior by the author accompanied by a sightless being with superhuman abilities or is it something a bit more 'Cloak and Dagger?' The author was a member of a secret society — The Masons? — and his journey to a "Hidden World" can only now be told. Come with the author as he probes an unseen universe that has a secret meaning for us all. SOME SAY IT IS A TESTAMENT TO THE TRUE NATURE OF THE CREATOR. – Over 300 large size pages — $22.00

☐ **The Secret Lost Diary of Admiral Richard E. Byrd and The Phantom of the Poles**

by Admiral Richard Byrd, William Reed, Commander X and Tim Swartz—TWO BOOKS IN ONE! In addition to the text of Admiral Byrd's diary is a rare, "long lost" manuscript by William Reed who puts forward his theory that we live on the outside of a hollow globe. Based upon the journals of various seafarers who have explored the regions around the poles, Reed puts forward the following questions: 1. Why is the earth flattened at the poles? 2. Why have the poles never been reached? 3. Why does the sun not appear for so long in winter near the supposed poles? 4. Assuming that the earth is hollow, the interior should be warmer. 5. Why does a compass refuse to work when drawing near the supposed poles? 6. Why are Meteors constantly falling near the supposed poles? 7. Why are great quantities of dust constantly found in the Arctic Ocean? 8. What produces the Aurora Borealis? 9. Why and how are icebergs formed? 10. What causes tidal waves? 11. What causes colored snow in the Arctic region? 12. Why are the nights so long in the polar regions? 13. What causes the great ice-pressure in the Arctic Ocean during still tide and calm weather? 14. Why is the ice filled with rock, gravel, and sand? This is a book that will intrigue and fascinate. It is like nothing you have ever encountered before! — $20.00

☐ **Subterranean Worlds Inside Earth (8th Edition)**

Authored by Timothy Green Beckley, Contributions by Richard Shaver—In "Subterranean Worlds Inside Earth," author Timothy Green Beckley has collected many stories from a vast wealth of sources on the subject of what is often called "The Inner Earth Theory." The theory holds that the Earth does not consist of molten metal at its core, as modern science tells us, but is instead quite hollow inside, and supports several different races of sentient beings as well as their impressive underground cities, said to be linked to one another by underground tunnels with above-ground openings that the occasional surface-dwelling mortal stumbles on to. Much of the information Beckley presents comes from Richard Shaver, who one day began to hear strange voices projected at him as he went about his work. Following the trail that began with that unearthly auditory experience, Shaver eventually came to the conclusion that the voices were coming from somewhere beneath the Earth, from a race of creatures he came to call the "Deros," (degenerate robots.) — $15.00

☐ **Inner Earth People — Outer Space People: A Minister Reveals The Truth About "Alien Beings."**

by William L Blessing —The author, is a full gospel minister who wants to share this vital information with you! Based on Scripture, Rev.Blessing is convinced that there are "three heavens that belong to the Earth. The Apostle Paul tells us that he was 'caught up to the third heaven' (II Cor. 12:2) and while in that heaven he 'heard unspeakable words which it is not lawful for a man to utter.' (II Cor. 12:4)." Blessing states that this area of "darkness" is inhabited by a very evil people. Beyond the darkness is the moon and then the asteroid or planetoid ring of places inhabited by the outer space people. Beyond this first heaven is a vaporous ring in which there are great quantities of ice." According to Blessing, "The Bible teaches us that there are people dwelling in the inside of the Earth. For want of a better name I shall call them Inner Earth People. I would estimate the population of the inner Earth to be ten billion, or about five times more than those of us who live on the surface of the earth. "There are 200,000,000 pilots in the flying saucers that circle the earth." Approx 300 pages. Published at $29.95 – NOW $25.00

☐ **Finding Lost Atlantis Inside The Hollow Earth**

by Brinsley Le Poer Trench, Introduction by Dennis Crenshaw— In addition to being the author of numerous books on UFOs and extraterrestrial archeology, Brinsley Le Poer Trench was for several decades the editor of the prestigious British Flying Saucer Review. But, his greatest influence came about as a member of England's House of Lords. Trench, who held the title Earl of Clancarty, long campaigned in the Halls of Parliament for the Crown to "come clean" on matters related to close encounters. While the Earl strongly endorsed the theory that aliens have been coming here since the dawn of creation, toward the end of his career, his ideas took on a stranger turn, encompassing the notion that an ancient "pre-deluge" civilization existed in what we commonly refer to as the Lost Continent of Atlantis. Intermingling with this Atlantean culture were space beings arriving regularly for various reasons, some beneficial, some destructive. "The result of which," says Brinsley, "is a long panoramic narrative in the form of legends and myths, telling us of gods that come from outer space, who ruled over Atlantis and were the progenitors of our own civilization who fought terrible wars, and made grotesque monsters and giants that turned upon the gods themselves." — $20.00

ALL BOOKS ARE LARGE FORMAT – EASY TO READ. ENJOY ONE OR MORE ITEMS, OR ORDER ALL FIVE INNER EARTH BOOKS FOR JUST $79.95 $6.00 S/H.

FREE DVD WITH ORDERS OF THREE TITLES OR MORE FROM THIS AD

**Timothy Beckley
Box 753
New Brunswick, NJ 08903
Pay Pal: Mrufo8@hotmail.com**

SEE THE COVERS ON PREVIOUS PAGE

ADVERTISEMENT

TIME TRAVEL IS A THING OF THE FUTURE!

ORDINARY PEOPLE HAVE TRAVELED BACK AND FORTH THROUGH THE CORRIDORS OF TIME AND SPACE – THIS COULD BE YOUR OPPORTUNITY TO DO SO AS WELL.

BONUS – ORDER ALL FOUR ITEMS AND RECEIVE BONUS TIME TRAVEL DVD

☐ **Plans For Time Travel Machines That Really Work - Revised And Updated Edition: How To Move Through Time And Space**—Authored by Patricia C Ress, Preliminary work by Steven Gibbs, with Nick Redfern, Commander X, Scott Corrales, Tim R. Swartz

They call Steven L. Gibbs, "The Rain Man Of Time Travel." — Jesse Ventura recently discussed Steven's invention on his TV show, Conspiracy Theory. — You have heard him on Coast to Coast speaking with Art Bell and George Noory — Now learn about some of his simplest devices for Time Travel that you can actually implement to visit the past as well as the future, as meticulously noted by researcher Patricia Ress, who has detailed and sketched out Steven's work at its very basics for all to utilize NOW! Yes! This large workbook and study guide — this is NOT a skimpy pamphlet like others dare to sell — contains actual usable diagrams for time travel machines you can construct in a reasonable amount of time. Most essential parts can be easily obtained in your own town for a modest fee. PLEASE NOTE — THIS MATERIAL IS NOT MEANT TO BE USED FOR UNLAWFUL OR IMMORAL PURPOSES. Furthermore, this book contains GOVERNMENT TIME TRAVEL SECRETS, the codes of which have been cracked by some of the top researchers in this fascinating field. This book is the only reference on the subject that thousands of truth seekers have long been asking for. RIDE THE WAVE OF THE FUTURE! — PERFECTLY SAFE — TRY FOR YOURSELF! — **$24.00**

☐ **Time Travel - Fact Not Fiction: Time Slips, Real Time Machines, And How-To Experiments**—by Commander X and Tim R. Swartz

EINSTEIN ONLY HAD PART OF THE EQUATION! ORDINARY PEOPLE HAVE TRAVELED BACKED AND FORTH THROUGH THE CORRIDOR OF TIME AND SPACE – AND THIS COULD BE YOUR OPPORTUNITY TO DO SO AS WELL. Up until recently it was thought that Einstein had revealed all there ever was to know about time and space and how we could never travel forward or backward in time without reaching the speed of light. Today those that have adopted the "string theory" of Physics have come to believe that everything in the universe exists at one time simultaneously. Retired Intelligence Operative Commander X and Emmy Award winning Tim R. Swartz have declared in this valuable book – written in easy to read terms – that we are not prisoners of Time and Space, but rather are prisoners of our physical bodies and the learned behaviors of existing in the material world. The Universe and its many mysteries await those who are not afraid to throw off the shackles of unawareness and begin the quest of exploration and learning. In TIME TRAVEL – FACT NOT FICTION!, a vastness of relevant topics are reviewed and discussed logically, including: Spontaneous Cases of Time Travel — People Caught In The Eddies Of Time — An Encounter With Spirits — Or A Brief Visit To The Past? — The Mystery of Time Slips — Doorways in Time — People, Buildings and Towns From Beyond Time — The Restaurant At The Edge Of Time — Flight Into The Future — Is Death a Jump in Time? — Are UFOs Time Machines? — The Philadelphia Experiment and the Montauk Project – Working Time Machines — Nikola Tesla's Time Travel Experiments — Human Time Machines — Techniques for mental time travel — UFOs and Time Distortion. — **$20.00**

☐ **UFOs, Time Slips, Other Realms, And The Science Of Fairies: Another World Awaits Just Beyond The Shadows Of Consciousness**

By Edward Sidney Hartland, Timothy Green Beckley, Sean Casteel, Brent Raynes, Tim R. Swartz

LITTLE MEN ARE NOT FROM MARS! CONSIDER THE FOLLOWING: The occupants of these craft come in all shapes and sizes and have the ability to mesmerize those they encounter...THEY are able to cloak themselves in various disguises and have made deceitful attempts to convince those who observe their activities that they are visitors from another planet; even if their claims are contrary to the evidence. A HUNDRED YEARS ago the good citizenry might have identified these denizens are fairies or leprechauns, whereas in this technological age the term "alien" might be more applicable. . . THESE BEINGS often behave more like specters, phantoms or spooks, rather than flesh and blood creatures from another planet. They can materialize as inter-dimensional shape-shifters able to change form at will. FREQUENTLY, THEY "abduct" humans and take them to "another land" where a slippage in time occurs. When the hapless mortals return to this "state of being" hundreds of years may have gone by, while to the experiencers it may seem like only a brief period of time has expired. THEY DELIGHT in tempting humans into sexual intercourse, often impregnating females, but later snatching up their offspring without warning, often in the dead of night, all the while making those who tell their stories seem delusional. Reality is not "static" but beings can be coming here through "Time Slips." — **$20.00**

☐ **Teleportation: A How to Guide: From Star Trek to Tesla**
By Commander X, Authored by Tim R. Swartz

NOW YOU CAN TRAVEL UP, UP and AWAY...INSTANTLY!

** Classified Experiments Concerning the Philadelphia Experiment, Time Travel and Area 51 are revealed FOR THE FIRST TIME! ** PROOF ALIENS HAVE LEFT BEHIND IMPORTANT TECHNOLOGICAL CLUES! ** IT IS POSSIBLE TO MASTER THE ART OF TELEPORTATION WITH A BIT OF PRACTICE ON THE PART OF THE READER!

Long thought to be the work of over imaginative writers, the author now takes the subject beyond the void of pure speculation and into the realm of 21st Century science. For according the COMMANDER X — a former military intelligence operative with connections to the CIA and Defense Department — on a number of occasions he witnessed the testing of highly classified super TOP SECRET black project aircraft engaged in maneuvers over Area 51 in the Nevada desert. Furthermore, the national whistle-blower claims he actually sat at the helm of one of these ships as it bio-located from one place to another...INSTANTLY! COMMANDER X further insists it is within the realm of possibility for the reader of this book to learn the fundamentals of teleportation and participate in experiments of their very own — no matter how outlandish this may seem! In detail, he describes his own work with the military in developing skills necessary to engage in spontaneous teleportation...skills that could very well lead you along the path to personal gratification and success. — **$20.00**

ALL BOOKS ARE LARGE FORMAT AND ARE FULLY ILLUSTRATED AND EASY TO UNDERSTAND
Enjoy one or more items, or order all four time travel books for just $64.00 + $5.00 S/H
BONUS! ORDERS FOR ALL FOUR ITEMS WILL INCLUDE A FREE TIME TRAVEL DVD

Timothy Beckley · Box 753 · New Brunswick, NJ 08903

ADVERTISEMENT

THE ULTRA-TERRESTRIAL INVASION OF EARTH HAS BEGUN!

BONUS: AUDIO CD

The Ultra-Terrestrials Are Here And They Are Walking Among Us!

Throughout history we have been surrounded by invisible beings who can upon occasion materialize and take up a variety of shapes and facades – even resembling humans so that they can walk on the surface undetected. Some of these beings may come in peace... while others are here for their own nefarious purposes, perhaps going so far as to control our minds, possess our body and do bloodcurdling experiments upon us. In 1966, a Gallipulis, Ohio, nurse saw a dome shaped UFO land in a remote field. She was compelled to walk toward the craft. Several seconds passed before a number of beings emerged from the UFO and walked up to the woman, who found herself unable to move. The woman said the aliens looked exactly like earthlings and spoke to her for several minutes in perfect English. Eventually, the ship departed and the woman wandered off in a daze. Months later, while walking along the street, she saw these same two men. She ran into the local sheriff's office in an attempt to drag him out to see the "space people" for himself. He refused. Since then she has been constantly ridiculed by her neighbors.

YES! They can pass for humans, but they are NOT and their true forms may be too horrific to comprehend.

PLUS! This volume contains dozens of strange cases taken from the files of "Mr UFO" over decades. Recently, Beckley – who is a frequent guest on Coast to Coast AM and the ParaCast.Com—appeared on William Shatner's Weird or What? TV show where he revealed the true origins of a strange little creature that had been captured in an animal trap in Mexico and mistaken for an "alien baby," which it definitely is NOT! Amazingly, Tim Beckley reveals how to contact the peaceful Guardians, and set up a telepathic bond with the Watchers.

FREE CD NARRATED BY BRAD STEIGER

As a BONUS anyone ordering this book will receive at no additional cost a 60 minute audio CD which discuses the various forms of alien contact and how to acquire the most positive benefits from a UFO sighting or close encounter.

( ) ORDER – **THE BOOK OF AUTHENTIC ULTRA-TERRESTRIAL CONTACTS**, $20.00 + $5.00 S/H

Also Recommended:
( ) <u>Round Trip To Hell In A Flying Saucer</u> - $22
( ) <u>Evil Empire Of The Ets</u> — $20
( ) <u>Trilogy of the Unknown</u> — $20
All Items This Ad Just — $72.00 + $8.00 S/H

Make All Payments To:
TIMOTHY G. BECKLEY · BOX 753
NEW BRUNSWICK, NJ 08903
PayPal: MRUFO8@hotmail.com

www.ingramcontent.com/pod-product-compliance
Lightning Source LLC
Chambersburg PA
CBHW081915170426
43200CB00014B/2735